WOLFGANG LAIB

WOLFGANG LAIB
A RETROSPECTIVE

KLAUS OTTMANN

WITH AN ESSAY BY
MARGIT ROWELL

AND A CONVERSATION BETWEEN THE ARTIST AND
HARALD SZEEMANN

AMERICAN FEDERATION OF ARTS
AND
HATJE CANTZ PUBLISHERS

This catalogue has been published in conjunction with *Wolfgang Laib: A Retrospective*, an exhibition organized by the American Federation of Arts. In-kind support of the exhibition was provided by Parmalat USA.

The American Federation of Arts is a nonprofit art museum service organization that provides traveling art exhibitions and educational, professional, and technical support programs developed in collaboration with the museum community.
Through these programs, the AFA seeks to strengthen the ability of museums to enrich the public's experience and understanding of art.

Cover: Laib sifting pollen, Centre Georges Pompidou, 1992.

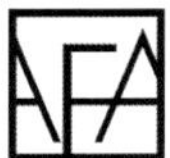

Published in 2000 by the American Federation of Arts and Hatje Cantz Publishers.

American Federation of Arts
41 East 65th Street, New York, NY 10021
(t) 212.988.7700 (f) 212.861.2487
www.afaweb.org

Hatje Cantz Publishers
Senefelderstr. 12
D–73760, Ostfildern/Ruit, Germany
(t) 49.7.11.4.4050 (f) 49.7.11.4.405220
www.hatjecantz.de

Trade distribution to the U.S.:
D.A.P., Distributed Art Publishers, Inc.,
155 Avenue of the Americas, Second Floor,
New York, NY 10013-1507
(t) 212.627.1999 (f) 212.627.9484
www.artbook.com

Library of Congress Cataloging-in-Publication Data

Ottmann, Klaus.
Wolfgang Laib : a retrospective /
Klaus Ottmann and Margit Rowell.
p. cm.
Published in conjunction with an exhibition organized by the American Federation of Arts and held at the Hirshhorn Museum & Sculpture Garden, Washington, D.C., and five other institutions between Oct. 26, 2000, and Jan. 2003.
Includes bibliographical references.
ISBN (trade) 3-7757-0945-2
ISBN (museum) 1-885444-14-1
1. Laib, Wolfgang, 1950—Exhibitions.
2. Conceptual art—Germany—Exhibitions.
3. Installations (Art)—Germany—Exhibitions. I. Laib, Wolfgang, 1950– II. Rowell, Margit.
III. American Federation of Arts.
IV. Hirshhorn Museum and Sculpture Garden. V. Title.

N6888.L29 A4 2000
709'.2—dc21

00-036269

EXHIBITION ITINERARY

Hirshhorn Museum & Sculpture Garden
Smithsonian Insititution
Washington, D.C.
October 26, 2000–January 22, 2001

Henry Art Gallery
Seattle, Washington
February 13–May 6, 2001

Dallas Museum of Art
Dallas, Texas
May 29–September 2, 2001

Scottsdale Museum of Contemporary Art
Scottsdale, Arizona
October 5–December 30, 2001

Museum of Contemporary Art,
San Diego
La Jolla and San Diego, California
January 25–April 21, 2002

Haus der Kunst
Munich, Germany
October 8, 2002–January 5, 2003

Publication Coordinator:
Michaelyn Mitchell
Book Design: Katy Homans
Editor: David Frankel
Printed in Germany
by Cantz

CONTENTS

ACKNOWLEDGMENTS

For more than two decades, Wolfgang Laib has been an important presence on the international art scene, creating an innovative body of installations and objects, as well as a superb group of drawings. Laib's work can be truly mesmerizing; however, while he has been represented in many group exhibitions all over the world and has had numerous solo exhibitions in Europe, this is the first in-depth presentation of his work in the United States.

Special thanks go to Klaus Ottmann, an independent curator who developed the project while a curator on the AFA staff, and who served as guest curator and author of this book. His commitment to the project has been untiring. We are grateful to Margit Rowell, formerly chief curator at the Department of Drawings at the Museum of Modern Art, New York, for her insightful essay in this book. We are also indebted to Harold Szeemann, director of the Venice Biennale and a curator who has worked on many exhibitions with Wolfgang Laib, for his part in the "Conversation" that constitutes such a valuable component of this book.

Numerous individuals at the AFA have been critical in the organization of *Wolfgang Laib*, in particular, Thomas Padon, director of exhibitions, whose support was instrumental in realizing the project; Robin Kaye Goodman, assistant curator of exhibitions, who oversaw all aspects of the organization of the exhibition; and Michaelyn Mitchell, head of publications, who supervised the editing and production of this book. Working with Ms. Goodman and Ms. Mitchell were Margaret Calvert, curatorial assistant, and Beth Huseman, editorial assistant, respectively. Karen Convertino, registrar, coordinated the shipping and receiving of loans; Lisbeth Mark, director of communications, disseminated information on the project to the national and local press; and Brian Boucher, interim head of education, created the educational materials.

Our collaboration with Hatje Cantz Publications has been especially productive, and we wish to acknowledge Markus Hartmann for this fruitful relationship. We would also like to thank David Frankel for his thorough editing of the publication, and Katy Homans for her handsome design.

We wish to recognize the museums that are participating in the exhibition: the Hirshhorn Museum & Sculpture Garden, Smithsonian Institution, Washington, D.C.; the Henry Art Gallery, Seattle; the Dallas Museum of Art; the Scottsdale Museum of Contemporary Art; the Museum of Contemporary Art, San Diego, which is presenting the exhibition at both its La Jolla and San Diego galleries; and the Haus der Kunst, Munich. To our colleagues at these institutions, we extend our deepest gratitude for their interest in and support of the project.

Our warmest thanks go to the lenders, institutional and private. We appreciate their willingness to part with the works in order that they may be included in this exhibition.

We are especially grateful to Parmalat USA for their in-kind donation of whole milk to all the U.S. venues.

Finally, but most importantly, I wish to express the AFA's great debt of gratitude to Wolfgang Laib himself. Mr. Laib has been extremely generous in the cooperation he has given us throughout the development of the project, and the staff has enjoyed working with him. We are pleased and proud to present this major exhibition of his work to a national audience and to affirm our support for the best of contemporary art.

SERENA RATTAZZI
Director
American Federation of Arts

What is great in man is that he is a bridge and not a goal:
what is lovable in man is that he is an overgoing *and a* downgoing.

I love those that know not how to live, except as downgoers, for they are the overgoers.

FRIEDRICH NIETZSCHE
Thus Spoke Zarathustra: A Book for All and None, 1883

Runge to Goethe: "Both white and black are opaque or solid. . . .
White water which is pure is as inconceivable as clear milk."

A surface-color is a quality of a surface.
One might (therefore) be tempted not to call it a pure color concept.
But then what would a pure one be?!

LUDWIG WITTGENSTEIN
Remarks on Color, 1950–51

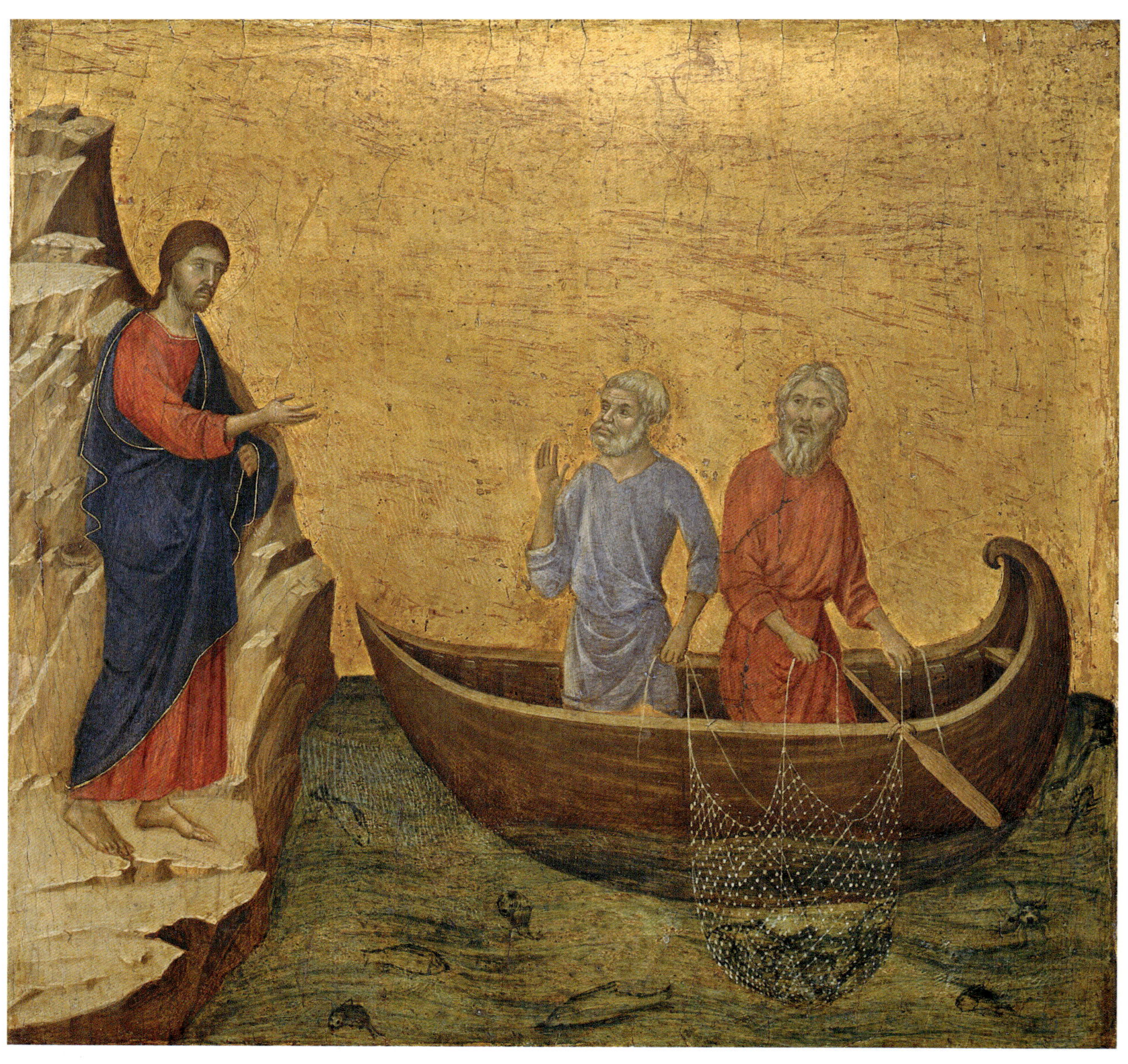

THE SOLID AND THE FLUID: PERCEIVING LAIB

KLAUS OTTMANN

A critic or art historian who is writing on an artist can choose among a variety of established methods: assessments of quality, analyses of style, discussions of pictorial traditions or of social contexts. These methods may include examinations of the conditions of the work's production and reception—tracing its sources, establishing its influences, and categorizing it into styles—and may also, particularly in recent years, involve biographical and ideological approaches that address issues of race, gender, and politics. There are artists, however, whose works are so completely their own that the established methodologies and approaches are inadequate to the task of the critic or art historian. In the postwar period, the roster of these few, highly autonomous artists would include the American artists James Lee Byars and Eva Hesse, and the German artists Joseph Beuys and Wolfgang Laib.

What makes Laib more singular than the others is that, unlike even such a radical artist as Beuys, he belongs to no school or movement, nor has he taught any students.[1] Laib also distances himself from Western European aesthetic traditions more generally: he sees himself as largely alone among his peers, for he has little interest in contemporary art apart from his own practice, which originates equally in the natural environment of his home, in a small village in southern Germany, and in his knowledge of non-Western art and religion. Relatively little influenced by other artists, and without formal art education, Laib is the absolute source for his own work. He has been true to his solitary art, and to his desire for a new artistic expression, for over twenty-five years.

Laib's work is characterized by a deep relationship with nature and a commitment to the purity and simplicity he finds in Eastern philosophies. Since the mid-1970s he has been creating objects and installations of austere beauty and delicacy, using naturally occurring elements such as milk, pollen, rice, beeswax, and marble. The son of a physician, Laib studied medicine but abandoned the profession to pursue his interests in religion and mysticism. He wants his art to share some of the formal and ceremonial qualities of non-Western art and ritual, particularly that of southern India, which he considers his spiritual home. Especially inspiring for Laib are the temple altars of the region, with their offerings of flowers and food and their portable bronze deities. Produced between the ninth and the thirteenth centuries, these figures are seen as participants in daily rituals and ceremonial processions, and are bathed, clothed, and given offerings of incense and food, including milk, which is often poured over them. Both Laib's milkstones and his rice houses, he says, are inspired by these rituals and cultural practices.

Laib still tries to spend part of every summer with his family in southern India, which continues to have a profound effect on his life and work. He has also explored the aesthetic practices of Turkey and Tibet. His experience of non-Western cultures has helped him to conceive of art in a radically individual way. By the standards of most Western artists today, the pace of his production is slow to the point of being artisanal; his methods are reclusive, circular, repetitive, and in certain respects ritualistic. Laib's art is eidetic, a term from the Greek *eidos*, for Plato the essential or universal form or idea underlying all experience. The work demands, then, that any appraisal of it begin with the work itself, rather than with its historical context.

How does one approach an artist who deliberately defies classification and denies dependence on any aesthetic precedent? One way would be to look at his work phenomenologically.[2] Simply put, phenomenology is the study of phenomena and appearances. That study is intended to allow an understanding of the world from the starting point of its "facticity"—its objective being. Phenomenology emerged as a philosophical discipline in the eighteenth century, in the form of a "theory of appearances," an examination of the objective and subjective sources of perception. At the start of the twentieth century, in the work of the German mathematician and philosopher Edmund Husserl, phenomenology came to involve an attempt to provide a description of the world as it is directly experienced, positing the individual as the absolute source of his or her own knowledge of the world. Husserl's aim was to uncover the essential structures and relationships describing phenomena.

The definitive method of phenomenology is the *epoche*, or phenomenological reduction, literally a restraint or suspension of participation or complicity in experience. Most simply, the reduction is a shift away from factuality and particularity and toward the essential and universal, a suspension of belief in the historical dimension of experience (also referred to as a "bracketing" of history), and a turning away from opinions (the preexisting theories of philosophers and historians) in favor of things themselves. This kind of suspension of or turning away from reality is precisely the experience called for by Laib's work. In *The Poetics of Space,* a book widely read by artists since its first publication, in 1958, the philosopher Gaston Bachelard writes that "the image, in its simplicity, has no need of scholarship. . . . To specify exactly what phenomenology of the image can be, to specify that the image comes before thought, we should say that poetry . . . is a phenomenology of the soul."[3] Maurice Merleau-Ponty, another influential phenomenologist and writer on art, remarked in an essay on Paul Cézanne that the painter remained "faithful to the phenomena" and painted "the lived perspective, that which we actually perceive," rather than the linear perspective established in the Renaissance. In the art of Cézanne, Merleau-Ponty saw a paradigm of the phenomenological *epoche*, which grants access to the consciousness of "lived experience": "By remaining faithful to the phenomena in his investigations of perspective, Cézanne discovered what recent psychologists have come to formulate: the lived perspective, that which we actually perceive, is not a geometric or photographic one."[4] Laib similarly leaves the perspectival principles of the Renaissance behind, turning instead to the lived perspective of non-Western and pre-Renaissance visual practices.

Laib began his work as an artist in 1972, when he was studying medicine and writing a dissertation on the hygiene of drinking water. His research led him to spend three months in southern India, where he had earlier spent time with his parents, so that, over the years, he had become acquainted with the simplicity and purity of the art and ceremony he saw there. Ultimately the experience of southern India inspired Laib to adopt the ceremonial as a continuing mode in both his life and his work, which were to become inseparable.

After returning to Germany, Laib decided to take time off from his medical studies. Discovering a large black rock, about three feet in length, in the countryside near where he lived, he brought it home and set to work on carving it into a perfect ovoid. During the three months he took to do this, it became clear to him that he was dissatisfied with medical science, which he felt addressed human needs only imperfectly, and that he wanted to turn to art instead. He eventually finished his dissertation, but he has never practiced medicine. The black oval stone has remained in his home ever since, the only artwork of his own creation that he has chosen to live with on a daily basis.

In 1973, on the 700th anniversary of the death of Jalal-ud-din Rumi (1207–1273), a Sufi poet and the leader of the Mevlevi order of whirling dervishes, Laib visited the Turkish town of Konya, where Rumi is buried. The

Mevlevi order is based on the pursuit of perfection, and of a mystical union with God through a form of spiritual ecstasy attained by a combination of music and dance. A former cloister in Konya remains an important place of worship for the order to this day, even though it was secularized by being turned into a museum in 1926. During his visit, Laib sculpted a second, larger ovoid stone from a block of red marble that he obtained at a nearby quarry. With the permission of the authorities, he placed this red stone in front of the museum as an act of reverence to the Sufi mystic. Years later Laib learned that many female visitors to the museum had sought out the stone, apparently believing that it was a meteorite, and that touching it would make them fertile. The authorities eventually moved the stone to the garden behind the museum, where public access is restricted. The stone is still there today.

In 1975, Laib made the first of his milkstones, a group of works that he continues to produce: each is a rectangular slab of polished white marble with a barely perceptible depression sanded into its upper surface. The artist fills this depression with milk, creating the illusion of a solid white object. Laib regards the act of pouring the milk into the hollow in the stone as a participatory ritual: he performs only the initial pouring; the owner of the work, or the staff of the gallery or museum where it is shown, must subsequently empty the stone at the end of each day, clean it, and refill it the next morning with fresh milk. Most of the milkstones are carved from a slightly yellow Macedonian marble, its warm color close to the color of milk. (Laib favors this marble for all of his marble sculptures, although he has on occasion used a cooler, bluish marble from Carrara, Italy.)

Laib created his first pollen field in 1977. Like the milkstones, the pollen fields involve a ceremonial, almost ritualistic process, and exhibit Laib's abiding interest in nature. Throughout the spring and summer months of each year, Laib collects pollen from the fields around his home. He moves with the cycles of the seasons, working on each tree or flower as it comes into bloom—first hazelnut, then dandelion, buttercup, and other pollens, ending with pine. Each pollen is distinctive in color and size: dandelion, for instance, is intensely orange and relatively coarse, while pine is lighter in color, and fine.

Laib collects the pollen in glass jars, where it will stay fresh indefinitely if kept dry and at a stable temperature. He often exhibits these jars, usually on a shelf. His second one-person exhibition in New York, at the Sperone Westwater gallery in 1981, consisted entirely of five jars of pollen, installed first on the gallery floor, later on a window ledge. Some types of pollen, such as buttercup and sorrel, are so scarce that Laib will exhibit them only in jars. Others he shapes into cones, or "mountains," that stand on the floor, either alone or alongside heaps of white rice next to the marble works he calls "rice houses." Laib considers his groups of cones, such as *The Five Mountains Not to Climb On*, of 1984—five hills of either buttercup or hazelnut pollen, each approximately three inches high—among his most important works. He may also sift pollen through muslin directly onto bare stone or concrete floors, creating fields in varying hues of yellow orange[5]; these are for a short time intensely fragrant, although the fragrance usually disappears after the first day. The dimension of each field depends on the type of pollen used and the amount of available space: pine pollen, which is quite abundant in Laib's region, leads to larger pieces, while dandelion, which is more scarce, permits only smaller works. At the end of each exhibition, the pollen is resifted through the muslin to separate it from the accumulated dust that has mingled with it on the floor, and is returned to a jar.

A common misconception about these pieces is that they exist as art only when the pollen is spread out or heaped into distinct forms on the floor. But Laib considers the pollen itself the work of art, even when he shows it in its jar. This is crucial to understanding his work. The jars, too, should not be seen merely as storage devices, in the way that paint jars are for painters; they are integral parts of the work.

Laib's notion of the autonomy of the pollen, as a substance apart from form, derives from pre-Renaissance art. Thirteenth-century Sienese painting, particularly that of Duccio di Buoninsegna (one of the painters Laib admires most), surpasses Byzantine art in its illusionism and naturalism, and is also characterized by its delicacy and fluidity of form. Duccio's overall compositions are to be thought of as visual dialogues between representation and void, figure and space, solid and fluid; between form—the silhouettes of the figures in the "foreground"—and formlessness, the shimmering gold plane in what the modern viewer perceives as the "background," although it is visually far more active than that word implies.[6] Defined by the lines surrounding the figures, the gold takes on a life of its own. The fact that it is as important as the foreground makes the painting a unified expression of form, color, line, and pattern.

During the Renaissance, however, a new visual hierarchy emerged, relegating the formless to a background understood as secondary, and ultimately replacing it with a perspectival landscape. The art historian Henri Focillon has discussed the naiveté of our faith in perspective: "The space of life is a known quantity to which life readily submits; the space of art is a plastic and changing material. We may find it difficult to admit this, so completely are we influenced by the rules of Albertian perspective. But many other perspectives exist as well."[7] The perspective of Renaissance art, in other words, is only one symbolic construction among others. In Focillon's view, form must be separated from signification, from any hierarchical reading: "Form signifies only itself."[8]

The paintings of Yves Klein, with their monochrome blues and pinks, or of Mark Rothko, with their floating rectangles of color, create meaning or emotion by alluding to or evoking some spiritual quality beyond the materiality of their pigment. Laib's pollen and milk works, on the other hand, concentrate on the material itself. In this sense they are closer to the Skyspaces of the American installation artist James Turrell, which frame the sky as their content, than to the art of such painters as Klein and Rothko. (Interestingly, Rothko felt a close affinity to the Renaissance painter Piero della Francesca, who in his view maintained "a perfectly balanced relationship" between objects and space, "one augmenting the dignity of the other"—a relationship not unlike the pre-Renaissance interdependence between form and formlessness to which Laib relates.[9]) Yet at the same time, Laib's pollen and milk have a physical impact that extends into an intermediate domain pertaining to neither their materiality nor their form. Instead it is located in what the philosopher F. W. J. von Schelling called "spiritual corporeality[10]": it produces a calm composure, a mood that Slavoj Žižek calls "pacified disengagement,"[11] a suspension of reality. The pollen fields and milkstones are directed outward; to use Lacanian terms, they take the Symbolic into the realm of the Real.[12]

Laib's wax rooms, on the other hand—life-sized chambers built out of large blocks of beeswax, illuminated by bare light bulbs hanging from their ceilings—are directed inward, forcing the viewer into a mental suspension of the Real. The intense smell and color of these rooms are overwhelming, almost to the point, should one stay inside long enough, where they induce a loss of awareness of self or place. Laib's relationship to the phenomenological *epoche* is most evident in this temporary suspension of the outside world, this experience of an inner "lived perspective." One enters a void space in which the gap between the Symbolic and the Real is closed—that is, in which desires are directly materialized.

Laib's wax rooms do not merely provide mental spaces into which one projects the truth about oneself. They constitute what Žižek calls "the Real of an absolute Otherness,"[13] like the mysterious "Zone" in Andrei Tarkovsky's science fiction film *Stalker* (1979), a forbidden space in which secret desires are said to be fulfilled. Žižek compares the "spiritual conversion" that takes place in Tarkovsky's Zone with what Lacan called "subjective destitution"—"a sudden awareness of the utter meaninglessness of our social links, the dissolution of our attachment to reality itself—all of a sudden, other people are derealized . . . so that we are no longer able to formulate our desires."[14] But the Zone is a paradox: it only functions for those who are able to believe with direct immediacy, that is, who know their *true* desires, those desires articulated in the state of pure faith or certitude. One of Laib's most recent wax rooms, from 1997, is titled *Somewhere Else—La Chambre des certitudes*, and a related drawing carries the title *La Chambre des certitudes—La Certitude c'est l'imaginaire* (*The Room of Certitudes—Certitude Is the Imaginary*). The term "imaginary" is strongly associated with Lacan, who, however, is not Laib's reference here; instead the artist is touching on his own mystical background. The word "certitude," as opposed to "certainty," implies a faith in something not needing objective proof, or not capable of it. Perhaps Laib's ultimate act of certitude is evoked by his plan to build a mountain sanctuary in the form of a wax room inside a granite rock in the Pyrenees—an ambition equal to Turrell's *Roden Crater Project* in the Arizona desert.

Beeswax ranges from yellow to near black in color, depending on such factors as the age and the diet of the bees. It has a honeylike odor, and its texture is soft to brittle. It is obtained by melting the honeycomb (after the honey has been harvested), straining the molten wax to remove impurities, and pressing the residue of the comb to extract any wax that remains. The purified liquid is then poured into molds to set.

To make his works in beeswax, Laib first fabricates molds, either of metal or of wood. (If the mold is wood, the surface is laminated so that no imprint of the grain will be visible in the wax.) He pours the wax in a local candle factory. Laib produces several kinds of work in wax, making panels that vary in dimensions and thickness with the use to which he intends to put them; the panels in the wax rooms are roughly one to two inches thick. He fixes them in place by pressing them against nails in a plywood wall. If the plates are to be shaped, the temperature has to be warm, and in the winter months Laib used to sculpt the wax in a heated room behind his studio. More recently he has taken to handling wax only during the summer months, working outside in the sun, which keeps the material malleable. When installing his wax sculptures in exhibitions, he uses a household iron to smooth the seams between the panels.

Laib also makes wax houses, sealed except for small openings. These works were originally made without internal support structures except for thin wax walls. This made them extremely fragile: the wax would soften with any rise in the ambient temperature, and the shape would shift under its own weight. It was important to Laib to keep these works pure wax, unlike the sculpture of the Italian artist Medardo Rosso, who, in the late nineteenth century, introduced the technique of modeling beeswax over plaster casts. Ultimately, however, Laib had to compromise, using a simple internal wooden structure to make the sculptures less fragile.

Laib works with other materials besides beeswax, milk, and pollen, and his choices help to make his art visually appealing: he also uses rice (he considers flour, another elementary food, too close in texture to pollen), brass (in the form of plates and cones from India), tin, silver, aluminum, and red sealing wax (still used in India to seal packages). *The Rice Meals* (1983) consists of piles of rice and pollen heaped on the brass plates commonly used in India to bring food and flowers to the temples. The rice houses—usually either sculpted in solid white marble and surrounded by rice, or made of red sealing wax and filled with rice—were inspired by Islamic cemeteries and medieval reliquaries but instead of bones contain rice, a literal symbol of food, of nourishment.

In addition to sculptural installations, Laib also makes drawings, a practice he began in 1983, when he was one of a number of artists asked to create a work on paper on the occasion of Johannes Cladders's sixtieth birthday. (Cladders was the curator who had shown Laib's work, together with that of the conceptual artist Hanne Darboven and the painter Gotthard Graupner, in the German Pavilion at the 1982 Venice Biennale, Laib's first major international exhibition.) Laib soon realized that on paper he could play with visual ideas that could not be expressed easily or at all in sculpture, such as that of a pyramid inside a mountain. Since then he has been creating exquisitely rendered, diaphanous drawings, which have a superficial relationship to his other works but are in fact independent of it: his specific mode of production makes preparatory drawings unnecessary (another trait he shares with Rosso).

The forms of Laib's works are as fragile as their materials. His work is inherently paradoxical: its sensual tactility invites the touch, but like most modern sculpture, it requires protective distance. (One thinks of the works of Constantin Brancusi, with their unexpectedly delicate surfaces, which can be damaged by the slightest touch of the hand.) How does one know whether what one perceives as the opaque surface of a sheet of marble is actually milk, unless one touches it? How can one be certain that a yellow substance is pollen, unless one blows on it? Yet these impulses, if acted upon, would harm the work. This perceptual dilemma recalls the quantum mathematician Werner Heisenberg's "uncertainty principle," according to which it is intrinsically impossible for an observer located within a system to give a complete description of that system, which must necessarily change through the act of being observed. Richard Feynman's remarks on this subject can easily be applied to the experience of Laib's "fuzzy" fields of pollen: the uncertainty principle, Feynman says,

> *describes an inherent fuzziness that must exist in any attempt to describe nature. Our most precise description of nature must be in terms of probabilities. . . . We can form an image of the hydrogen atom by imagining a "cloud" whose density is proportional to the probability density for observing the electron. . . . Thus our best "picture" of a hydrogen atom is a nucleus surrounded by an "electronic cloud" (although we really mean a "probability cloud"). . . . In its efforts to learn as much as possible about nature, modern physics has found that certain things can never be "known" with certainty. Much of our knowledge must always remain uncertain. The most we can know is in terms of probabilities.*[15]

In addition to requiring physical distance, Laib's works demand stillness and quiet. This often becomes evident in the large group exhibitions in which he has been invited to participate, such as the 1997 Venice Biennale, where his sculpture, to its detriment, shared space with a deliberately disordered installation by Jason Rhoades, and with the performances of Vanessa Beecroft. The maintenance of his works can also be a challenge for museums and their staff, as became evident in *Objects of Desire: The Modern Still Life*, at the Museum of Modern Art, New York, in 1997: for budgetary reasons, Laib's milkstone in this exhibition remained unfilled during the weekends, a practice he apparently permitted but did not condone.

The art historian Wilhelm Worringer distinguished between two poles of artistic experience: "empathy," or the enjoyment activated by a sensuous object; and "abstraction," the approximation of an object to its material individuality "to purify it of whatever it has of life and temporality and make it independent of the external world and of the subject."[16] Worringer associated empathy with "naturalism," which he defined as the

> *approximation to the organic and that which is true to life, but not because the artist desired to depict a natural object true to life in its corporeality, not because he desired to give the illusion of a living object, but because the feeling for the beauty of organic form that is true to life had been aroused and because the artist desired to give satisfaction to this feeling, which dominated the absolute artistic volition* (Kunstwollen). *It was the happiness of the organically alive, not that of truth to life, which was striven after.*[17]

To the concept of naturalism Worringer contrasted the concept of "stylization," which he associated with the urge toward abstraction and toward "tranquility and felicitation," and with a preference for abstract and geometric forms, "purified of all dependence upon the things of the outer world."[18] According to Worringer, most cultures are predisposed toward the one (empathic naturalism) or the other (stylized abstraction). One might say, however, that Laib's "spiritual materiality" felicitously combines both—the "happiness of the organically alive" and the purification of abstract forms.

When Laib was growing up, he never intended to become an artist. But his feeling for the beauty and serenity of nature, which he saw materialized in pollen and milk, awoke that desire in him—or, rather, awoke in him not so much the desire to become an artist as the desire to participate in the beauty of nature. (On a recent visit to his studio I took a photograph of him walking toward me through flowers and trees in the field between his home and his studio (p. 184); a slight, unassuming figure, clothed in loose cotton fabrics, with a shaved head and simple wire-frame glasses, he seemed almost invisible—in perfect harmony with his surroundings.) Laib considers the attempt to *create* beauty the tragic failure of most art. For him, art is an act of participation and sharing—participating in nature and sharing that experience with others. The milk in the milkstones is not simply a white surface; it is a living organic thing, just as the pollen is. Nor is the pollen simply a yellow rectangle: it has no definite border, no strict, clean separation from the world outside it. Laib's works are not merely visual experiences but serve as his contributions to social and spiritual change. For him, the *spiritual* reality of the work is embedded in its *materiality*—the two cannot be separated. He wants to present the structure of the world as a totality. To show a piece of marble as an artwork might have a certain powerful intellectual simplicity, but without the milk it would remain purely visual. Yet the milk, and the pollen, in Laib's work are not just about nature; they restore to the modern "world picture" what Husserl called the "life-world," the naive, "natural" ground of conscious life, which is always already there, pregiven, prior to any theoretical activity.

To equate Laib's phenomenological reduction with ascetic denial, however, would be to miss the point. A pursuit of simplicity as a means of order, it relates to cultural practices and religions around the world: Japanese Zen Buddhism, Chinese Buddhism, the teachings of Saint Francis of Assisi, American Quakerism. The sensibility of simplicity can be invited through a variety of rituals—Japanese bathing practices, for example—while rhythmic repetitions and universal forms (squares, circles, spheres, triangles, cones, pyramids) are everywhere used to instill a sense of order, discipline, and repose. The eighteenth-century Japanese painter Gibon Sengai, an itinerant Zen priest, illustrated the universe with nothing more than a circle, a triangle, and a square.

In using some of these shapes and forms, Laib's pollen fields, milkstones, and wax sculptures superficially share a formal language with Minimalist art, and with certain abstract painting. But to present his work as an offshoot of Minimalism is inadequate; it is more appropriately understood in the context of pre-Renaissance and non-Western aesthetics. There is Asian and particularly Indian art that reveals the aesthetic qualities Laib strives for in his work—simplicity, purity, and the transgressive power temporarily to suspend reality. As Didier Semin has written of Laib's pollen fields, "The pantheistic ritual inherited from India does not replace the avant-garde quest for a fusion of art and the world: it joins together with it and extends it by confronting it with elements it had never even imagined."[19]

It should also be remembered that Laib's work is as essentially phenomenological as Minimalism is structuralist. Unlike phenomenology, structuralism does not render the world as it finds it; it looks at the world's *functionality*, at the rules that describe its parts. Roland Barthes defines structuralist activity as a "controlled succession of a certain number of mental operations" whose goal it is "to reconstruct an 'object' in such a way as to manifest thereby the rules of functioning (the 'functions') of this object."[20] Ultimately structuralism is concerned not with meaning but with the *fabrication* of meaning. Similarly, Minimalism replaces essence in art with presence and place: it relies on the void, the space around it, the space that since the Renaissance has been seen as distinct and separate from the art object. Minimalist sculpture, by its very definition, affects and interacts with the space it occupies, to the extent that the architectural space surrounding it is an intrinsic part of it. One of Laib's fields of pollen, on the other hand, may affect the walls of the surrounding space by casting its intense color onto them (especially if they are white), but this reflection is never part of the work itself, and may be entirely absent in a different installation—when, for example, the pollen is presented in jars.

Laib's work is often compared with Joel Shapiro's Post-Minimalist cast-iron houses, first produced in 1973. These structures—some painted, most of them no more than a few inches high, and ranging from basic forms to more expansive objects that extend into fields or driveways—question issues of size, color, and relative placement, and often suggest both architecture and children's blocks. Their geometry, and their location on the floor rather than on a base or pedestal, bespeak their Minimalist heritage. The similarities to Laib's houses are striking, but Laib rejects any comparison of his work with Shapiro's. It is interesting to note, however, that Shapiro spent nearly two years (from 1965 to 1967) teaching in southern India.

It should be pointed out that while seriality features prominently in Laib's more recent installations, and also in his drawings, it relates less to the serial arrangements of Minimalism than to non-Western notions of repetition: the idea of the eternal recurrence of the same is central to Buddhism. In Laib's words, repetition is "the most beautiful thing that exists."[21] In works such as *Durchgang—Übergang* (*Passageway-Overgoing*, 1996, a title referring loosely to Nietzsche's *Thus Spoke Zarathustra*), *You Will Go Somewhere Else* (1995), and *Ich bin nicht hier* (*I Am Not Here*, 1997–99), Laib repeats the forms of beeswax "ships" anywhere from five to ten times. (The wax ships are a continuation of the wax houses, being the same form turned upside-down, and are often installed in serial progressions on wooden scaffolding, which was inspired by Laib's visits to Tibetan monasteries where sacred scriptures are stored on freestanding elevated shelves. Many of his drawings also feature repeating images of ship- and houselike forms.) The idea of progress, and consequently of time as linear, has been at the core of Western culture and history, and is pointedly expressed by the late-nineteenth-century Viennese philosopher Otto Weininger, the infamous author of the misogynist study *Sex and Character:* "The backward motion is the quintessential unethical motion. . . . It is unethical to say the same thing twice."[22] Yet Laib continues to create milkstones and pollen fields in forms virtually unchanged since the mid-1970s. His art resists classification into separate, chronologically sequential bodies of work: "The pollen mountains," he says, "will survive the '90s and I can still make them in twenty years. Even if people find it old-fashioned, I don't care."[23] Alluding to its continuous recycling into new works, Laib once referred to the pollen as "a detail of the infinity."[24]

The artist Max Beckmann once wrote, "The artist can know nothing of religion, politics, and life. He must not forget that sylphlike presence that he is, his only purpose consisting of sprinkling the world with brightly colored pollen."[25] Laib disproves Beckmann's ironic statement, insinuating the beauty of nature in his art and creating immediate sensations that expand our understanding of life, politics, and religion. His modesty gives his art a sense of grace, serenity, and transcendence.

I would like to thank the following people for their advice, inspiration, and help during the writing of this essay: Wolfgang Laib, Leslie Tonkonow, Sheryl Conkelton, Peter Anders, Donna Gustafson, David Frankel, and Slavoj Žižek.

1. Wolfgang Laib admits only a "very open" connection with Joseph Beuys. He shares with Beuys a belief in the therapeutic power of art, but where Beuys's social sculpture politicizes public desires, in a fusion of art, science, and religion, Laib's work is directed more toward private, noncollective experience, and toward stillness. The literal stillness of the milk in his milkstones was one reason for the inclusion of one of these works in *Objects of Desire: The Modern Still Life*, curated by Margit Rowell at the Museum of Modern Art, New York, in May–August 1997.

2. So far as I know, Laib has never referred to phenomenology in discussing his work. But it is not necessary that an artist be familiar with a particular critical model for a writer to consider that model applicable to his or her work.

3. Gaston Bachelard, *The Poetics of Space* (Boston: Beacon Press, 1969), p. xvi.

4. Maurice Merleau-Ponty, "Cézanne's Doubt," in *The Merleau-Ponty Aesthetics Reader: Philosophy and Painting*, ed. and with an introduction by Galen A. Johnson (Evanston, Ill.: Northwestern University Press, 1993), p. 64.

5. Laib will not install pollen on wood-grained or carpeted floors: both would cause precious pollen to be lost, and would interfere with its texture and color. In the case of stone floors that are porous or contain cracks, Laib has occasionally used a layer of gesso underneath the pollen.

6. For a discussion of the rediscovery of the notion of formlessness in twentieth-century art, see Yve-Alain Bois and Rosalind E. Krauss, *Formless: A User's Guide* (New York: Zone Books, 1997).

7. Henri Focillon, *The Life of Forms in Art* (New York: Zone Books, 1992), p. 69.

8. Ibid., p. 34.

9. Mark Rothko, in his "Scribble Book," a collection of notes from the 1930s. Quoted in James Breslin, *Mark Rothko: A Biography* (Chicago: at the Chicago University Press, 1993), p. 134.

10. Friedrich Wilhelm Joseph von Schelling, *Clara: Über den Zusammenhang der Natur mit der Geisterwelt* (1810), and Slavoj Žižek, *The Invisible Remainder: An Essay on Schelling and Related Matters* (London: Verso, 1996), pp. 4, 152.

11. Žižek, "The Thing from Inner Space," unpublished ms.

12. For Jacques Lacan, need, demand, and desire are expressions or effects of orders of human existence that can be defined as the "Real," the "Imaginary," and the "Symbolic"—the raw materials of psychoanalysis. See Lacan, "The Function and Field of Speech and Language in Psychoanalysis: Report to the Rome Congress held at the Istituto di Psicologia della Università di Roma, 26 and 27 September 1953," in *Ecrits: A Selection* (New York and London: W. W. Norton & Co., 1977).

13. Žižek, "The Thing from Inner Space."

14. Ibid.

15. Richard P. Feynman, *Lectures on Physics* (Reading, Mass.: Addison-Wesley Publishing Company, 1963), pp. 6–10.

16. Wilhelm Worringer, *Abstraction and Empathy: A Contribution to the Psychology of Style* (Chicago: Ivan R. Dee, Publisher, 1997), p. 44.

17. Ibid., p. 28.

18. Ibid., pp. 35, 37.

19. Didier Semin, "A Piece by Wolfgang Laib at the Centre Pompidou," *Parkett* 39 (1994): 75.

20. Roland Barthes, "The Structuralist Activity," in Richard and Fernande DeGeorge, eds., *The Structuralists from Marx to Lévi-Strauss* (Garden City, N.Y.: Doubleday & Co., 1972), p. 149.

21. Laib, in a conversation with the author at Laib's studio in the summer of 1998.

22. Otto Weininger, "Uber die Einsinnigkeit der Zeit," in *Über die letzten Dinge* (Munich: Matthes & Seitz Verlag, 1980), p. 111. Translated from the German by the author.

23. Laib, in a conversation with the author at Laib's studio in the summer of 1998.

24. Laib, in a conversation with the author at Laib's studio in the summer of 1999.

25. Max Beckmann, *Self-Portrait in Words: Collected Writings and Statements, 1903–1950*, ed. and annotated by Barbara Copeland Buenger (Chicago: University of Chicago Press, 1996), p. 282.

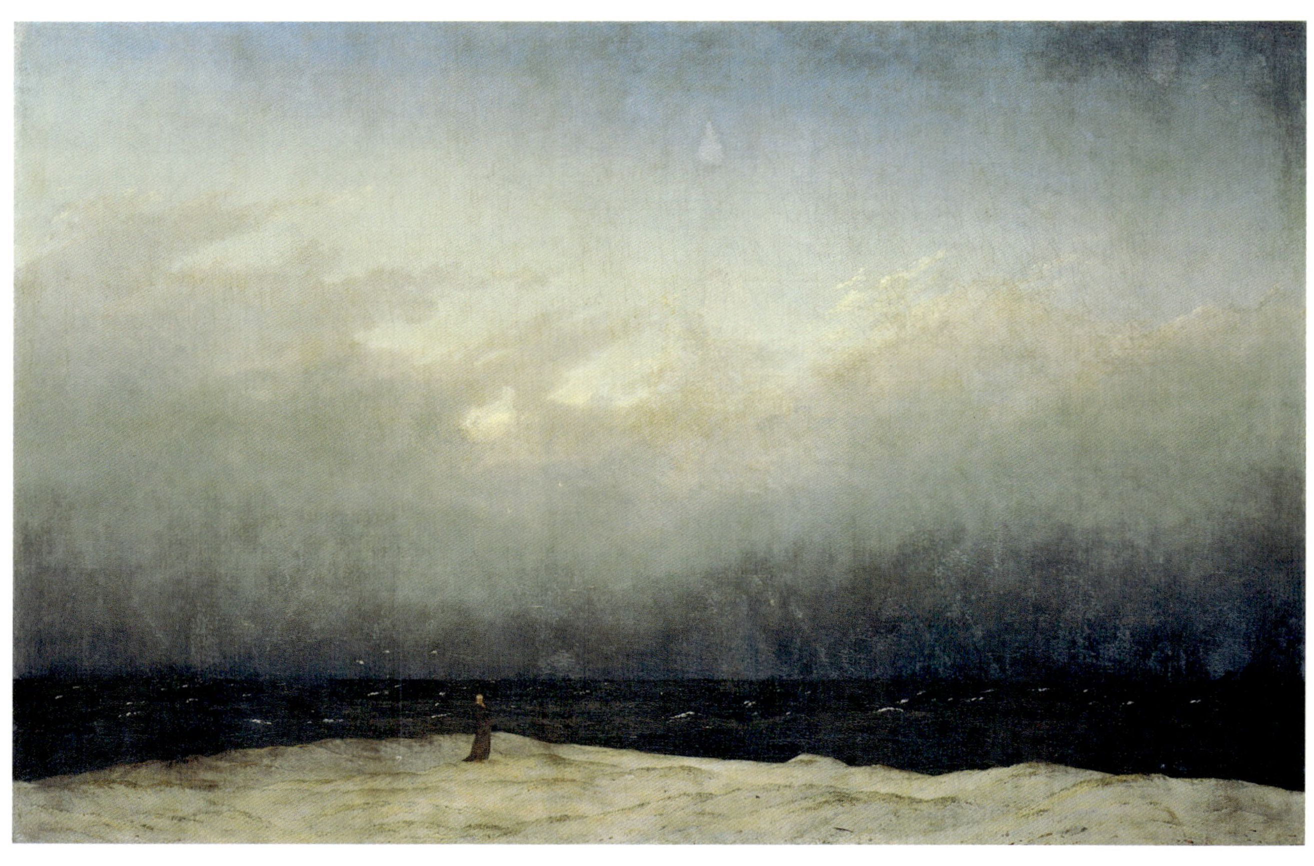

MODEST PROPOSITIONS

MARGIT ROWELL

I

Milk: *creamy white, shimmering, fluid yet still, contained in a pool by its organic structure and substance.*
Marble: *cool white, opalescent, solid; mat, or glowing with a silky sheen.*
Pollen: *yellow, powdery, incandescent; coarse or fine; dandelion (deep orange gold), buttercup (bright and pure), pine (with an infinitesimal tint of green), moss (the finest and palest of all).*
Beeswax: *rich, milky tints from ocher to deepest amber, unexpectedly scented.*
Rice: *white or gray, streaked, pearlescent, its grains clumped or strewn.*

These are Wolfgang Laib's chosen mediums: energetic, generative substances from the world of nature, from its active cycles, its essence, its vitality.

White rectangles: *milk on marble, white on white. Visions of purity.*
Yellow rectangles: *powdery hues sifted evenly and flat on the floor, feathered at the edges. Visions of radiant light.*
Houses: *small, elongated, with pitched roofs, in beeswax, sealing wax, aluminum, marble. Visions of enclosure and protection, in life or death.*
Cones: *of rice, nestling against the houses, or isolated, sometimes in brass bowls; of pollen, alone or in lines or in clusters. Visions of spiritual nourishment.*
Corridors and chambers: *of giant slabs of amber beeswax, narrow, barely lit, leading to a blank wall or opening on space. Evocations of a journey.*
Ships: *of beeswax, one behind the other, high above us on fragile scaffoldings, sailing we know not where. Too large to be precious objects, too small to be actual vessels, their surfaces stained and scarred. Evocations of other journeys.*
Ziggurats or stepped pyramids: *once again in beeswax; hand polished, patinated, oxidizing; large or small. Evocations of other places.*

These are Laib's chosen images. Archetypal shapes cast from richly tactile natural materials, they produce in the viewer an experience of immediate sensuous pleasure and an equally immediate effect of spiritual mystery, quite foreign to both our common experience of ordinary reality and the extra-ordinary illusions of works of art.

The first impression is that of color: saturated, uncanny, but at the same time pure and natural. The second impression is that of texture: tangible, yet too fragile to be touched. These elemental colors and textures should be familiar yet are somehow mysterious, their meaning obscure. The third impression is cued to size: the works are modest, one would be tempted to say domestic, in their dimensions, and relate to human scale. They may be small, miniature; medium, encompassed at a glance; or large, for the eyes to admire from a distance, or for the body to enter. Yet ultimately their scale is unimportant, for they are emblematic presences and their aura cannot be measured or contained.

A further effect derives from placement. Laib's early works are horizontal, flush to the floor. Later works—the corridors, for example—invite us to enter them. Still others, such as the ships or some of the small houses, float above us, in an essential contradiction of their identity. Inasmuch as the placement of all of these works defies logic and convention, it suggests that their meaning is clearly other.

Finally, their titles—*Passage, Nowhere, Elsewhere, A Taciturn House, You Will Go Somewhere Else, Meals for a Stone, The Five Mountains Not to Climb*—elicit the ideas of a transmutation of substance, a transmigration of meaning, or an initiatory journey.

II

Laib's latest catalogue, at this writing, appeared on the occasion of a retrospective exhibition at the Carré d'Art in Nîmes.[1] As in all the publications conceived and realized by the artist, the book's color photographs are centered in and framed by the whiteness of the page, and have a pristine presence. An opening sequence shows field, forest, and mountain scenes, sometimes including the tiny silhouette of the artist. Incorporated in fields of color, whether radiant or muted—a meadow of dandelions, a carpet of moss—he is collecting pollen. Yet this discrete human presence seems to exist in consonance with the subtle movements of nature, leaving its integrity inviolate.

The second series of photographs is devoted to Laib's art: large rectangles or tiny cones of luminous pollen, mirrors of milk slipped across a cool marble surface, roughly hewn marble houses amid small mounds of rice, dimly glowing corridors, ziggurats, or boats made out of beeswax. First nature, then art; first the source, then the source transformed by the creative act. There is a simplicity to this art, yet everything about it surprises.

Consider the use of natural materials in this technological age; the choice of generic abstract forms in an artistic period largely dominated by figuration; the ritual discipline and repetition of creative gestures at a time when few ritual practices survive; the relative anonymity of the works in an age of hyperindividualism and signature styles; and the unashamed emphasis on contemplation, beauty, spirituality, sensuousness, and feeling at the close of a century in which these notions, although they do exist, are rarely central to an artist's endeavor. The question that begs to be asked, then, is how to situate Laib and his art in the context of contemporary expression.

III

An artist builds on his or her history and experience, and Laib is no exception. Yet little in his social demeanor or in his art seems to identify him (at least superficially) with his native country—he was born and still lives in Germany—or with his countrymen. His delicate frame, his near-shaved head, his simple (often yellow) cotton clothing, his soft-spoken manner, and his ingenuous smile have earned him the epithets of a "monk" or "Western Buddhist." His art, produced by sifting pollen, pouring milk, casting beeswax, or heaping rice, reinforces the impression of a man who has chosen to live in another context of experience, and of an artist engaged in a singular relationship to the modern world.

Laib's appropriately succinct biography relates that he was born in southern Germany in 1950. His father was a doctor and a modest but knowledgeable art collector. Starting in his mid-teens, Laib traveled regularly to India and several Islamic countries with his parents. He studied medicine in Tübingen and completed his examinations to become a doctor in 1974. Upon finishing his dissertation, on the purity of drinking water, he concluded that nothing is pure, for purity is a mental concept that exists solely in the mind. Immediately thereafter he abandoned medicine and decided to become an artist, and shortly after that, in 1975, he made his first milkstone.

Laib has said that he has tried to escape the historical, cultural, and social traditions of his country—his Germanness, so to speak.[2] It has therefore been easy to assume, as the popular (critical) imagination would have it, that, influenced by his far-flung travels, he has turned his back on his northern European birthright to become a "Western Buddhist." According to this perception, his regular trips to the Orient nourish his continuing search for a spiritual absolute, distinct from the materialist and rationalist premises of Western European society; and his knowledge of Eastern religions and cultures has provided the inspiration and models for a totally non-Western art. Yet a closer study of Laib's art, its motivations and its context, prove these allegations to be superficial at best. Indeed the search for absolute truth belongs to a long German tradition, present in the writings of German mystics such as Meister Eckhart and Jakob Boehme, and is also germane to eighteenth-century Romanticism. Even the idea of the initiatory journey to a distant place is found more often in German cultural history than in those of its Mediterranean neighbors. So, paradoxically, one might suggest that Laib's frequent journeys and his immersion in Asian cultures—which, it must be said, have served to confirm and intensify his creative incentives—reveal his Northern European heritage at the same time as they seem to deny it.

The notion of Germanness, as indeed of any national identity, is an abstract and relative concept. Nonetheless, every country has a history that cannot be eradicated or forgotten. Recent history, bracketed by the memory of living generations, is easy enough to call to mind; but remote history too is everywhere present, in monuments of art, architecture, literature, and music, in religious traditions and linguistic patterns, in geography, in works of history, philosophy, and science. This explicit and implicit knowledge subtly shapes our inner consciousness. When Laib asserts that he has tried to escape his Germanness, he is presumably referring to all these aspects of his history—the immediate historical past that most postwar German artists cannot fail to address, and, more broadly, certain Western values and conventions in the formulation of which Germany and Northern Europe played a major role. It is in reference to all of these contexts, both specific and general, that, one might argue, only a European of Germanic origin would have undertaken the artistic journey that Laib has chosen.

German Protestantism may be considered one factor of Laib's heritage that propelled him outward toward the "elsewhere" of his artistic journey. He has admitted that, growing up in a dominantly Protestant part of southern Germany, he was uncomfortable with the rigors and proscriptions of his community, in which most aspects of social behavior and values were governed by religious doctrine. In his view, Protestant dogma is an arbitrary system of rules designed for the rigorous control of many human impulses, desires, and emotions. Its constraints are compounded by a denial of beauty and a denigration of the senses.

Although the Reformation seems far behind us, traces of its teachings survive in most Protestant societies. Max Weber's book *The Protestant Ethic and the Spirit of Capitalism*, first published in 1904–5, offers a chilling image of the Protestant society invented and propagated in the sixteenth century by Martin Luther, and reinforced by John Calvin and his followers. For Weber, "the Reformation meant not the elimination of the Church's control over everyday life, but rather the substitution of a new form of control for the previous one. It meant the repudiation of a control which was very lax . . . in favor of a regulation of the whole of conduct which, penetrating to all departments of private and public life, was infinitely burdensome and earnestly enforced."[3] Protestants, unlike Catholics, could not atone for their sins through prayer, confession, or a retreat to monastic asceticism. On the contrary, they would be judged for eternity by the extent to which they devoted their worldly life to labor, brotherly love, and denial of the flesh (including beauty and pleasure). The result was a standardization of society in which all activity was measured in moral terms. Hard work precluded leisure, and also bodily temptation. Art and culture were useless unless they served the glory of God. The material gain and social success to which work led were not perceived as against the will of God but on the contrary as signs of a virtuous life. Those who failed in business obviously did not enjoy God's grace.

The negative relationship of Reformation theology to images, and in particular to the elaborate paintings, sculptures, and stained-glass windows that adorned Catholic churches in the Middle Ages, is well known. In pre-Reformation Europe, these sacred images wove dramatic narratives around familiar scriptural themes, and their expressive deformations and atmospheric effects were intended to convince the viewer that he or she was in the actual presence of God's miracles. The viewer was to respond not only intellectually ("reading" the familiar story) but emotionally, reacting to the awesome mysteries of a world beyond this world. The religious rituals—the Latin mass, the sacraments—that provided the context for these images reinforced their auratic power and sustained the irrational hope of receiving God's grace.

These suggestions of divine presence, immanence, and revelation were contrary to Luther's doctrines, as were many other trappings of the Catholic Church. In translating the Bible into German, denying the cult of saints, discarding most of the sacraments (except baptism and Communion), and divesting the clergy of its functions in these ritual offices, Luther sought to establish a direct communication between the human and the divine. In his eyes, the beauty and sensuousness of sacred images corresponded to idolatry and superstition.

Stripping the churches of their images helped to destroy the mysterious and emotional impact of the religious experience, transmitted through the senses, and to expel irrational hopes and illusions of salvation. God's teachings were to be transmitted through the reading of the scriptures; the miraculous scenes of art were to be replaced by the written word.

The primacy of the word and of rational discourse, and distrust of the irrational and instinctive, have dominated Western culture ever since. We live in a society in which truth is measured by supposedly objective data. In our secular world, even aesthetic experience is generally approached with an analytical eye for formal premises, technical prowess, historical or topical referents, and perhaps moral intent, instead of with the spontaneous openness and receptivity that pre-Reformation Christians brought to the miracle of revelation.

The experience of a work by Laib, however, defies the rational or cognitive approach. Although this may be true of works of art in general, Laib's works are even more recalcitrant than most. A search for historical or social content, technical invention, or moral significance is irrelevant here: this art must be physically confronted to be understood. It invokes the power of revelation through direct perception, the victory of the senses and emotion over the intellect, the revenge of the image over the word. Laib's refutation of German Protestantism has produced some of the most unstructured, autonomous, and uncommonly spiritual images of the last decades of the twentieth century, and has reintroduced the notion of "aura" to the work of art.

What is being suggested, then, is that if Laib's creative activity seems superficially remote from the mainstream of postwar Modernism, this is not because it is fundamentally non-Western but, on the contrary, because it draws its force from a deeper subsoil of his Northern European heritage. This indeed tends to set him apart from those late-twentieth-century artists for whom recent historical events (World War II, for example), or contemporary cultural or social conditions (capitalism, materialism, industrialization, and their consequences), are preferred subjects. Laib's inspiration is both more general and more generic. In his search to liberate a natural and spontaneous spirituality repressed by centuries of sociocultural conventions, Laib is reacting not only to his Protestant heritage but to the vast movement of secularization that characterizes modern Western civilization.

That secularization reached its peak in eighteenth-century France and Germany, the period of the Enlightenment, or *Aufklärung*. Defined historically as an age of rationalism, empiricism, and scientific materialism (but also of liberalism and political emancipation), the Enlightenment placed man at the center of the universe, in control of his destiny, where previously he had considered himself subservient to the will of God. Not only Christianity but the abstract metaphysical systems of the seventeenth century, indeed all belief systems with claims to revelation and transcendence, were subordinated to the scientific investigation and classification of the physical world. The sources of knowledge and truth were now thought to lie in the natural sciences, and humanity's social order to reflect universal scientific laws. Art and literature were desacralized.

The German Romantic movement, which emerged in the late eighteenth century, was born in reaction to Enlightenment thinking, and also in response to a collapse in the authority of the Protestant Church. Although the Romantic artists and writers were mostly Protestants, they sought to transgress the Protestant code. According to Luther, the divine spirit could not be circumscribed, and thus could not be represented in visible form; according to Enlightenment philosophy, the divine spirit simply did not exist. For the German Romantics, on the other hand, the divine spirit was visibly manifest in nature. In consonance with earlier Christian practice, and indeed nostalgic for mysteries of religion that had been all but abolished by Enlightenment society, they believed that the contemplation of images would awaken the viewer to a more intense spiritual life. Nature would be their subject and their model.

In the German Romantic view, the reality determined by the presumably objective data derived from the intellect and the senses was an unacceptable representation of authentic experience. The Romantic reality was that of the subjective imagination, an inner dimension free of the externally imposed rules and classifications of analytical reason and social and historical convention. Returning to a state of *Ursprünglichkeit*, or origins, people would reconnect with their instincts and intuitions and gain a visionary awareness of the universe in its primitive clarity and sublime unity. For the Romantic poets and painters, nature was at once phenomenon and essence; it was the manifestation of the divine spirit in a perpetual movement of change and becoming, within a timeless and eternal design.

The landscape paintings of Caspar David Friedrich, arguably the greatest painter of the Romantic tradition, seem to represent, with a pristine, crystalline clarity, a vast primeval world prior to any human presence. Friedrich eliminated the accepted formulas of the landscape genre. Few perspectival indications chart his paintings; the point of view is in most cases centered and frontal; human figures, where they exist, are abstract ciphers, or foils to the immensity of Friedrich's visionary landscapes. These rigorously contemplative works are clearly something other than the fruit of a spontaneous response to a subjective inner vision—they are the products of a highly disciplined mind and a controlled execution. Friedrich sketched out his canvases, first in pencil, then in ink, and subsequently built up a surface of superimposed glazes, achieving an effect of flat translucent planes without, however, precluding a suggestion of unfathomable depth.[4] The color is unmodulated, and there is no visible brushstroke. The individual hand is deliberately absent from this creation, which reflects not only the divine essence of nature but the spirit's longing to lose itself in nature. Immersed in these vast expanses of color and light, individual existence is forgotten, effaced, subsumed in a heightened awareness of the universal spirit. In Romantic thought, this oneness with nature was humanity's highest destiny.

The Romantic tendency, with its desire for communion with nature and its nostalgia for primitive experience, is an integral part of Northern European cultural history. In the early twentieth century, many artistic movements emerged whose idealism and mysticism bore its imprint—from Die Brücke, German Expressionism, and the Blaue Reiter, to Suprematism, Neo-Plasticism, and even the utopian Bauhaus. These movements emphasized instinct and intuition, the irrational and the visionary, the inner life and "inner necessity," not to mention a belief in the vitalism of cosmic energies and in the universal stability of cosmic structures. Artists such as Vasily Kandinsky, František Kupka, Kasimir Malevich, and Piet Mondrian, to mention only a few, turned to abstraction as the purest, most immaterial manifestation of cosmic laws and the incarnation of the universal spirit. Although recent writings have pointed out the appeal of Romanticism for a number of postwar German artists,[5] Laib has rarely been discussed in this context. Yet it seems evident that his work relates to this heritage, both formally and in the intentions behind it.

Nature, in its purest and most intimate manifestations, is Laib's subject and vehicle of expression. As living, organic substances, his mediums contain the potential of the infinite in the detail, the eternal in the transitory, the macrocosm in the microcosm. At the same time that they manifest the phenomenon of nature, they have an extraordinary physical presence and a spiritual aura that is difficult to define. Laib arrives at his forms through a discipline of complete concentration in which he is no longer separate from the world of nature but a participant in its organic process. As he sifts pollen through a sieve, or pours milk and lets it flow, the work takes shape according to the substance's own powers of dispersion and coalescence under the force of gravity. Similarly, the weight of rice produces the cones and mounds in which it stands; and the resistance of marble or the density of beeswax dictate the choice and facture of their forms.

Laib's virtually geometric configurations realize archetypal structures in archetypal natural substances. The anonymity and austerity of the works summon an extra-ordinary dimension of experience, yet at the same time, these objects are of this world; they are physical, and obey natural laws. This dialectic between the abstract and the real, the timeless and the immediate, the sensuous and the metaphysical, is what makes Laib's art elusive, ineffable, and, finally, Romantic.

IV

Laib's search for a natural spirituality, a transcendent beauty, and a communion with nature, it may be argued, reflect the legacy of Romanticism, and constitute a reaction to the constraints of Protestantism and the anthropocentric positivism of the Enlightenment—all constituents in the cultural strains of "Germanness." Laib's response may run counter to the Western ideal of rational objectivity, but a revolt against the tyranny of reason, and an election of the instinctive and the spiritual, have their own rich history in European culture. Finally, the idea of the initiatory journey to an elsewhere, beyond the here and now of Western bourgeois values, also has a long tradition, and has often led to the East. To the Romantic imagination and its descendants, the East or Orient represented a source of primal spirituality in which beauty and mysticism, the real and the ideal, the individual and the principle of the divine spirit in nature, were undivided. The lyric verse of the eighteenth-century German poet Novalis is filled with evocations of journeys to an imaginary East, in search of an absolute truth. Another Romantic poet, Friedrich von Schlegel, would state, "For the acme of Romanticism, we must look to the Orient."[6]

The quest for the spiritual dimension that was attributed to Eastern cultures found an eloquent twentieth-century voice in the work of the German writer Hermann Hesse, who was born into a family of Indian missionaries of strict Protestant (Pietist) persuasion. Hesse's mature writings illustrate the attempt of a modern Western consciousness to achieve self-knowledge through an assimilation of Eastern thought. Whereas his early work shows the strong influence of German Romanticism (in his yearning for an idyllic harmony with nature), his later writings integrate Eastern myths to his search for an inner self. His allegorical tale *Siddhartha*, for example, recounts the story of a Brahmin youth who, refusing the dogma of the Buddha (a teaching transmitted by the word), eventually attains self-knowledge, redemption, and peace by observing simple people and their modest yet profound bonds to nature.[7] The moral lesson is that wisdom cannot be taught by the spoken word, only gleaned from an intense participation in the world. Siddhartha's model is a boatman, and the novella's prevailing metaphor is the river, perpetually moving and becoming, showing the simultaneous transitoriness and permanence of its eternal life.

Hesse's real and ideal journey may be compared with that of Laib in only a superficial way, but it is worth citing here simply to show the existence of precedents in German culture for the artist's orientation. Laib's early travels to the East cannot be compared to the Romantic metaphor of an exotic voyage, or to Hesse's moral parable, for they had no metaphysical purpose, but occurred as part of his normal existence—in the context of his father's annual sojourns as a doctor in an Indian village. There Laib encountered a reality very different from that of his native environment. These initial journeys made a number of distinct impressions on him: one was the simplicity and economy of Indian life, the measured gestures, the modest scale, the close bonds to the natural world. Sensuality and beauty were everywhere revered, whether in nature, the secular environment, or the precincts of the sacred. Spirituality was pervasively present in all aspects of daily life, and the same ritual patterns governed both domestic and religious activities. (As an example, the same dishes were used for meals and sacred offerings.) Laib was struck by the fact that almost all activities were performed seated or kneeling on the ground, in a contemplative, nonaggressive posture, close to the energies of the earth and on an equal level with plant and animal life. He was further impressed by the uncluttered emptiness of sacred and secular spaces, an emptiness that was nonetheless pregnant with spiritual resonance. And finally he saw that there were things in life, in nature, that were considered too fragile, too precious, to be touched.

It was therefore natural that the young Laib decided to study Sanskrit, philosophy, and religion in order the better to apprehend and articulate the lifestyle he had observed in India. His studies of Buddhism and Jainism ran parallel to his medical studies in Tübingen, and he immediately perceived the gulf between these doctrines and disciplines. Western thought, he came to believe, tends to be anthropocentric, and to accent logical reasoning, the power of the human will, and the importance of the material body. It is built on abstract systems having little to do with spiritual needs and the forces of the natural environment. Eastern philosophies and religions, on the other hand, are neither anthropocentric nor rational, but are based on the idea of the dissolution of the ego in the universal spirit that orders and moves all things. In this scheme that is traced for eternity, the physical body and will of the individual are impotent. To Laib, Eastern philosophy seemed designed to perpetuate a spiritually fulfilled, unegotistical, and fully integrated way of life. It may be suggested that his childhood and youth in Protestant Germany prepared his sensibility to receive the lessons and visions provided by his early travels to India; surely he discovered a more sympathetic worldview and lifestyle during his regular sojourns there, first with his parents, later on his own. Unconsciously at first, and then consciously, he allowed this exposure to reorder his existential priorities and to contribute to the art he practices today, an art in which an intense sensuality and an indisputable mysticism are not in contradiction.

Indian art is a traditional art based on ritual and convention. The Indian artist, like the yogi, works in a state of concentration and devotion, in order to capture the undivided principle that rules both internal and external human life. The Indian icon is a vehicle of sacred energies; it furthermore represents an ideal vision, symbolizes a permanent condition of wholeness and latent becoming. In tantric art, it is devoid of narrative and of references to historical or personal contingencies, and is often brightly (and symbolically) colored, geometric, and emblematically abstract.

Many aspects of Laib's creativity are comparable to these practices, and furthermore might evoke a tantric aesthetic. His works are without figuration or deliberately personal expression; they are free of accident, visible subject matter, or topicality; and they eschew all Western techniques and iconographic conventions. His physical activities—polishing marble, pouring milk, collecting pollen and sifting it into luminous rectangles or squares, casting beeswax—demand intense concentration, discipline, and devotion; these are virtually ceremonial acts. Laib's materials, drawn directly from natural phenomena, are common and modest, never exceptional or exotic. They are presented as they exist, as ends in themselves, unrelated to any willed human purpose. His gestures in making his works are simple, almost domestic, and show a spontaneity combining freedom and control. His simple repeated shapes mirror an ideal vision; even when they present familiar forms (houses, ziggurats, ships, mountains), they are never a likeness of something seen, but represent the abstract idea or species of a thing. Analogical, exemplary, they correspond to an idea of permanence, yet their organic life makes them never twice the same.

V

The hypothesis that Laib's activity corresponds to that of a Western sensibility fecundated by the experience and beliefs of Eastern cultures, or by a subtle dialogue between East and West, does not completely answer the question posed at the outset, of how to situate his ambitions in the context of contemporary Western art.

Laib came of age in the mid-1970s, a decade aesthetically marked by Joseph Beuys, the Zero Group, Arte Povera, Minimal art, "process" art, and Conceptual art. Indeed by the late 1960s, the landscape of Western art was undergoing radical change. In an attempt to move away from the stretched canvas and the discrete sculptural object, from representation and relational composition, from industrial fabrication and from what was seen as a commodification of art, a new generation of artists was seeking to expand the field of artistic endeavor, drawing inspiration from untapped areas of human experience.

Many American artists of this generation, reacting against the formal codes of Pop art and Minimalism, adopted the detritus of the industrialized urban landscape as their medium, which they draped, dropped, and scattered with presumably casual abandon on wall or floor. Many European artists, on the contrary, turned their attention toward more natural processes (such as exposure to fire, smoke, or sunlight) or toward organic materials (including wood, honey, and wax). Horizontal or floor pieces began to appear more frequently, in opposition to the conventional vertical (and anthropocentric) mode of art; and the use of random or natural processes began to increase, replacing the artist's personal authority and control with the innate potentials of materials—their structure, their weight, their reaction to the force of gravity. Further options included the investigation of concepts and mental systems through diagrams, charts, maps, words, numbers, and other schematic markings or signs. It was a widely shared belief among artists that process should take precedence over the desire for a finished object, "attitude" over "form."[8] Although these artists differ from Laib in their intentions, their "expanded field"[9] of art produced a context that was hospitable to his work, and that remains vital today.

Laib's avowed interest in Beuys (which should not, however, be overemphasized) is understandable. Beuys's conviction that the vocation of art was to combat rationalism and materialism, his belief that art, like nature, commanded deep spiritual and therapeutic powers, his concept of the artist as a visionary—all this continued the discourse of Romanticism, at the same time that Beuys distanced himself from the canons of historical

Modernism. His attitude to materials was central to his project: his chosen mediums were not just vehicles for content but its embodiment. Choosing elemental substances such as iron, felt, fat, honey, and wax, he drew on their structural morphology, contained energy, and latent powers of metamorphosis in their raw state, and underscored their mythical potential in a modern social context. Art for Beuys had a timeless spiritual dimension. It also had a sociopolitical objective: to change the world. The role of the artist was that of a teacher or mentor, transmuting matter into an experience of the spirit, and rational objectivity into irrational belief.

Beuys's message to the generations that followed him was potent and pervasive. Yet despite superficial analogies, Laib's methods and effects are extremely different from his. Beuys's art, and the performancelike works he called "actions," were often presented in scenarios that required a captive audience, whereas Laib's works propose a solitary, contemplative participation. Beuys's charismatic persona was central to his work; Laib's persona is near invisible. Beuys's objects were woven into narrative accounts and performances, from which they survived as the residue. Laib's processes of making are private; there are no public demonstrations. The photographs of his process found in his catalogues are the only visual testimony of how the pieces are made. Beuys's choices of materials were said to relate to his personal history (whether real, legendary, or mythic), and it follows that his pieces carry the imprint of their maker, his biography, his ideas, his hand, his passage; Laib's materials are impersonal, generic, universal, and his works are in a sense anonymous—indeed anyone can make them. Their aura is not defined by the individual who made them, but generated by the organic substance itself. Yet a general culture connects the two artists, reflected in the deliberate choice of raw or organic materials to serve the redemptive vocation of art, and in an attitude: an open-ended artistic (and even existential) process that creates spiritually charged artistic forms.

Interestingly, Beuys's maxim, "Every man an artist," appears less appropriate to his own endeavor than to Laib's. Because intrinsic to Laib's design is that others must participate in the life of the work. During the course of an exhibition, the pollen gradually disperses with the movement of the air, and must be swept up and laid down again. The milk, so as not to sour and turn acid, must be emptied daily from its marble slab and replaced, poured with the same control and dedication that the artist originally displayed. One is reminded of the activity of the gardener who, with simple yet disciplined gestures, rakes the sand in ripples around a Zen temple, participating in the daily maintenance of a symbolic purity. So that whereas Beuys's objects, without the magic of his personal touch, seem to lose some of their metaphysical charge, Laib's organic forms and textures degenerate according to each element's life cycle but then are born again, authentic and pristine, though the work is executed by someone else.

VI

During his many travels in Europe, Asia, and America, Laib has seen pools of water appear in the desert after a sudden torrential rain, fragile, fleeting, miraculously manifesting and as miraculously gone, evaporated into the scorched sand. He has experienced the discovery of a clearing in the forest, its bright illumination cradled in the dark underbrush. Water in a waterless land, a velvet carpet in a wilderness, these scenes appear as miracles of nature, places of sustenance and relief in an otherwise rude environment.

Pollen and milk we cannot touch, infinitesimal mountains we cannot climb, passages and houses we cannot enter, ships in which we cannot sail; these modest propositions address neither the physical body nor the rational mind but the inner spirit, soliciting us to pause before these images, to take stock of the world and ourselves and, ultimately, to find sustenance and relief. They invite us to journey outward, and inward, to another dimension of experience, another place, not so much exotic as familiar—that place so aptly described by the German Romantic poet Heinrich von Kleist as "the locked and barred paradise to which we can never return except, perhaps, from behind, after a laborious journey around the world."[10]

NOTES

1. *Wolfgang Laib, Ailleurs*, exh. cat. (Nîmes: Carré d'Art, Musée d'art contemporain de Nîmes, 1999).

2. See for example Clare Farrow, *Wolfgang Laib: A Journey* (Ostfildern-Ruit: Cantz, 1996), p. 64; Laib has also remarked to this effect in many conversations with the present author.

3. Max Weber, *The Protestant Ethic and the Spirit of Capitalism*, 1904–5 (London and New York: Routledge, 1996), p. 36.

4. See Wieland Schmied, "Faces of Romanticism: Friedrich, Delacroix, Turner, Constable," in *The Romantic Spirit in German Art 1790–1990*, exh. cat. (Edinburgh: Scottish National Gallery of Modern Art, and London: Hayward Gallery, South Bank Center, 1994), pp. 31–32.

5. Several essays in *The Romantic Spirit in German Art 1790–1990* are devoted precisely to this theme.

6. Friedrich von Schlegel, quoted in ibid., p. 30.

7. Hermann Hesse, *Siddhartha*, 1922, Eng. trans. Joachim Neugroschel (New York: Penguin Putnam Inc., 1999). Begun in 1919, first published in 1922; republished with three other novellas in the volume *The Way Within* in 1933.

8. I refer to the title of Harald Szeemann's landmark exhibition *When Attitudes Become Form*, at the Kunsthalle Bern in 1969.

9. The term was coined by Rosalind E. Krauss in her essay "Sculpture in the Expanded Field," collected in Krauss, *The Originality of the Avant-Garde and Other Modernist Myths* (Cambridge, Mass.: The MIT Press, 1985).

10. Heinrich von Kleist, as paraphrased in Angelika Wesenberg, "Origin and Archetype," in *The Romantic Spirit in German Art*, p. 115.

CATALOGUE

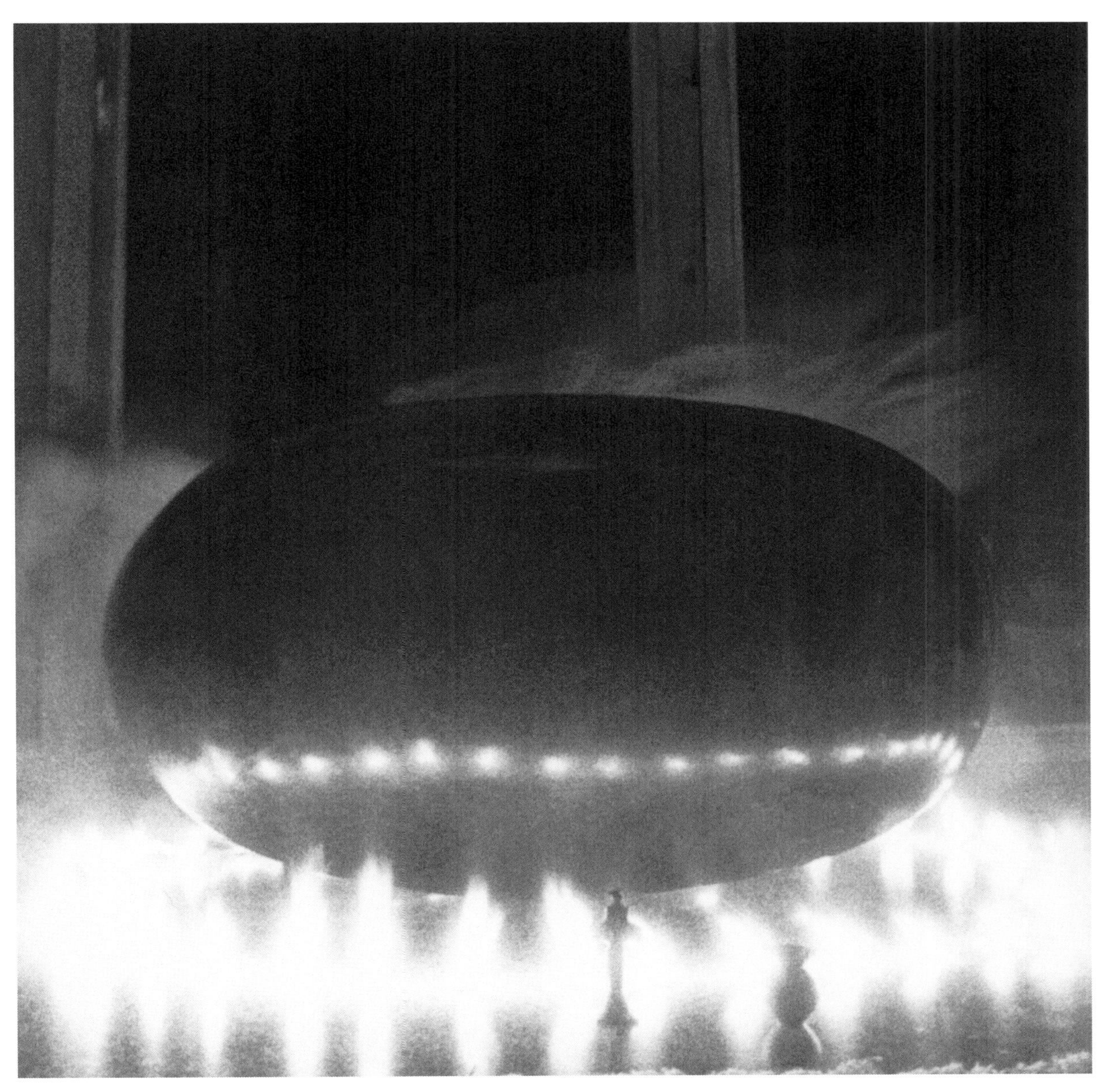

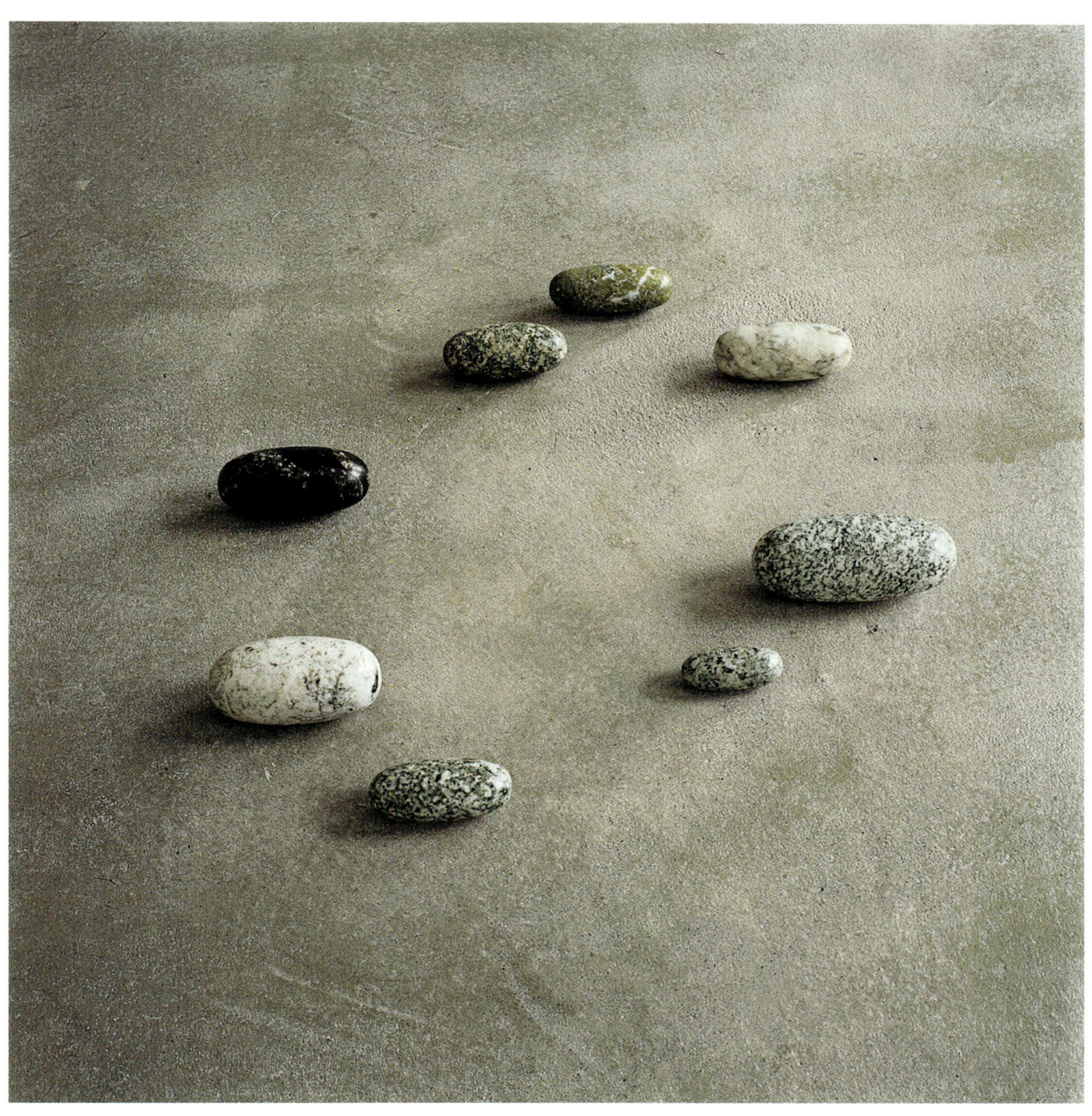

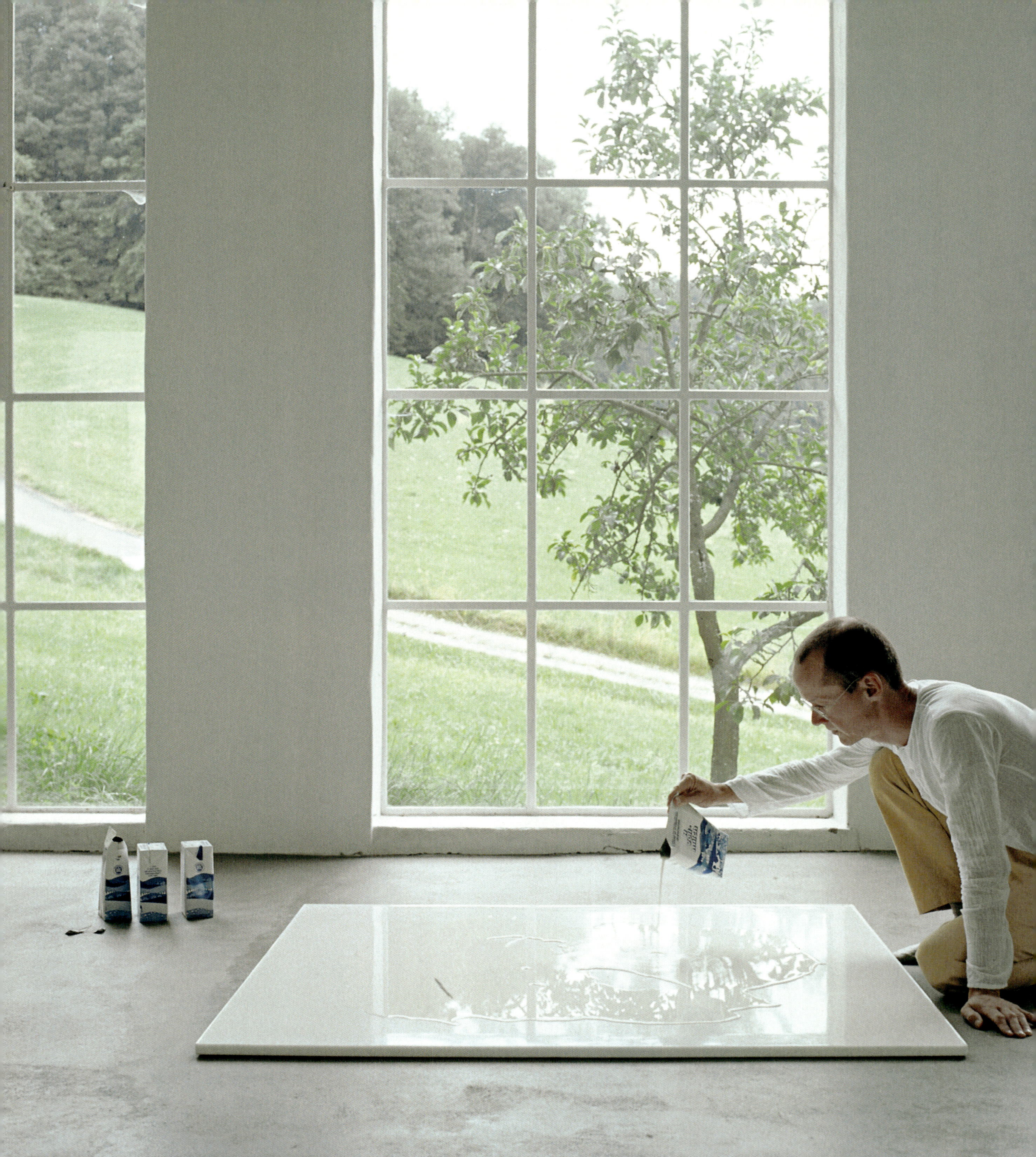

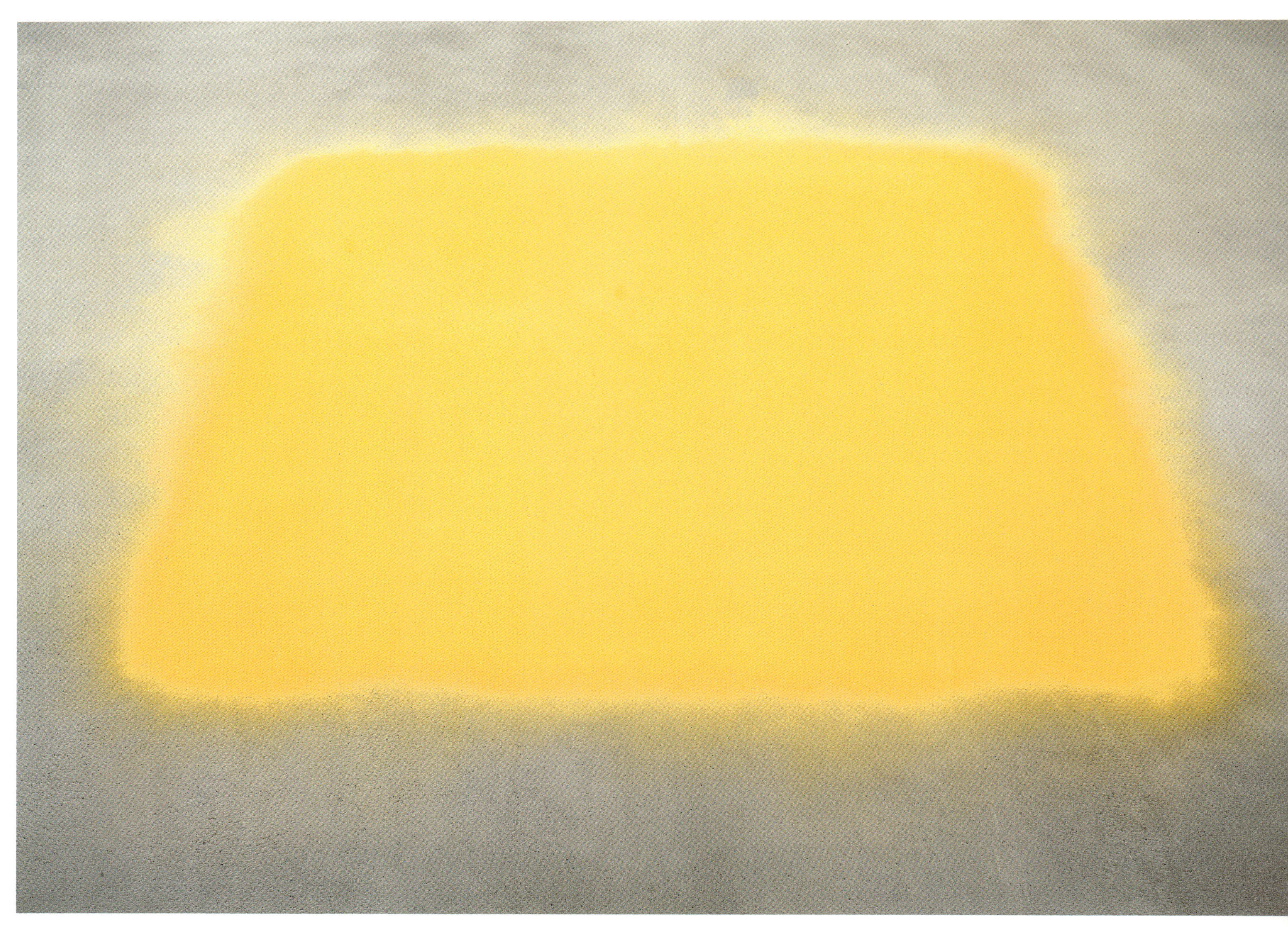

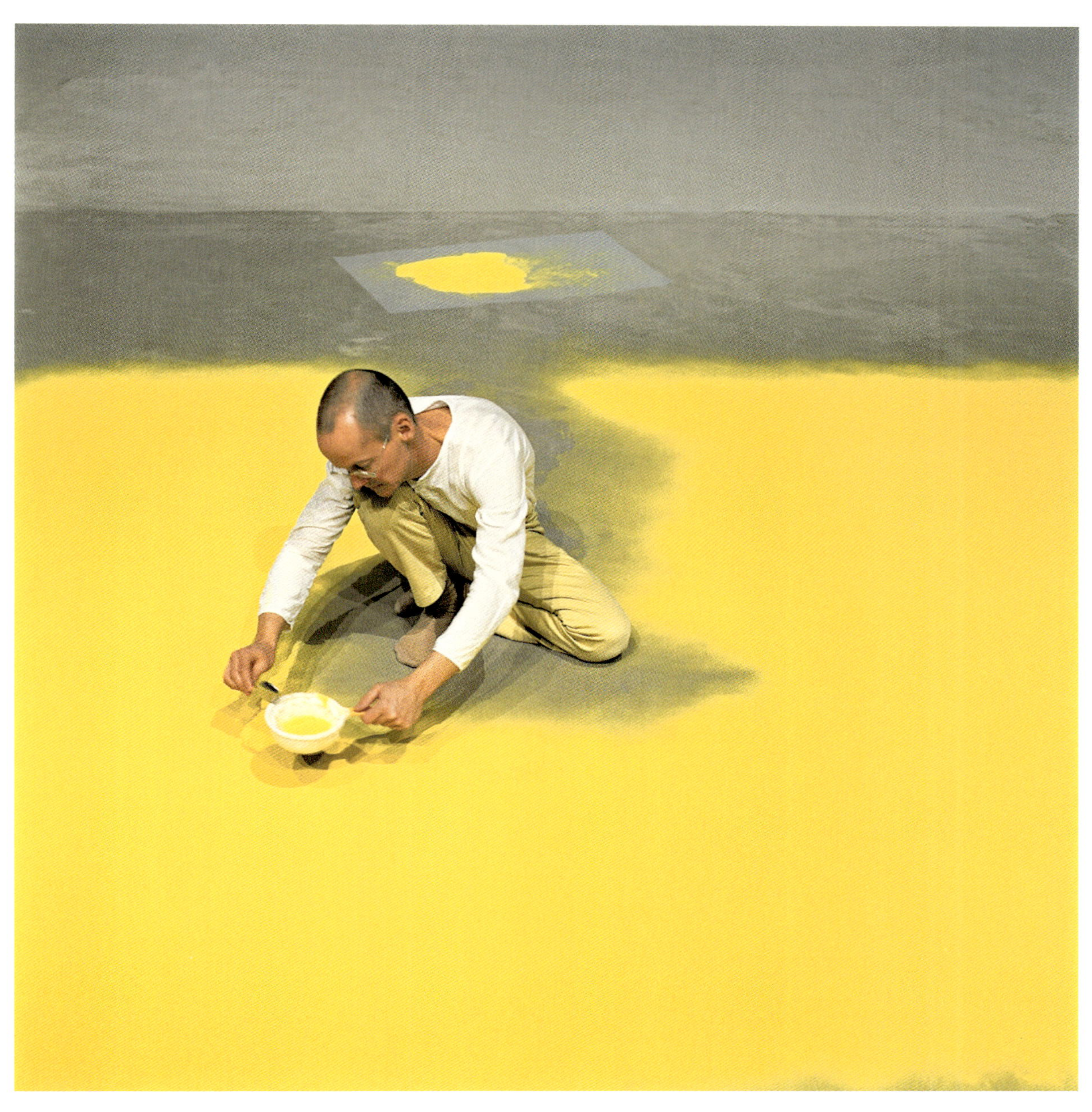

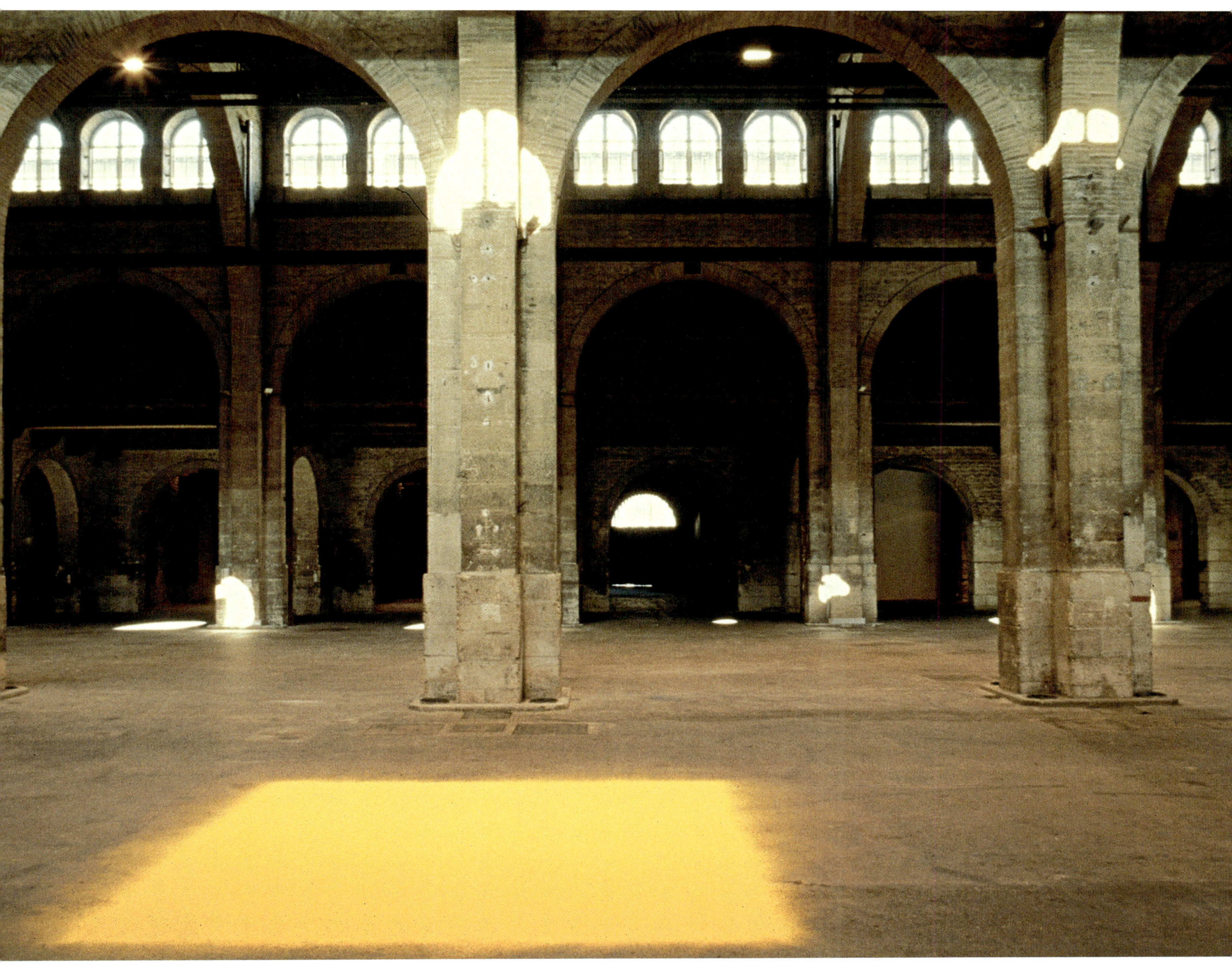

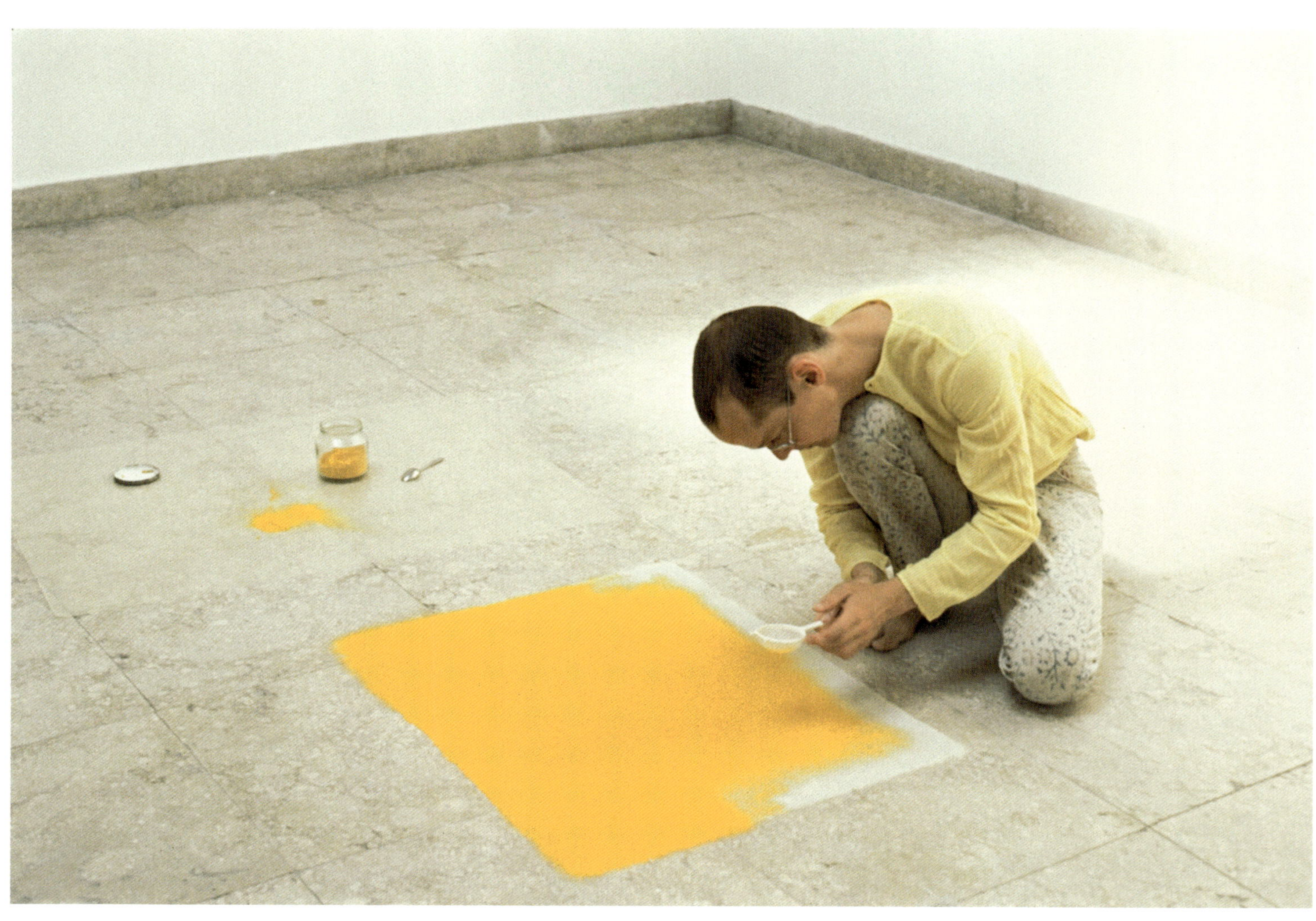

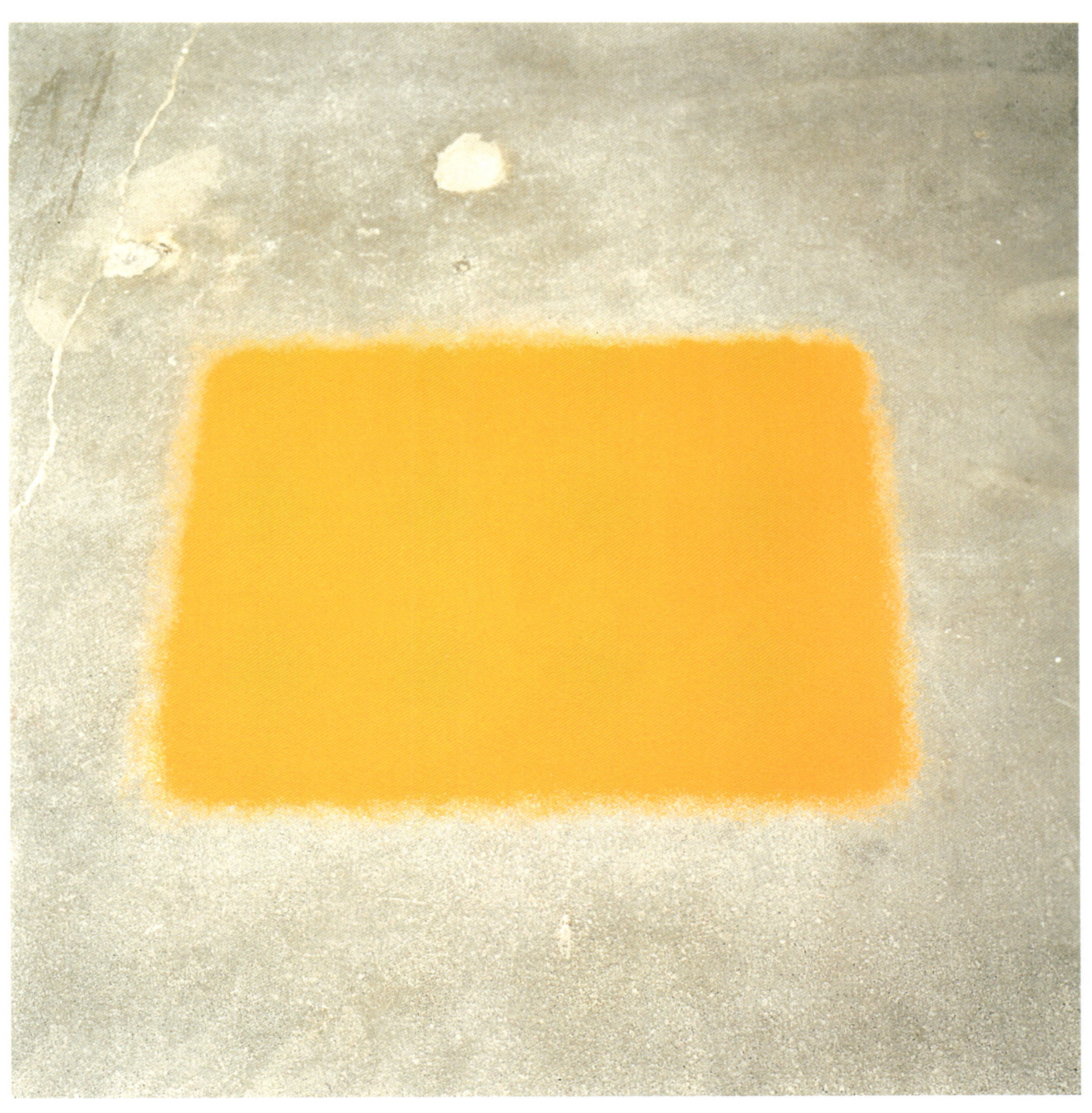

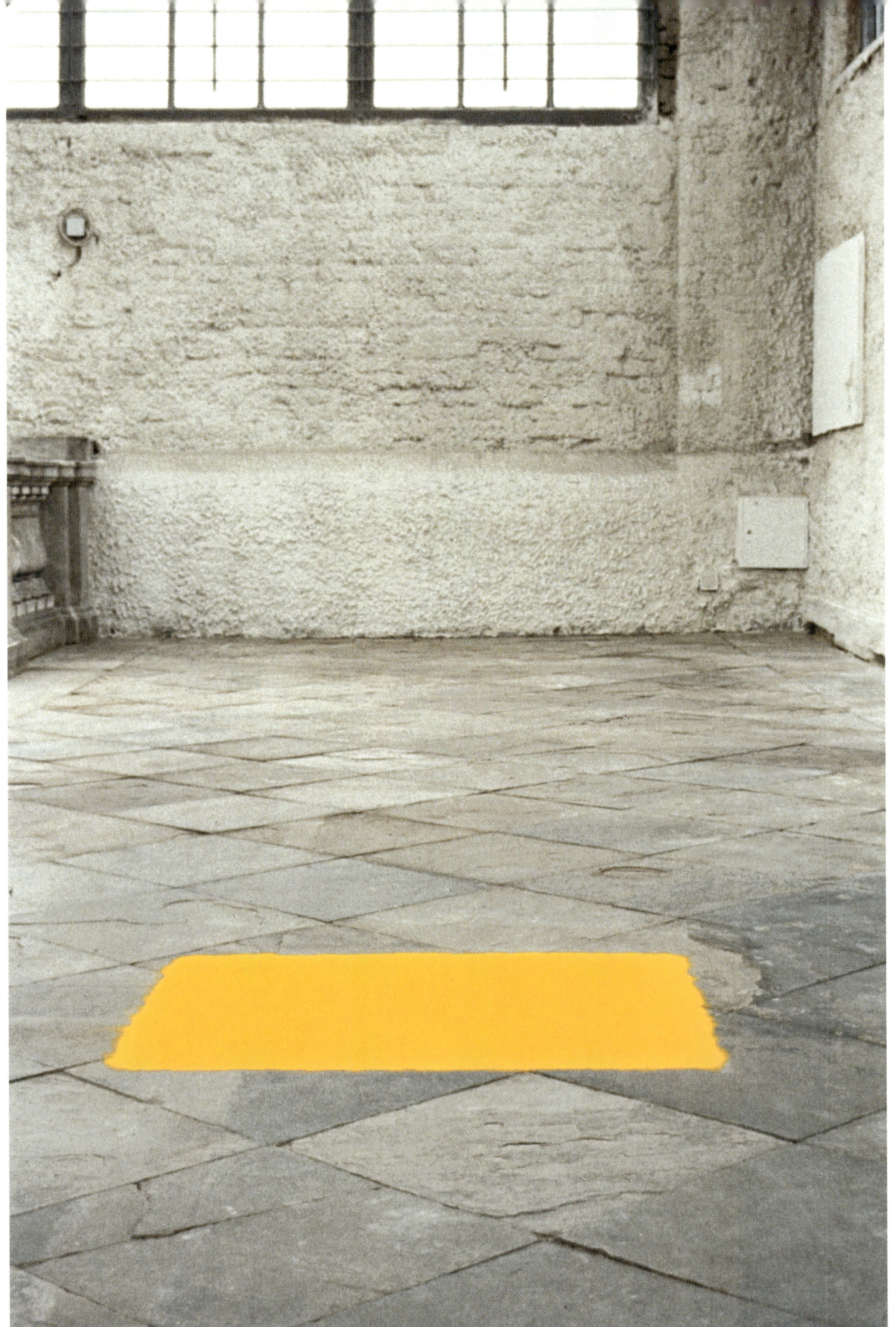

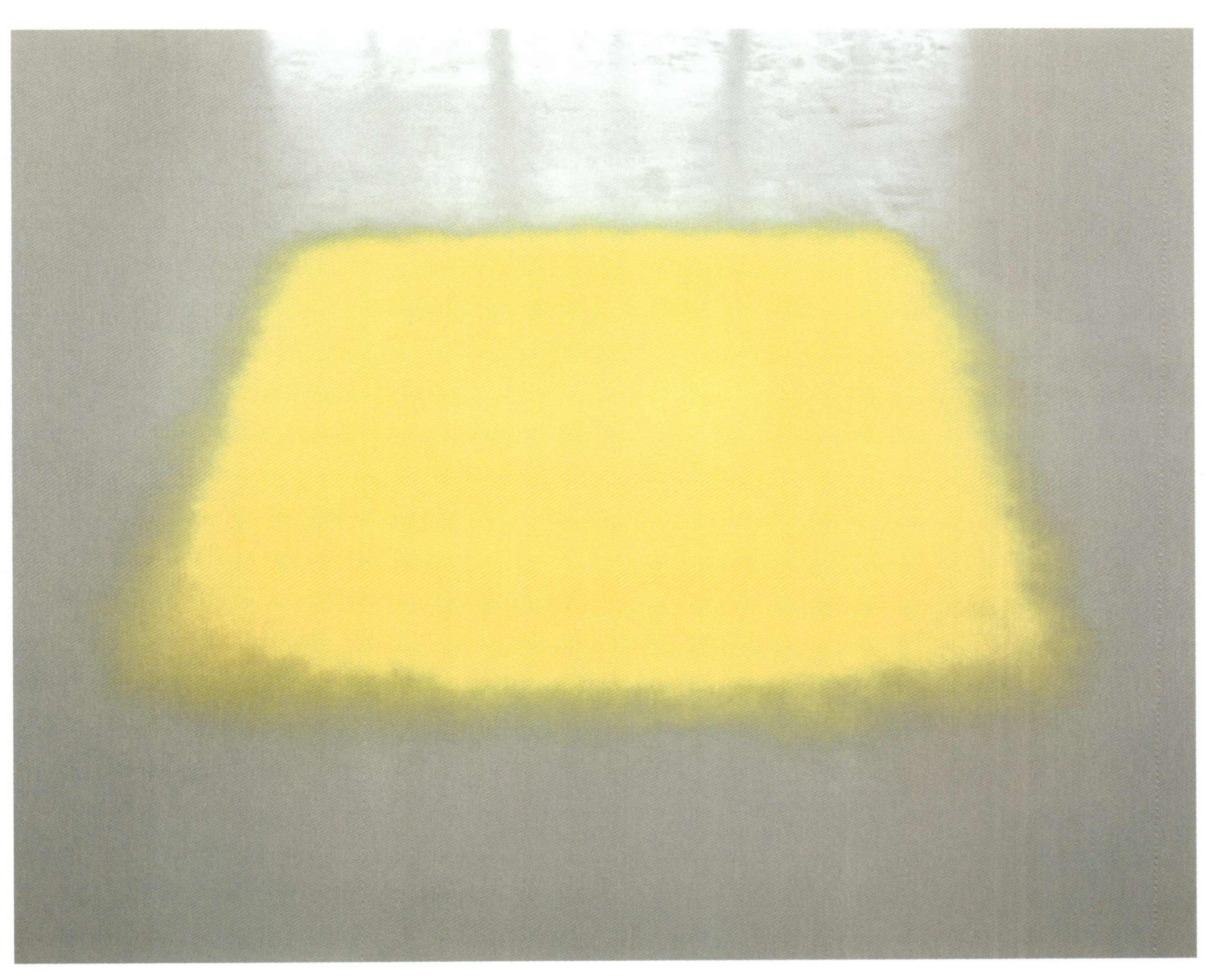

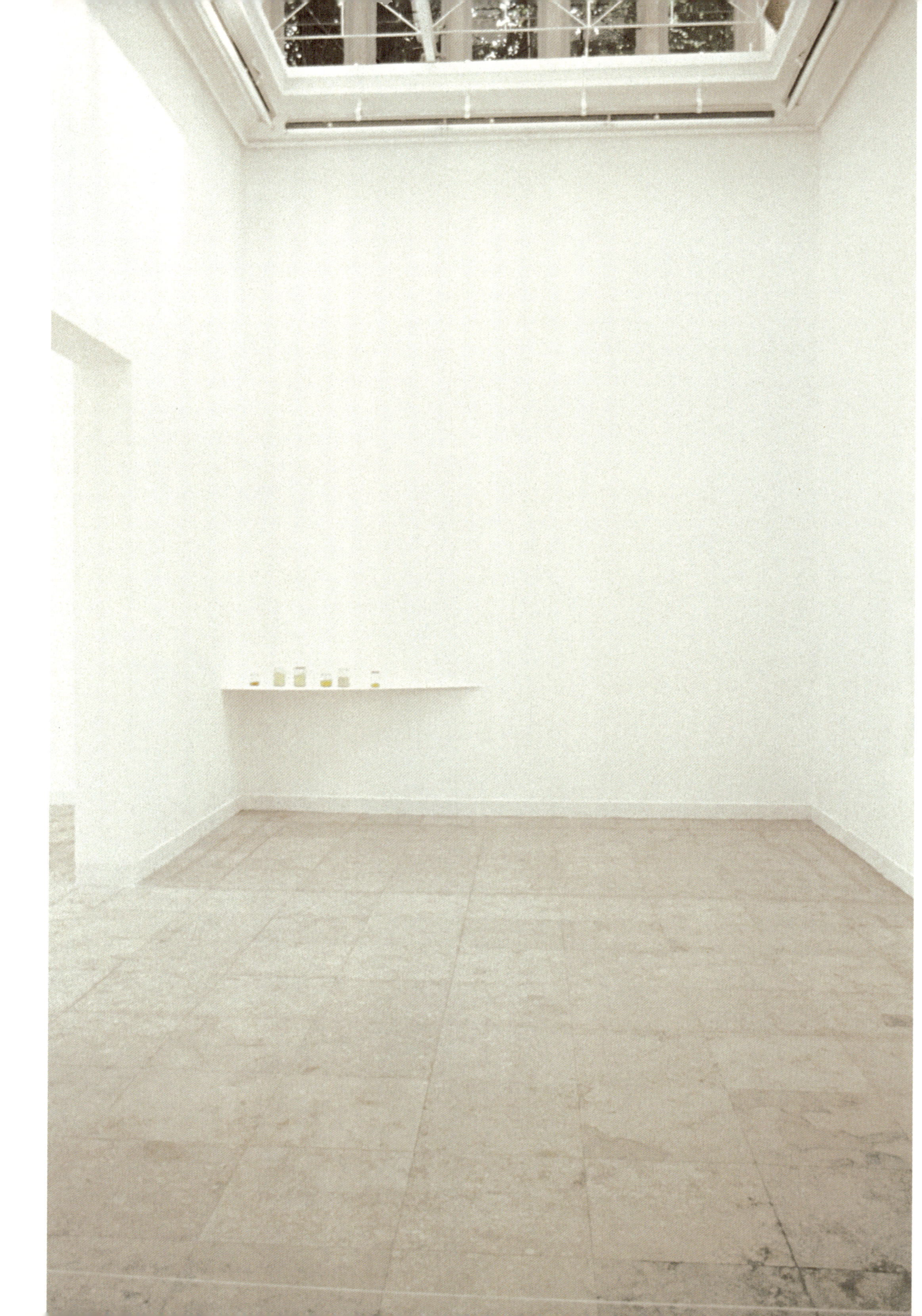

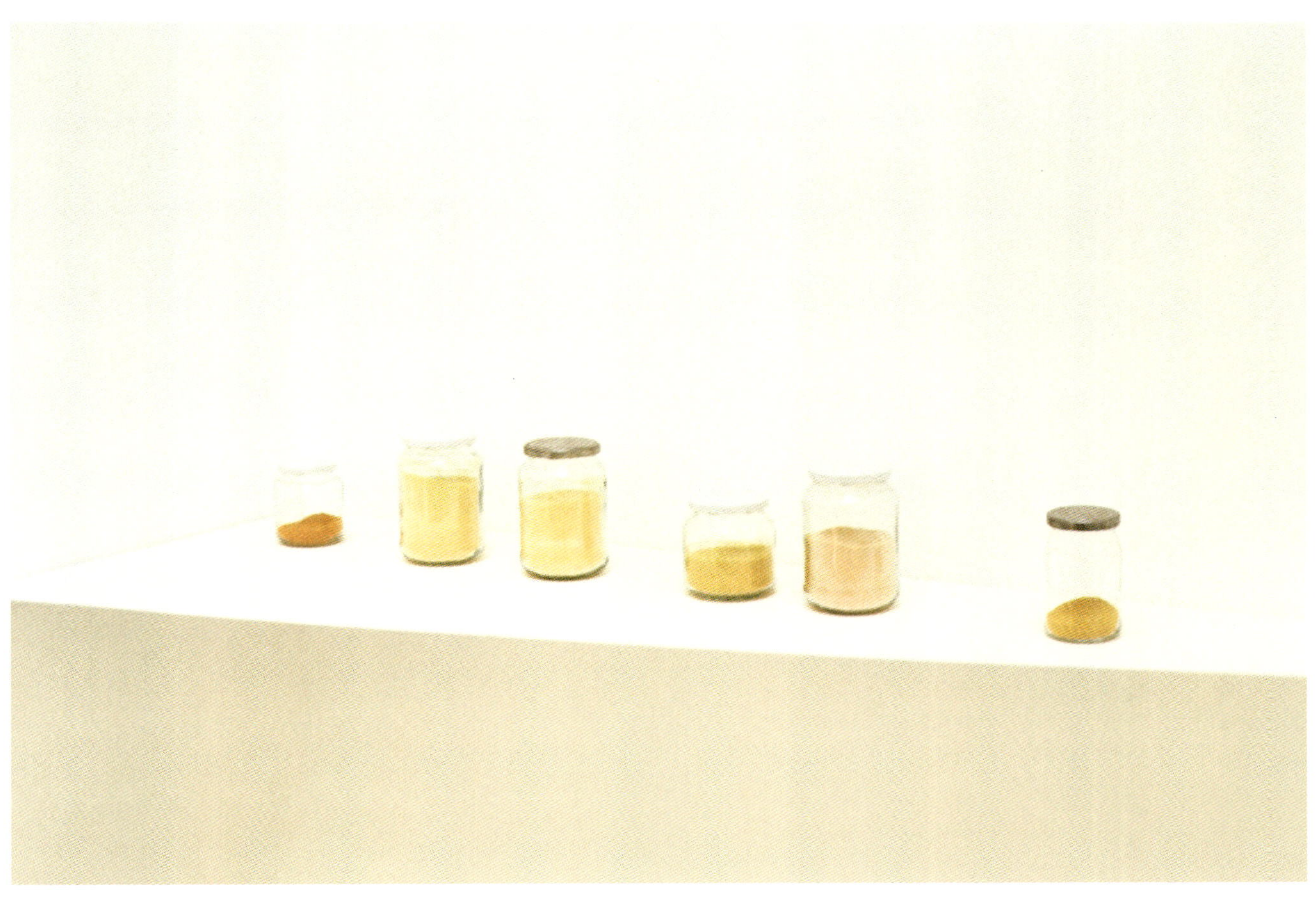

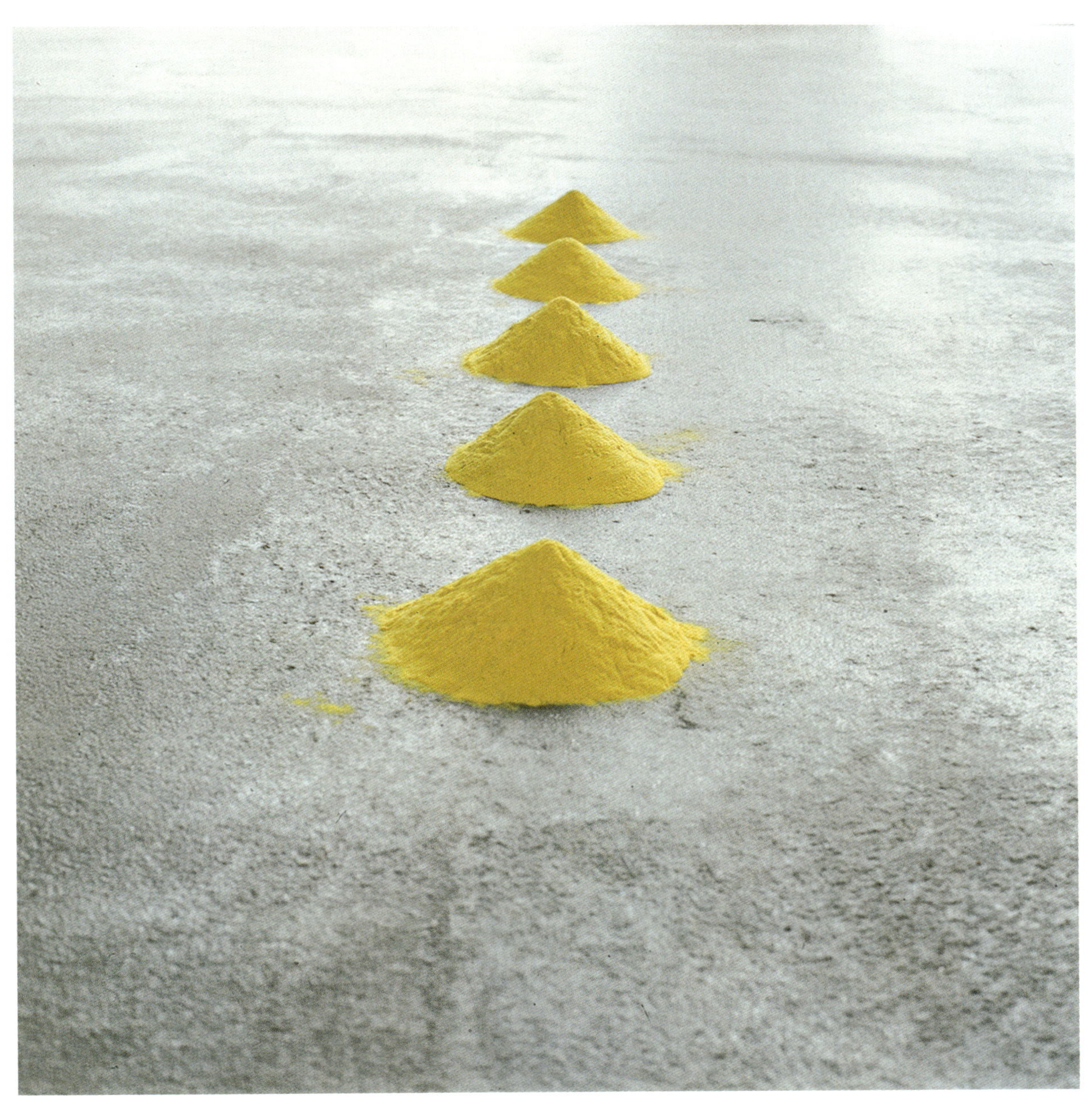

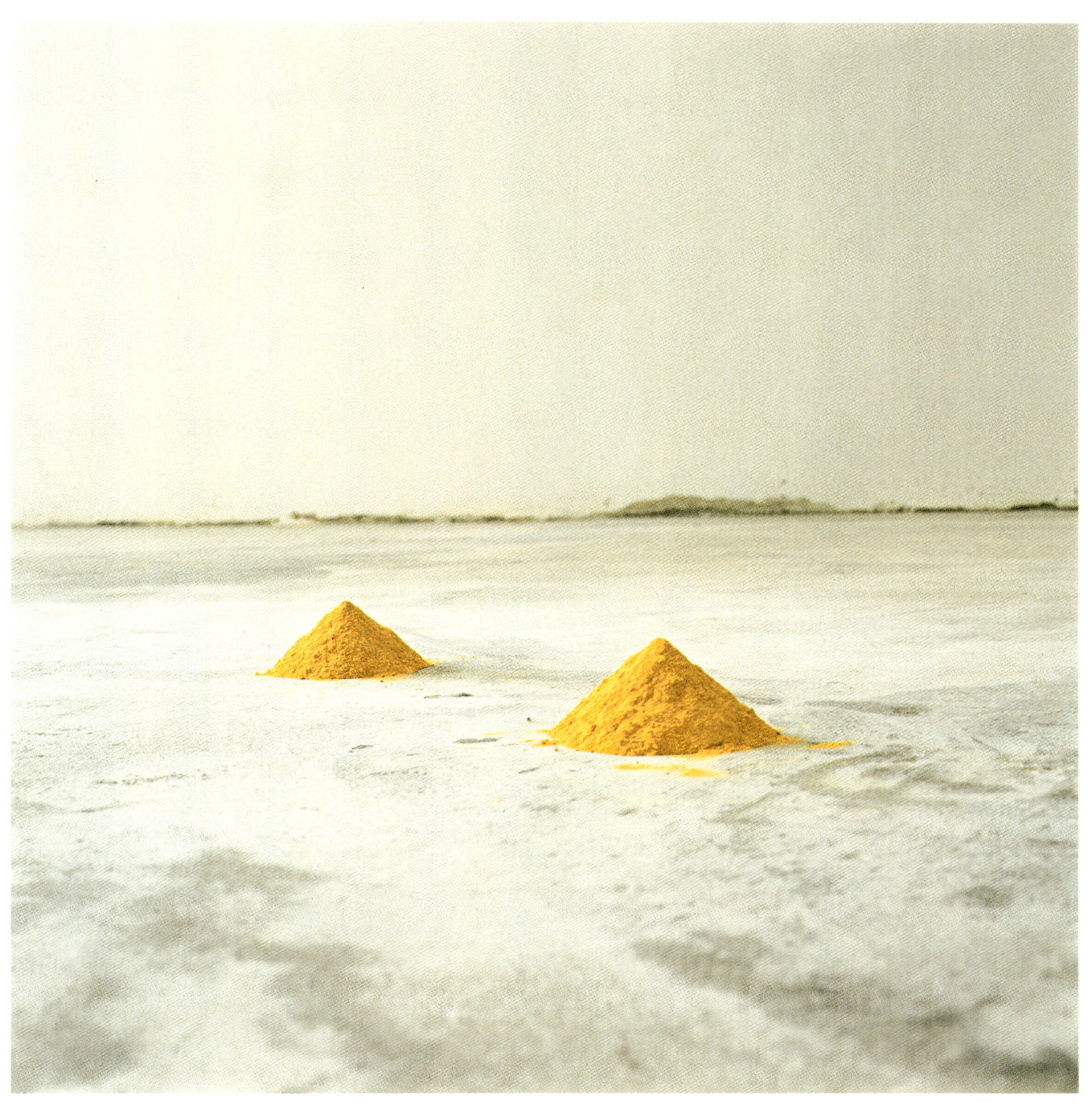

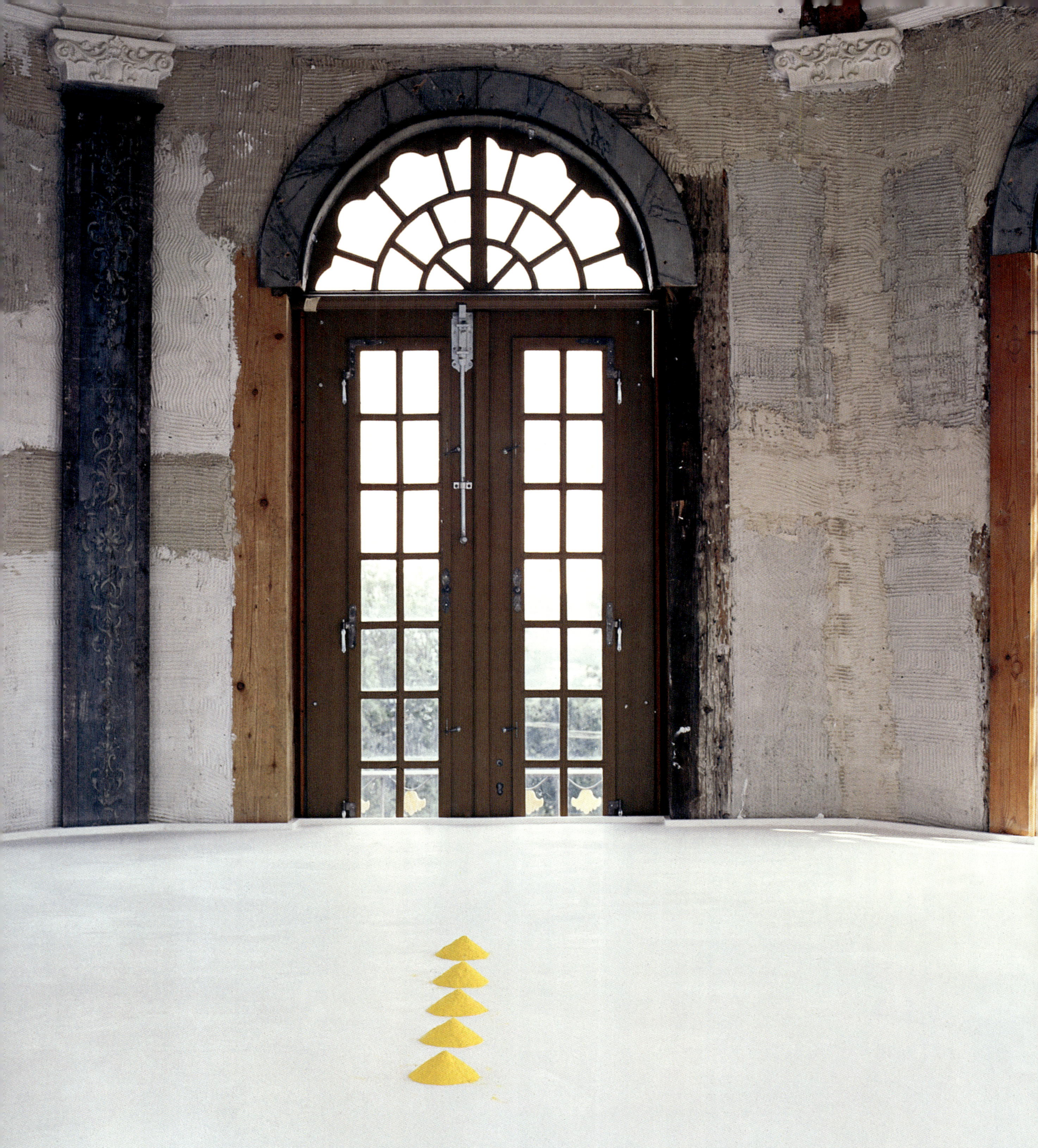

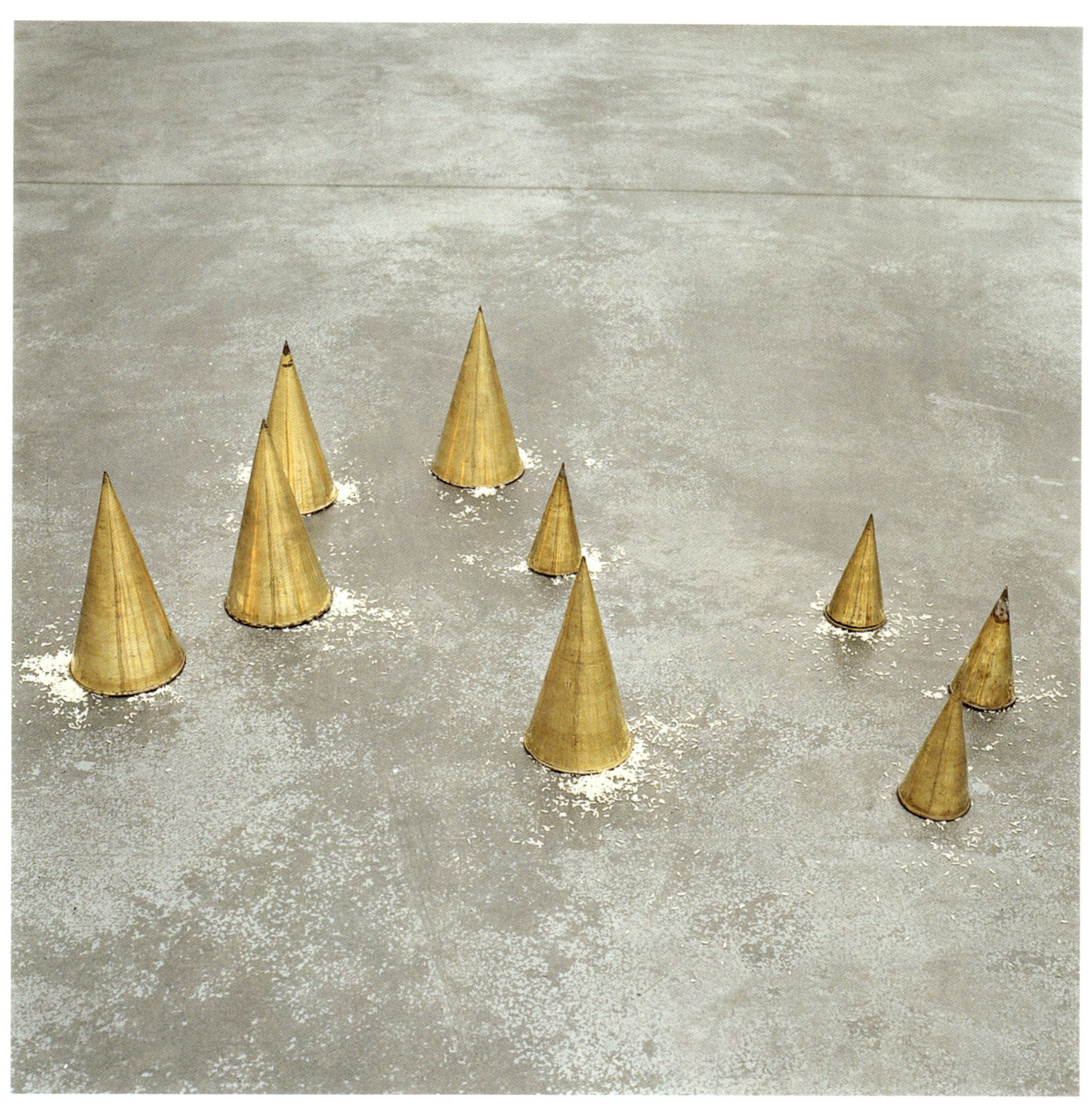

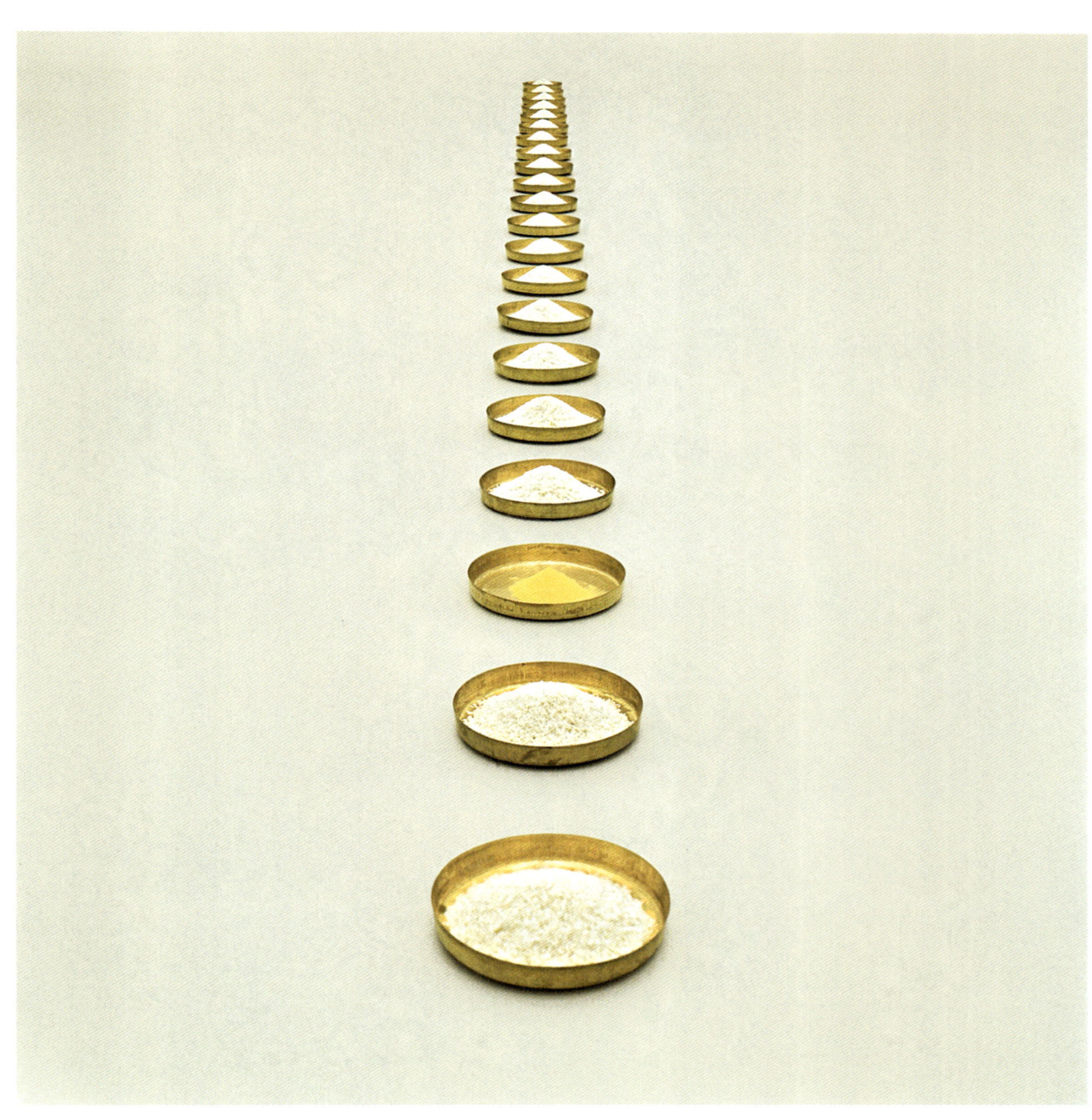

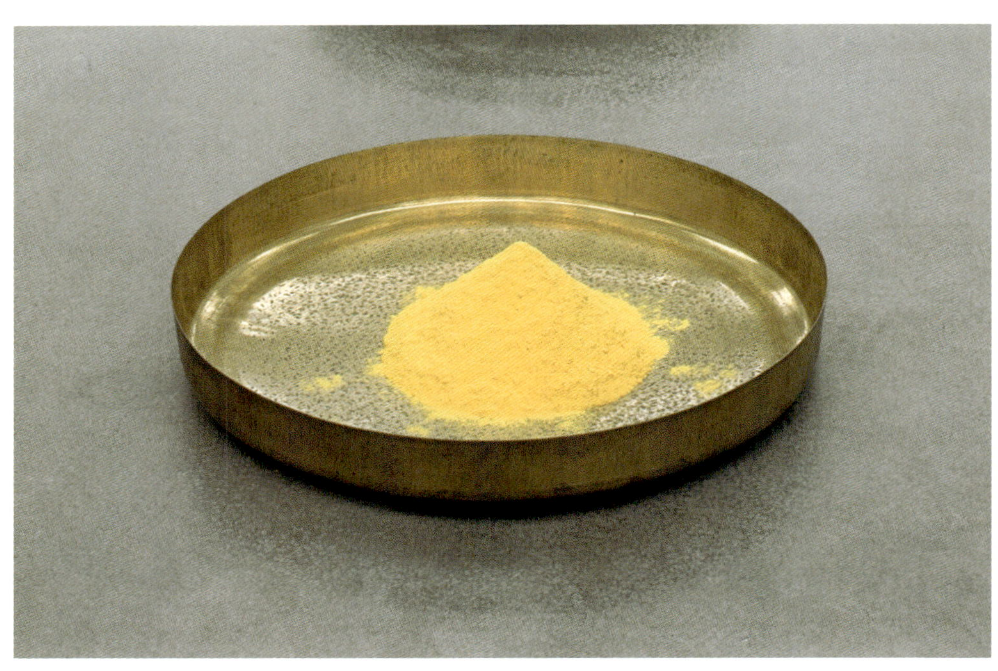

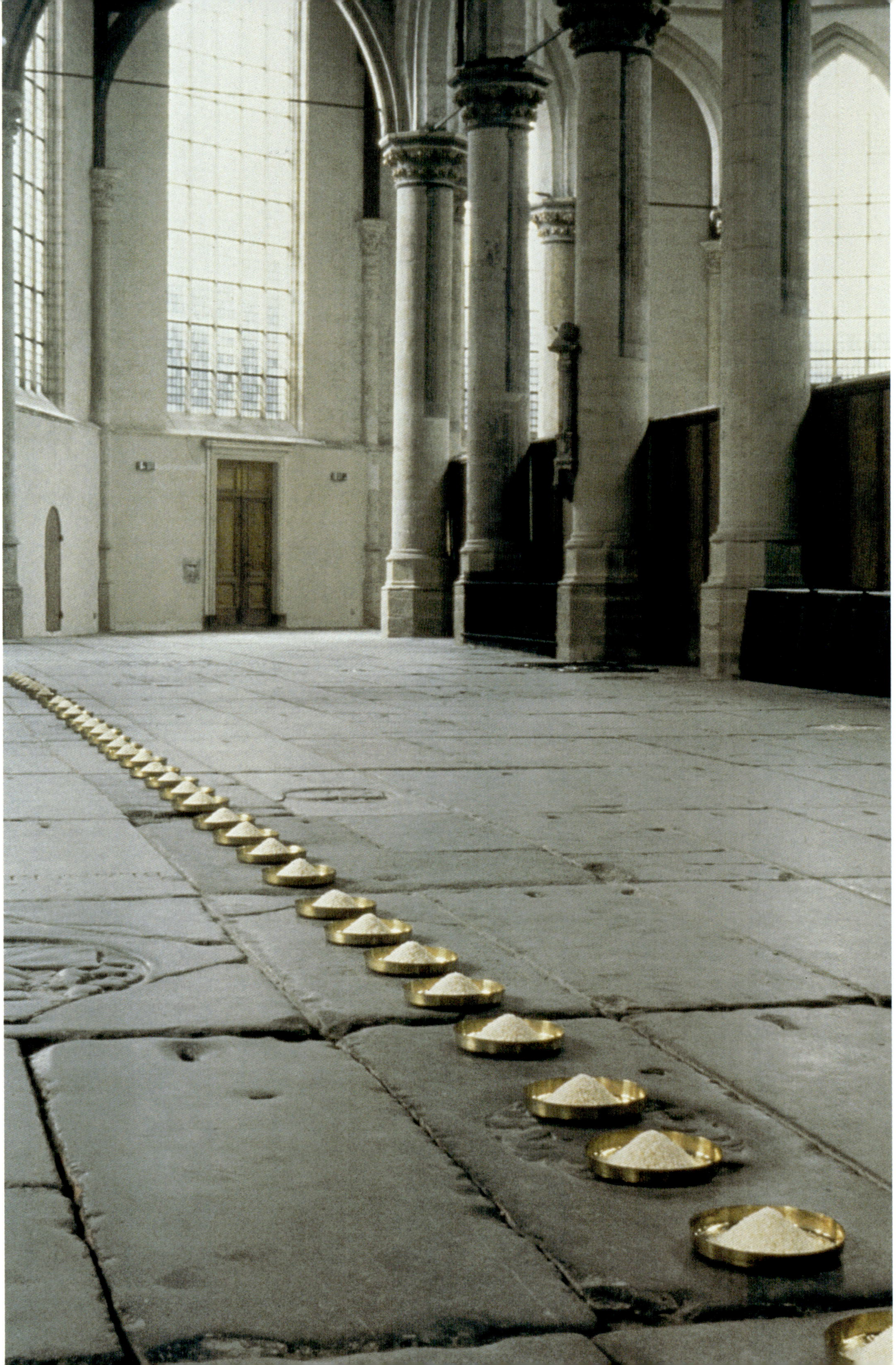

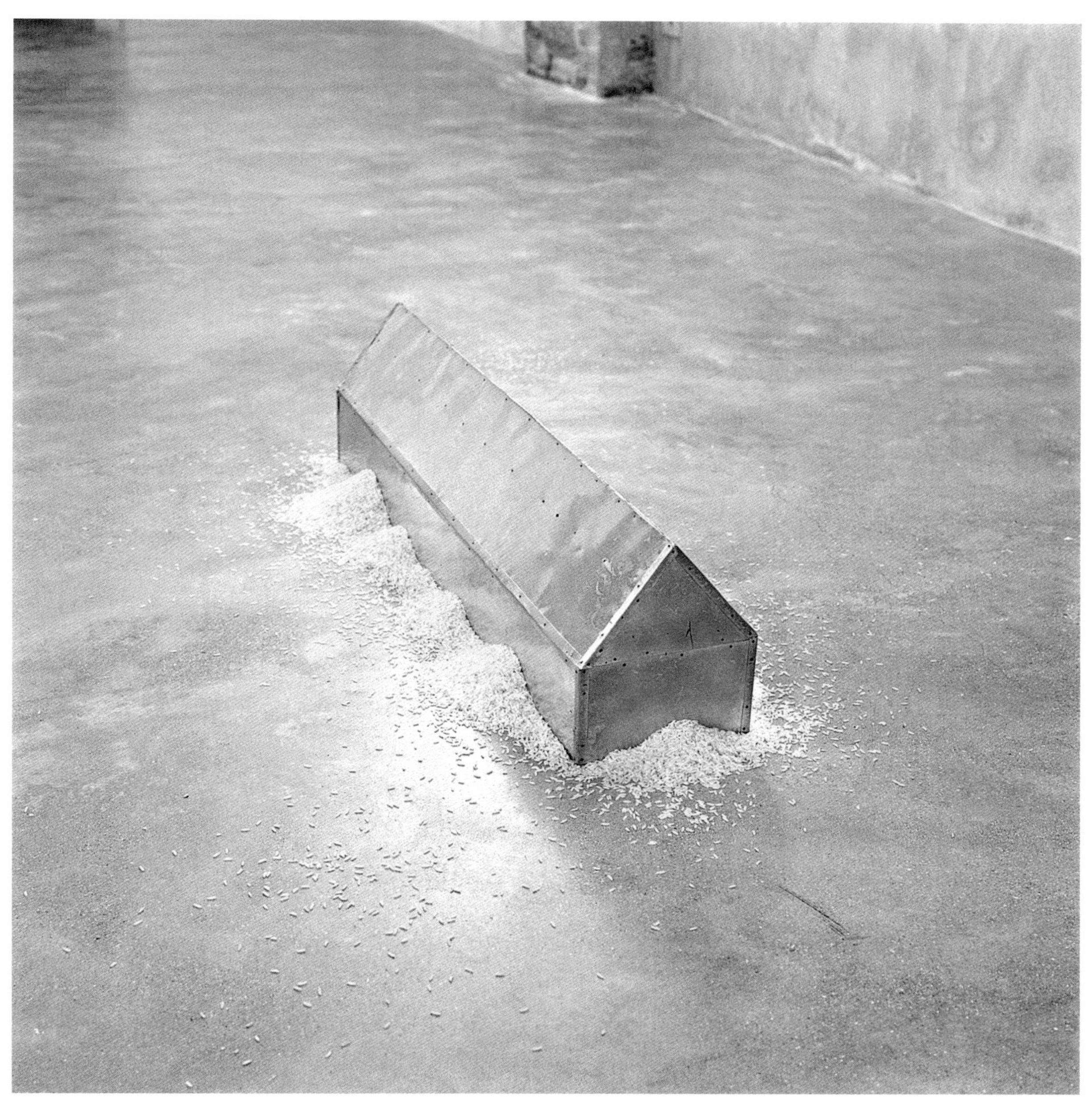

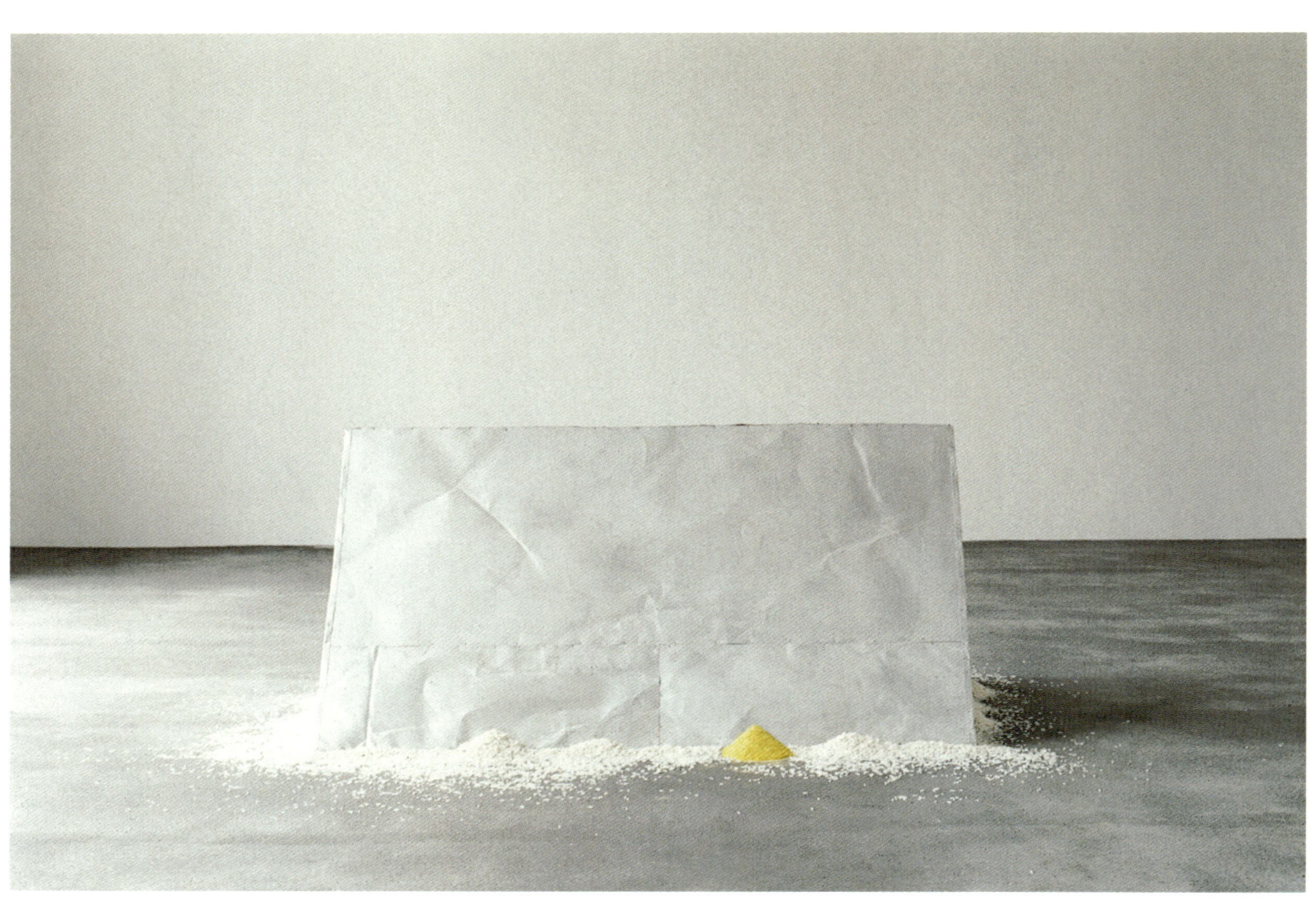

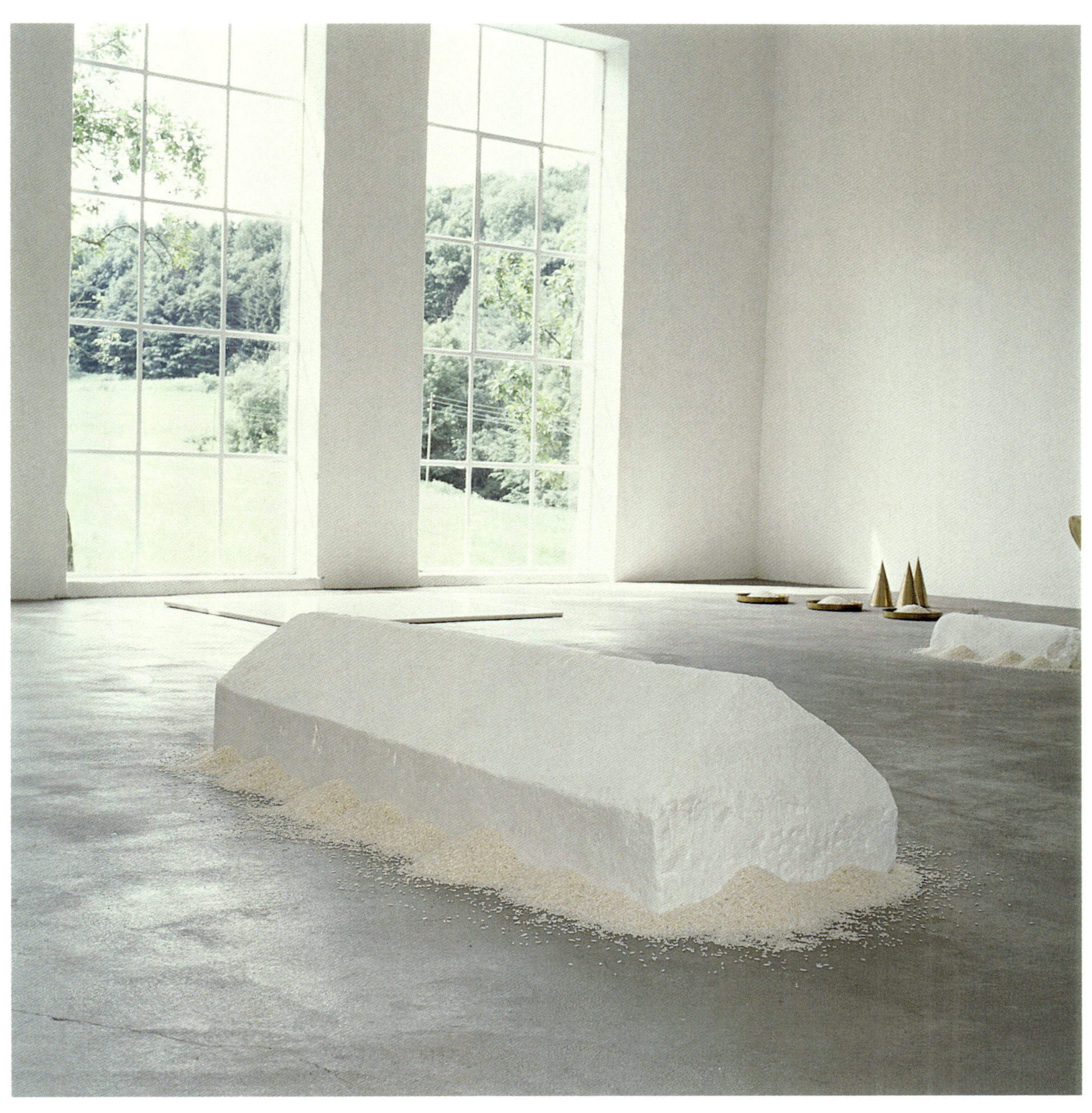

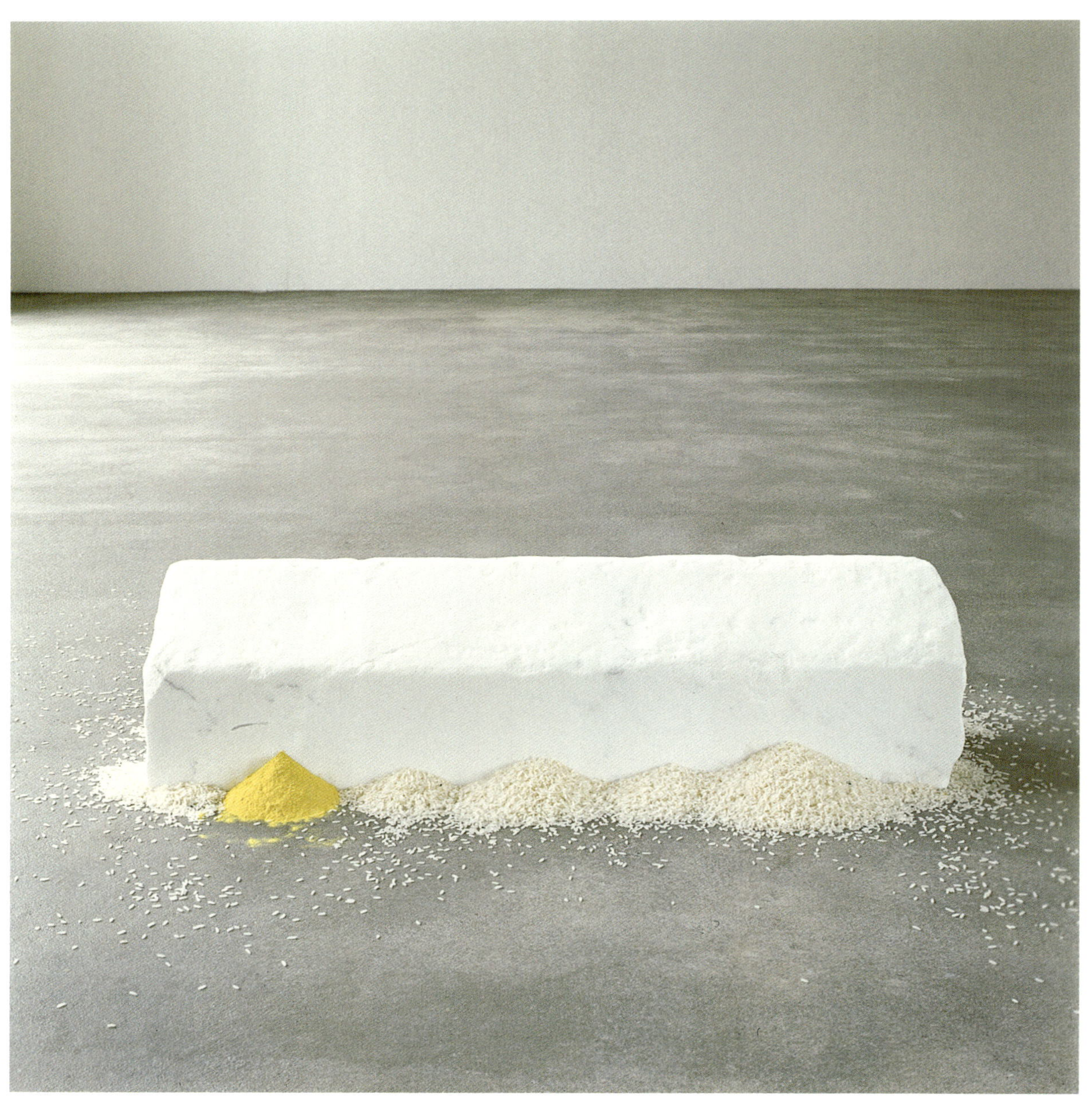

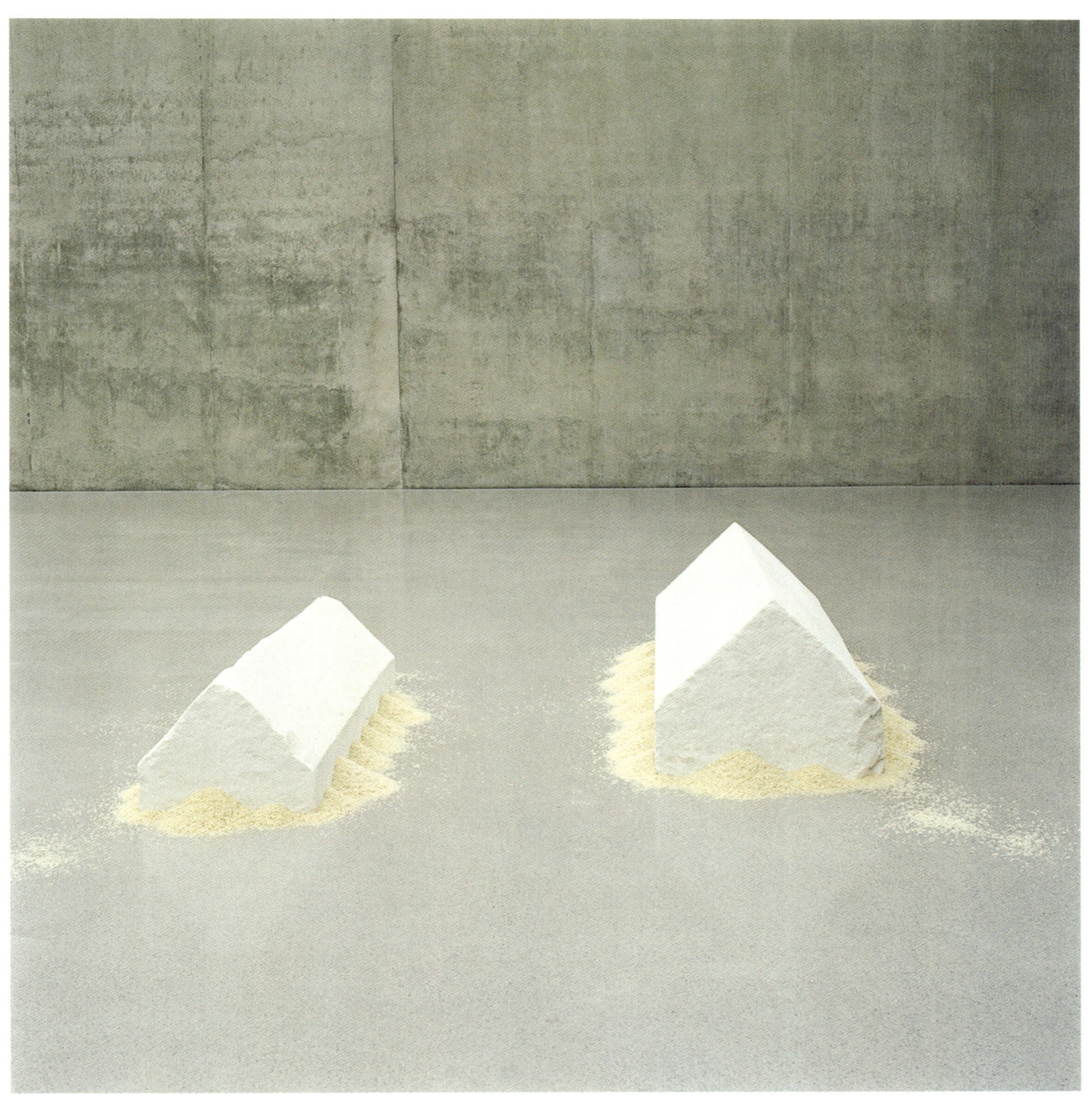

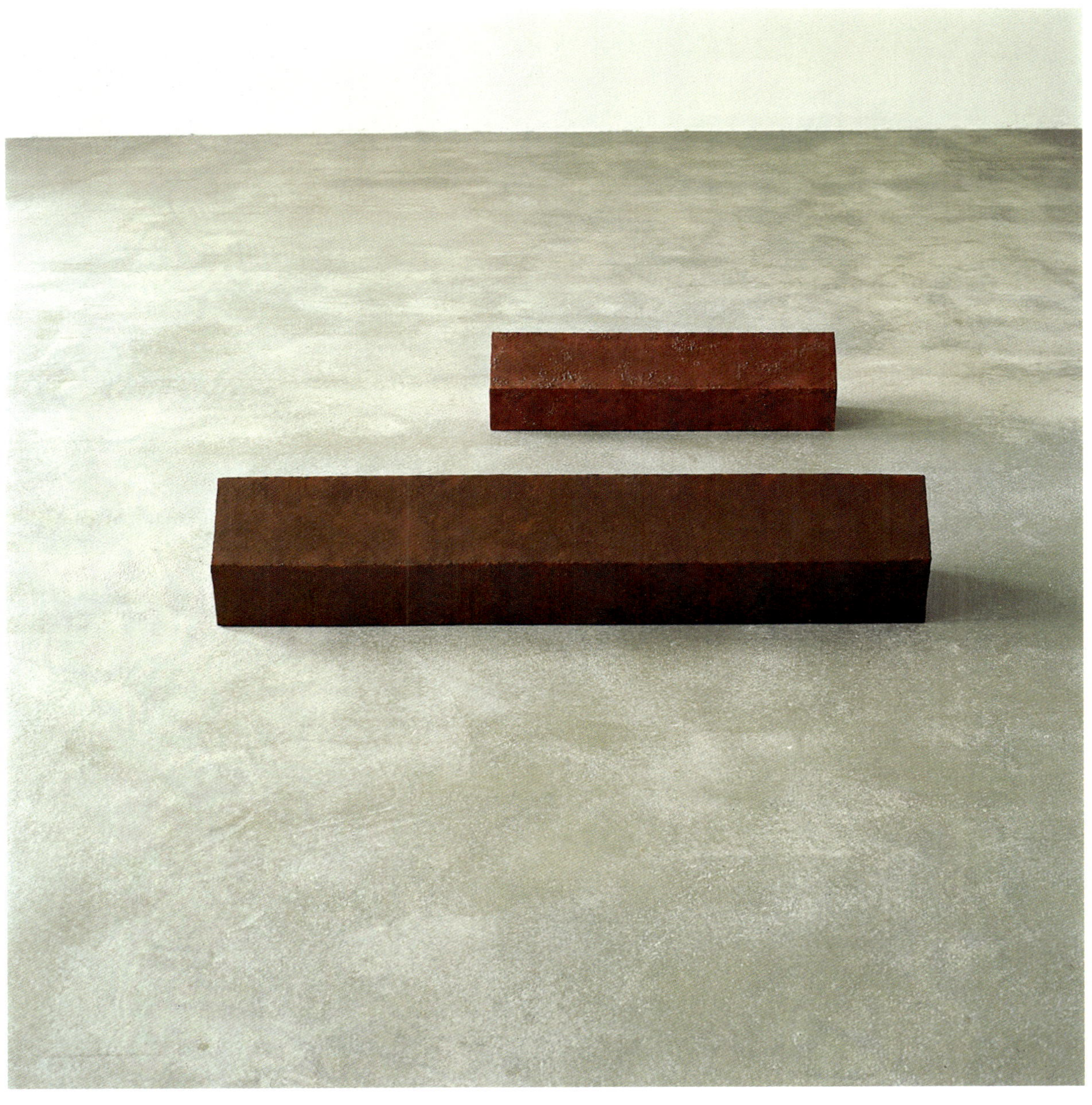

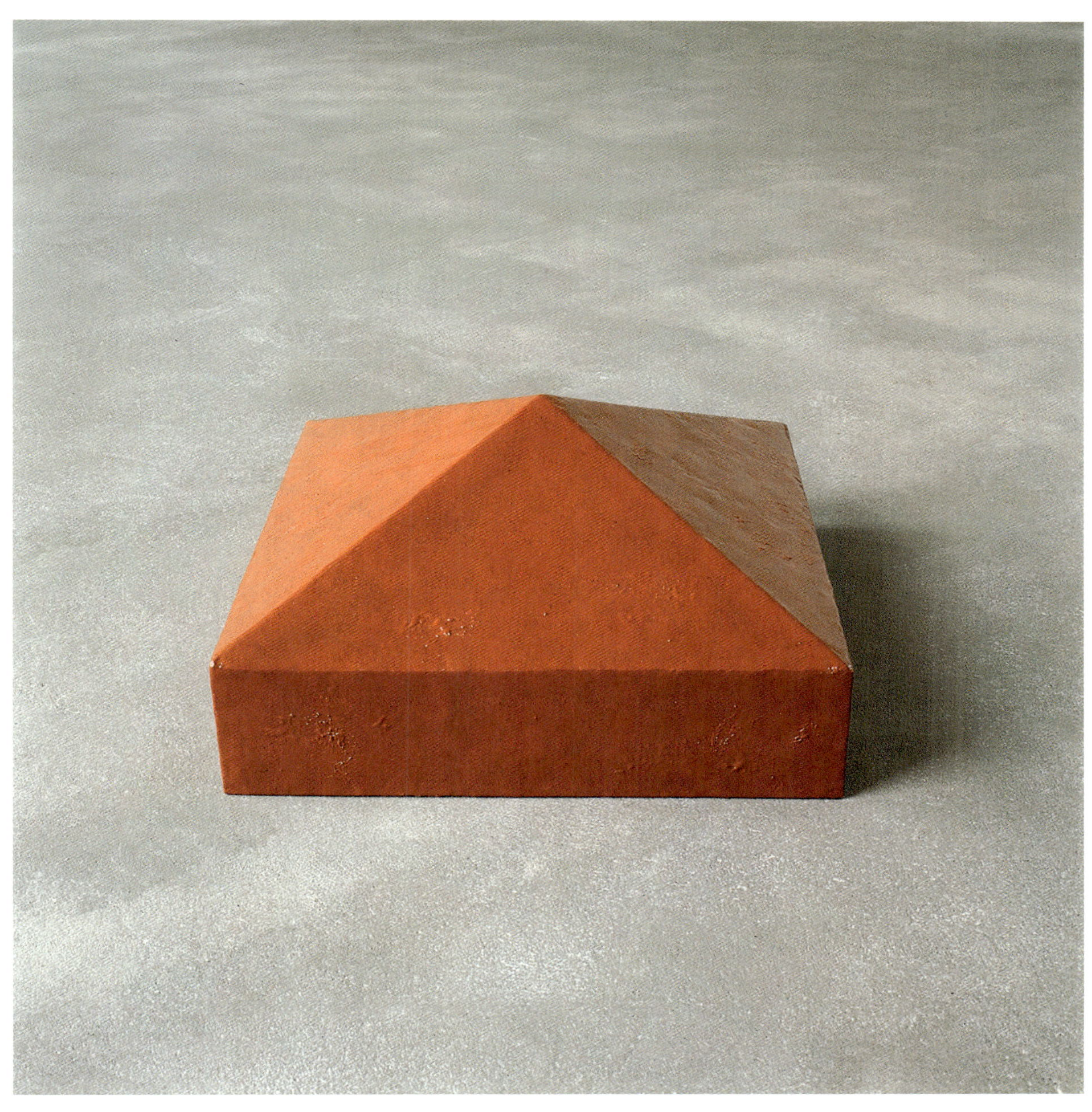

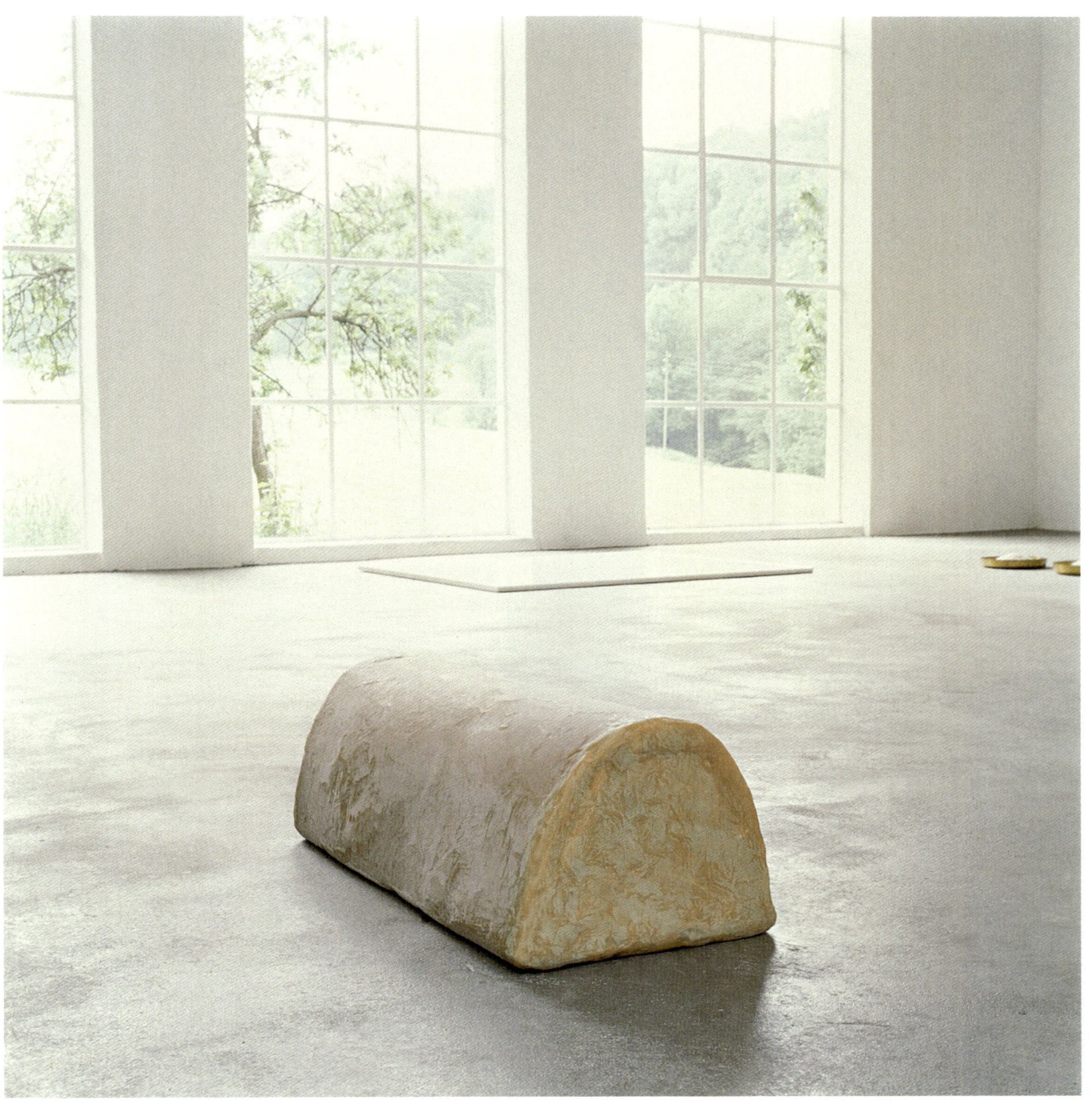

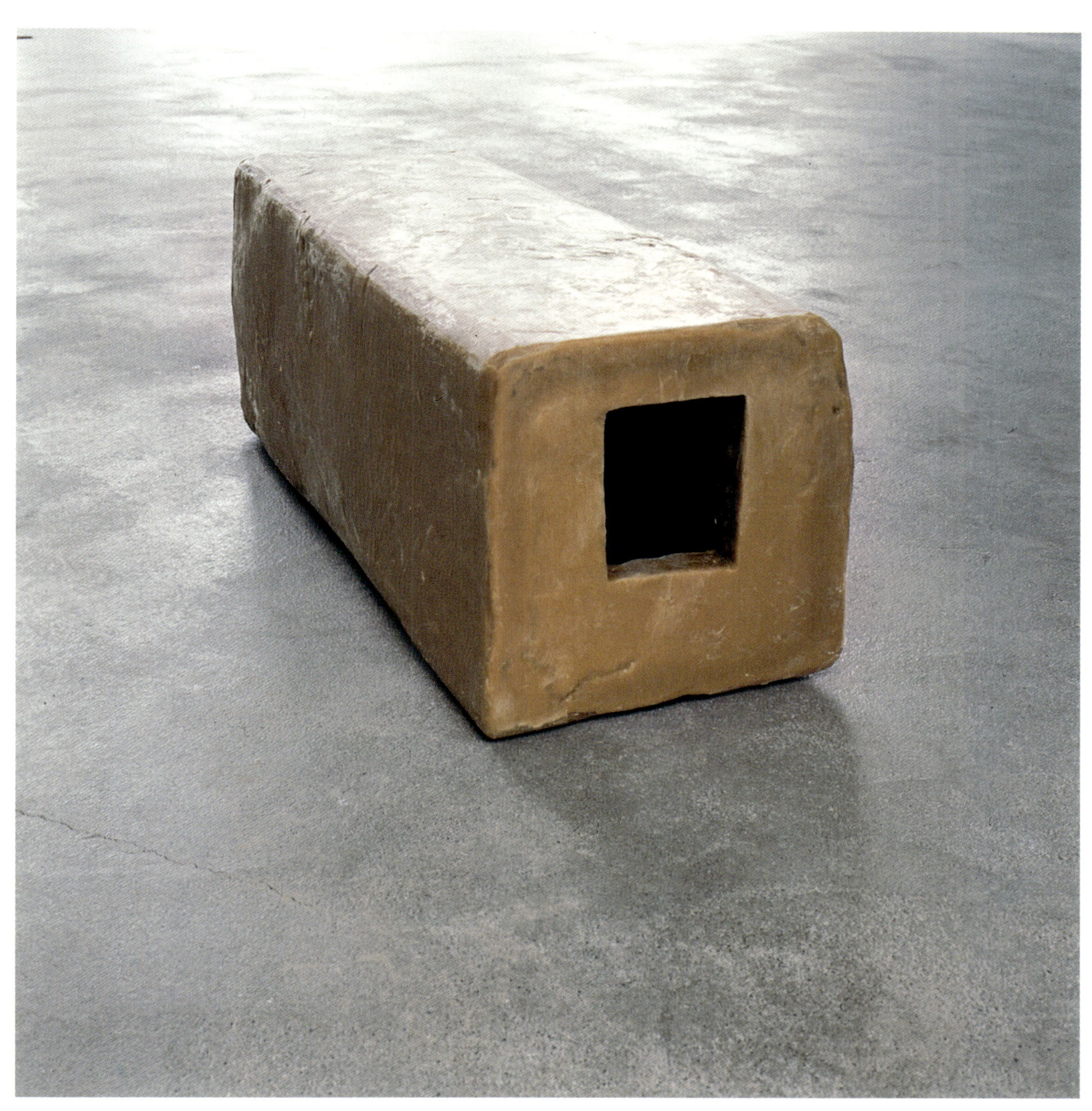

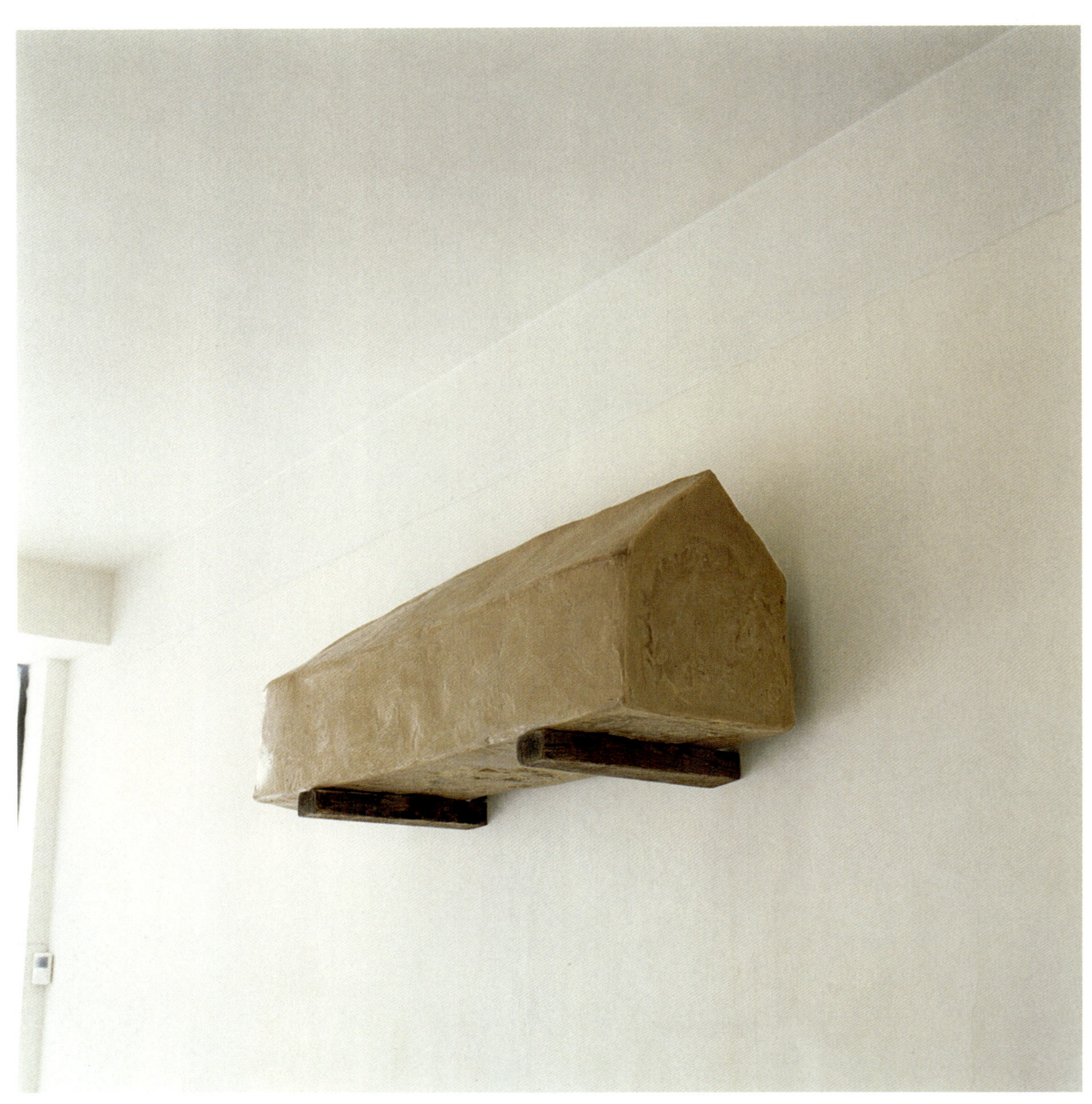

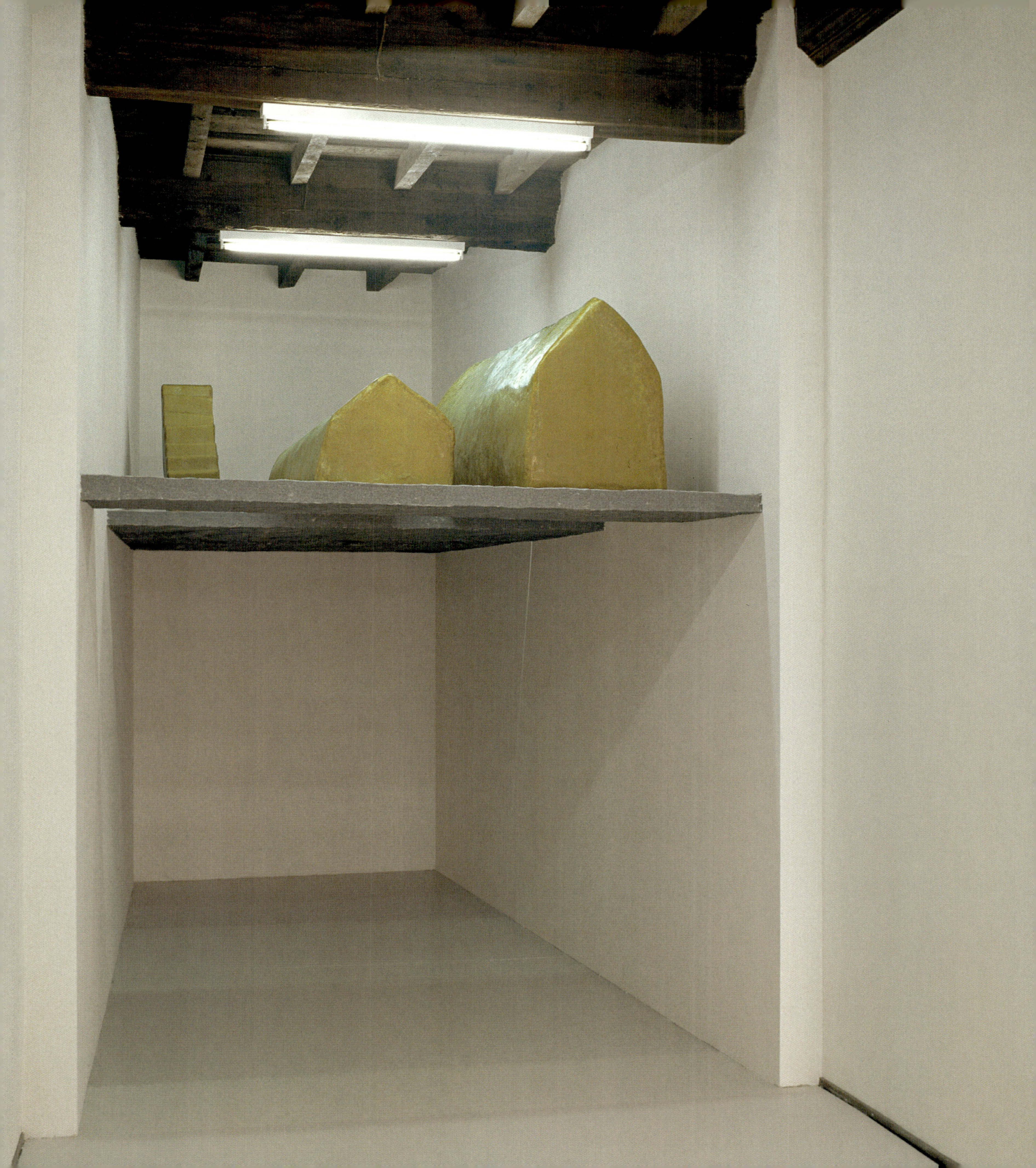

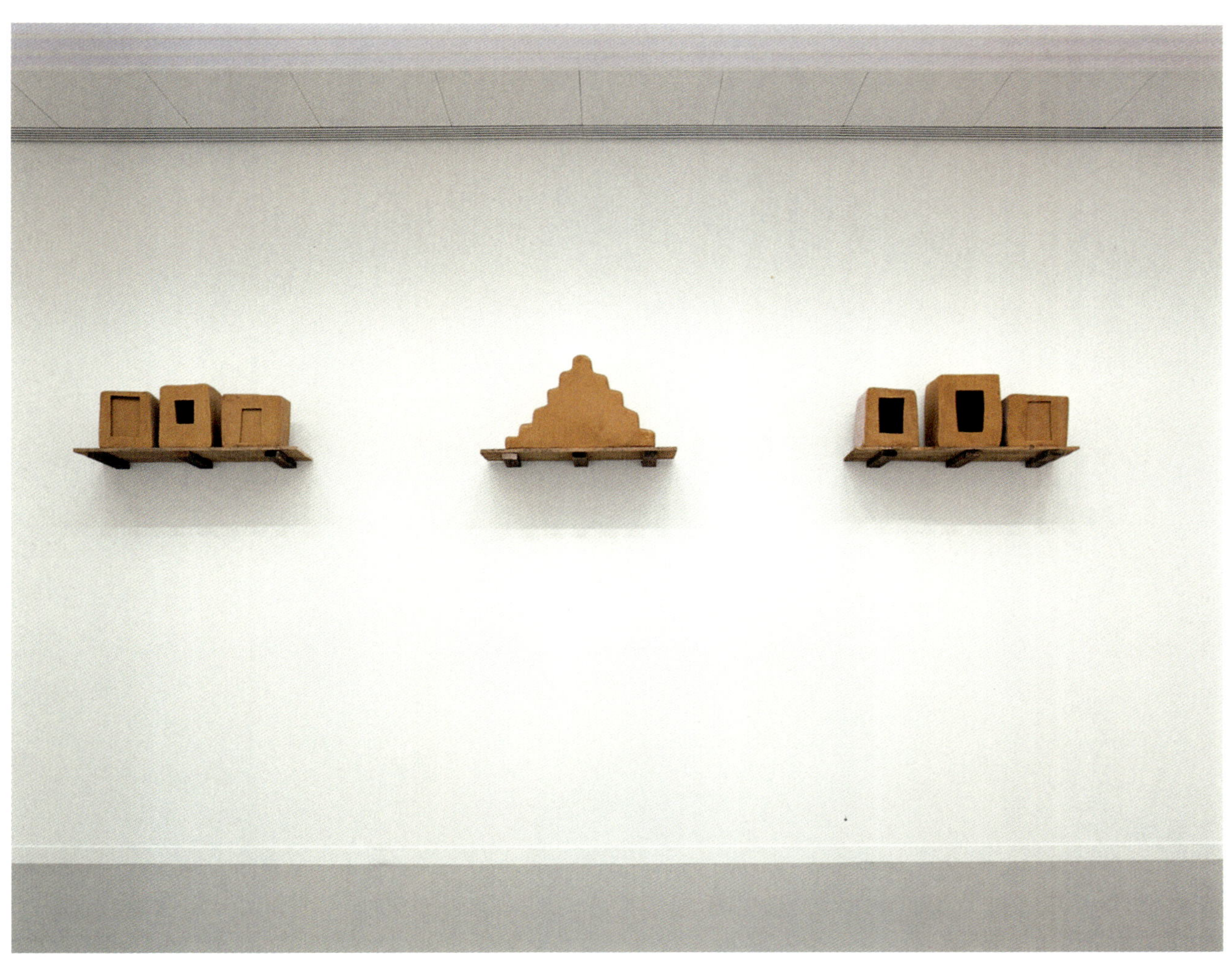

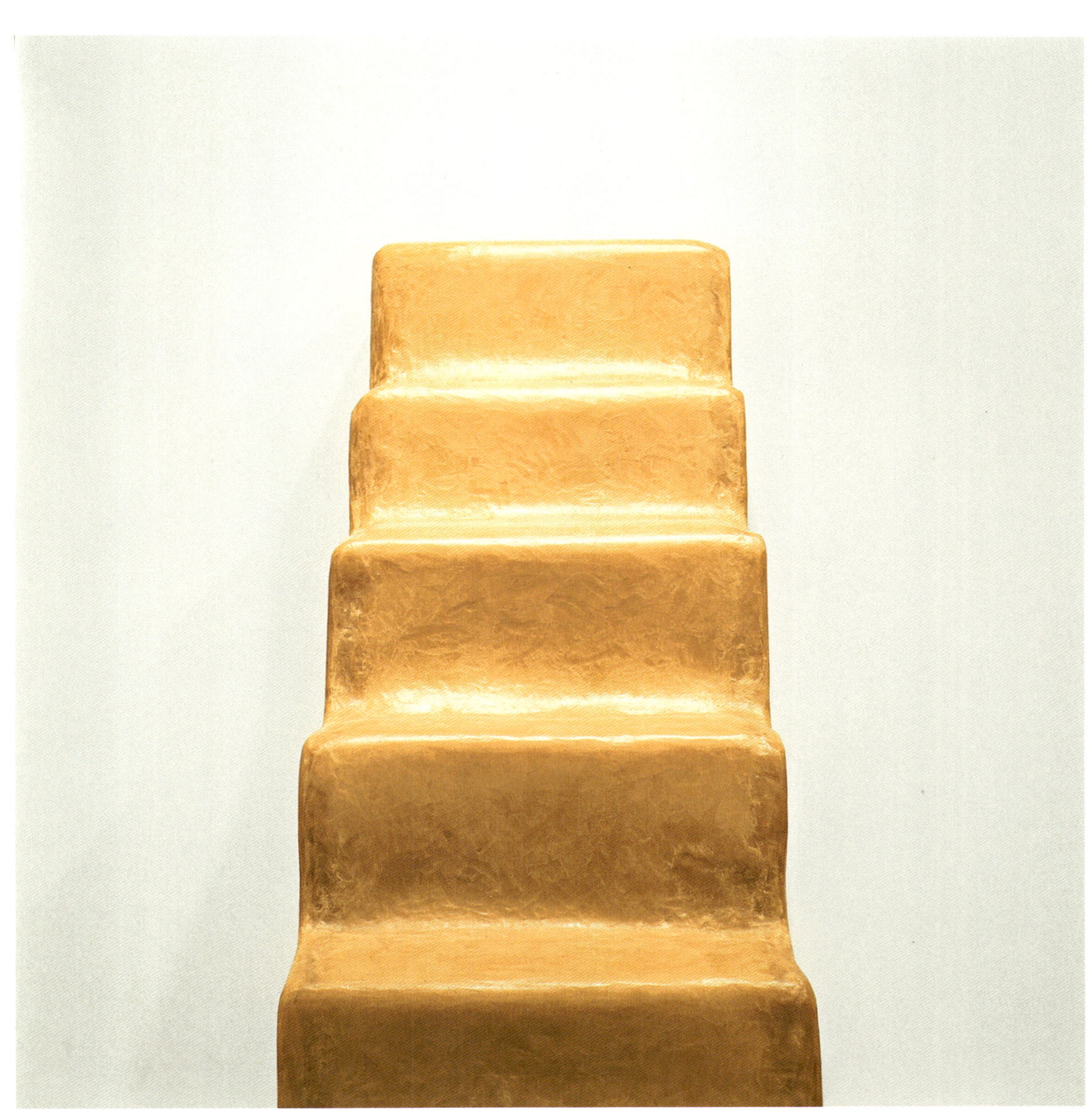

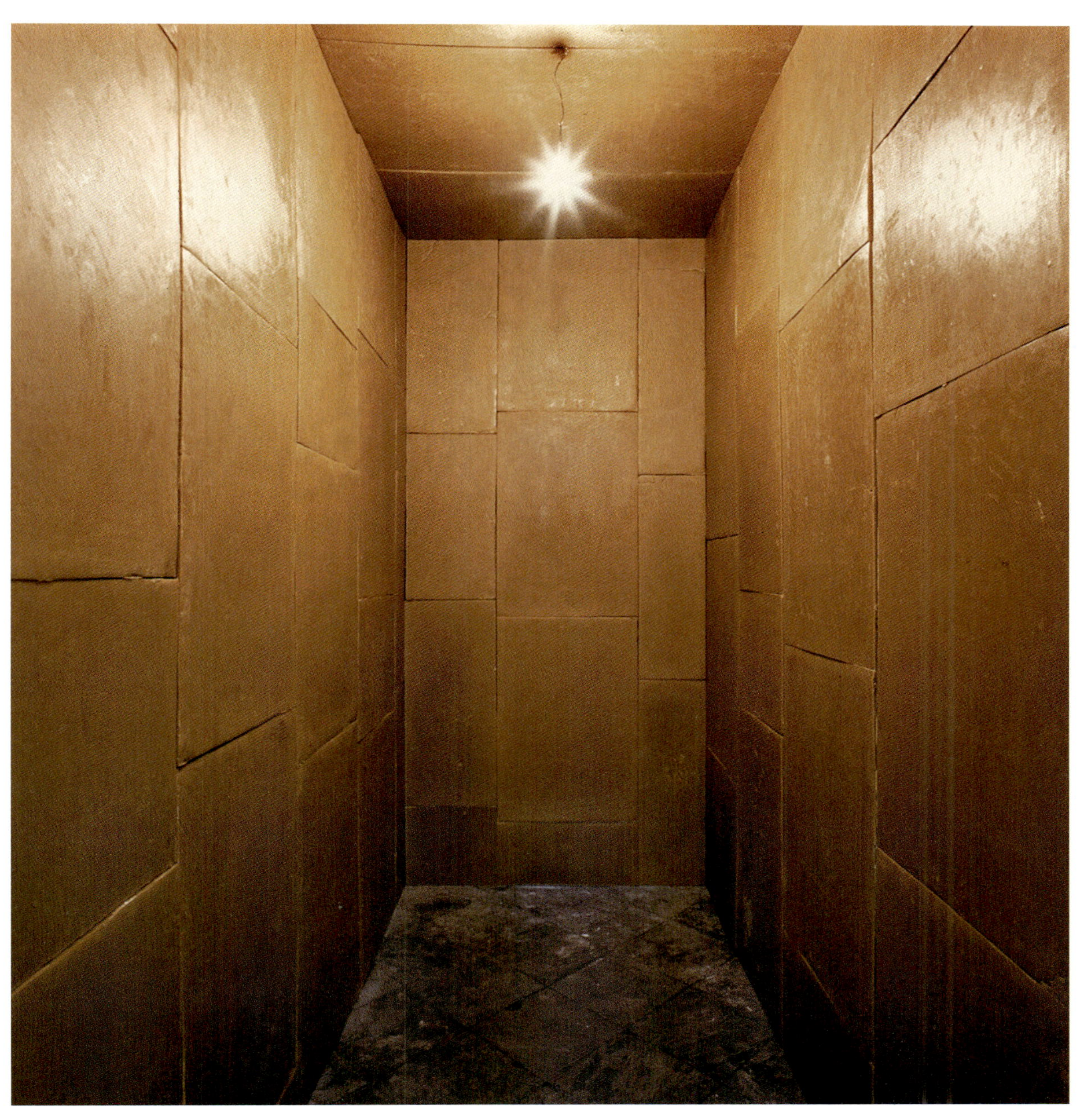

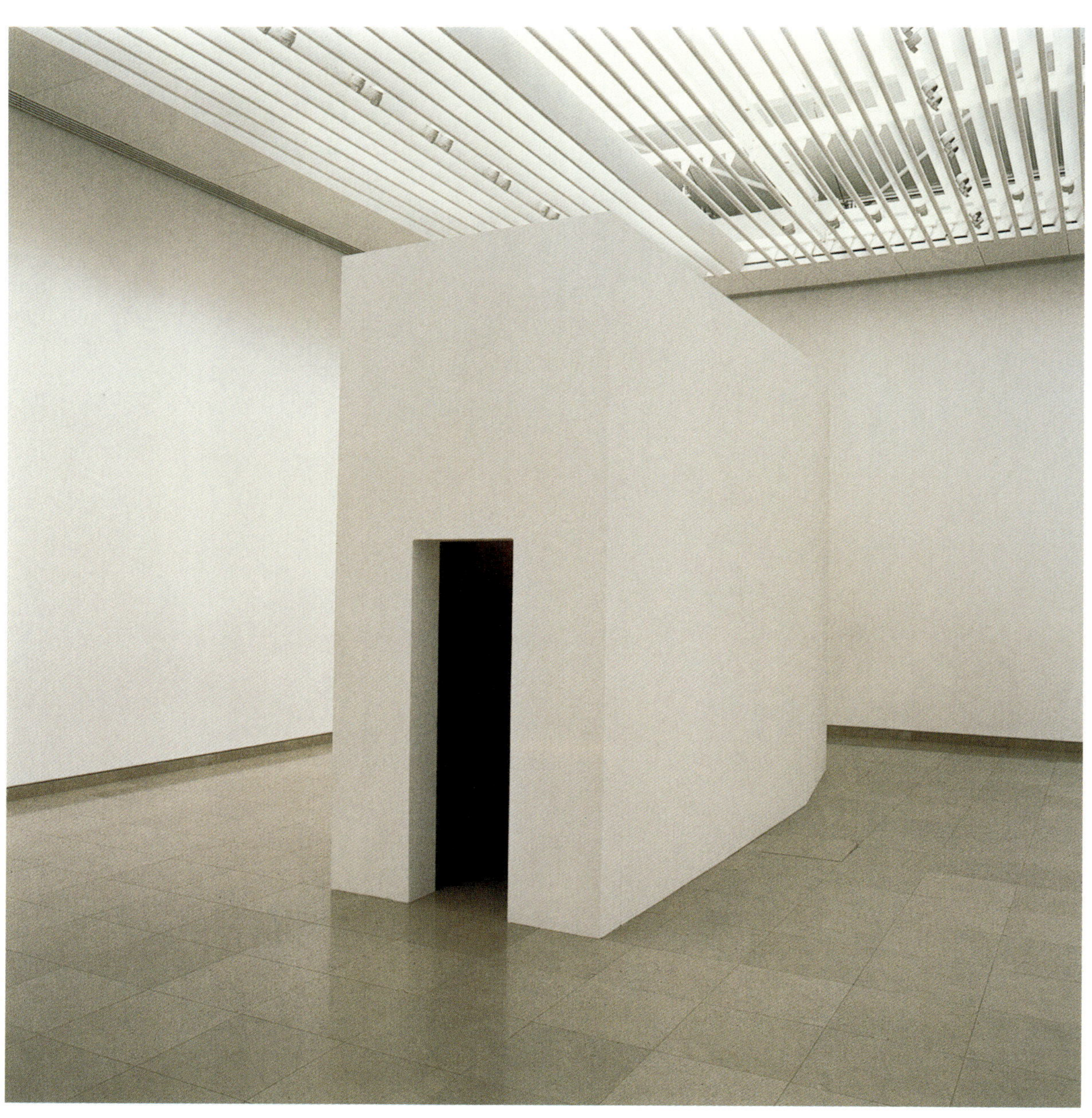

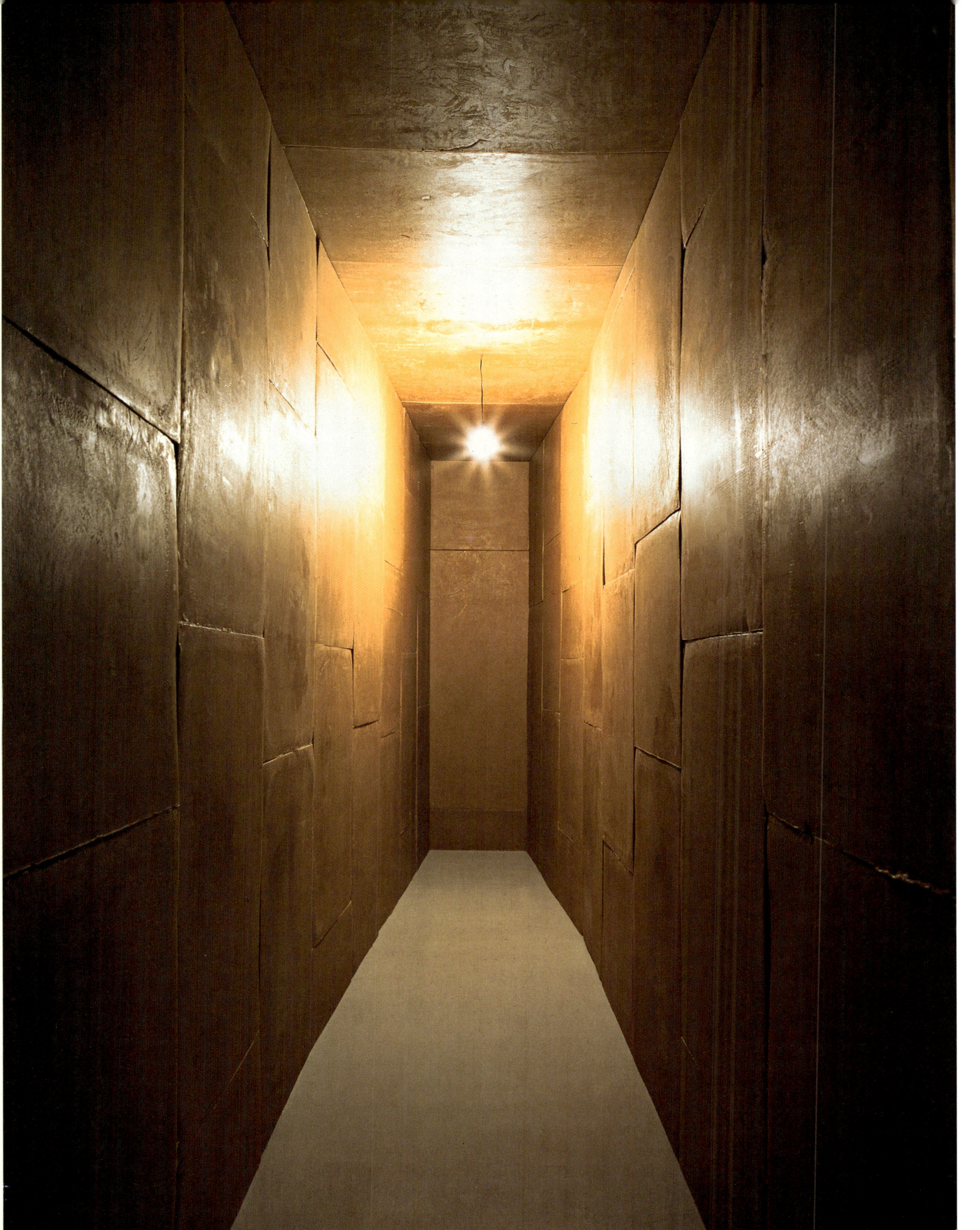

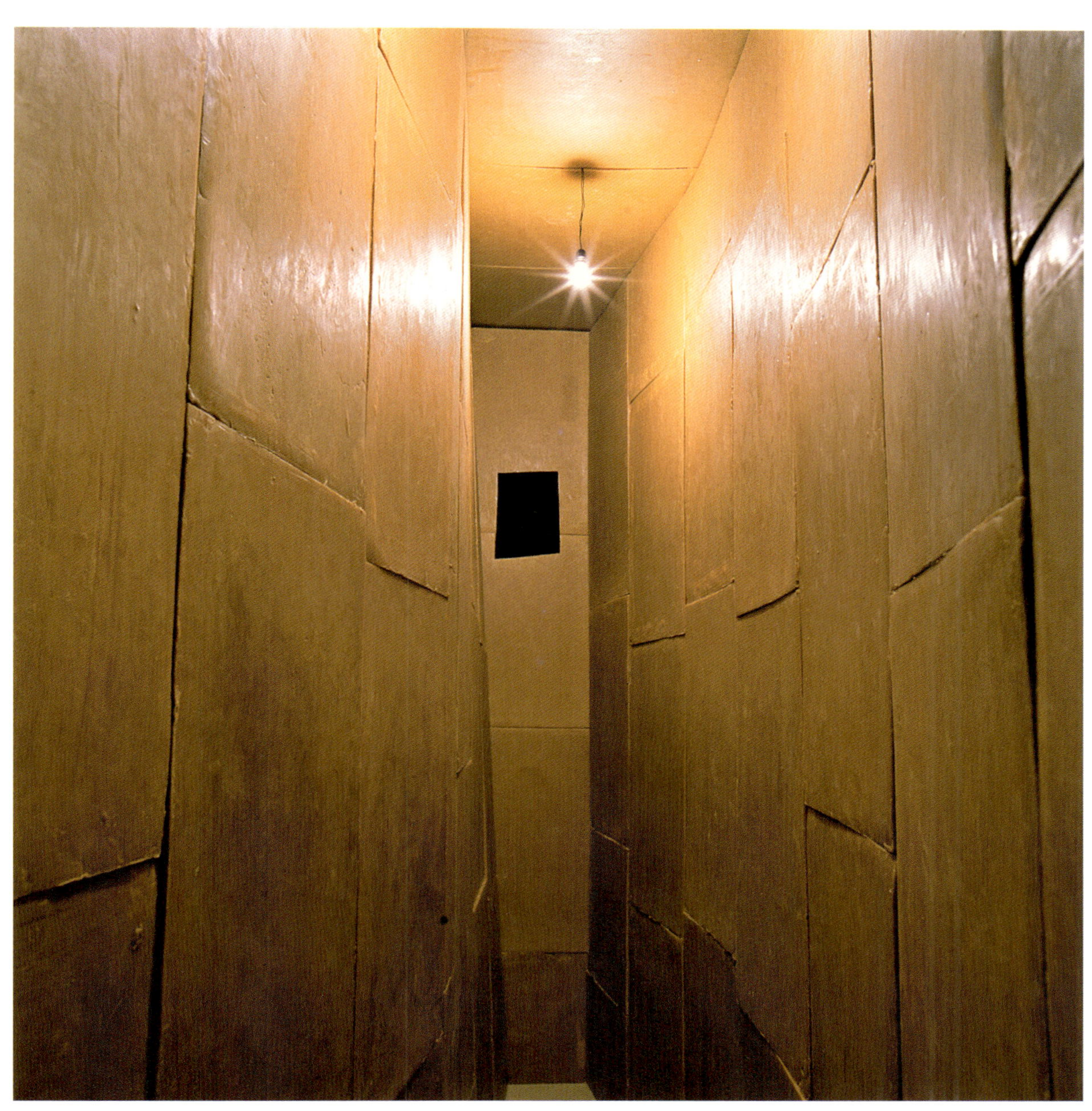

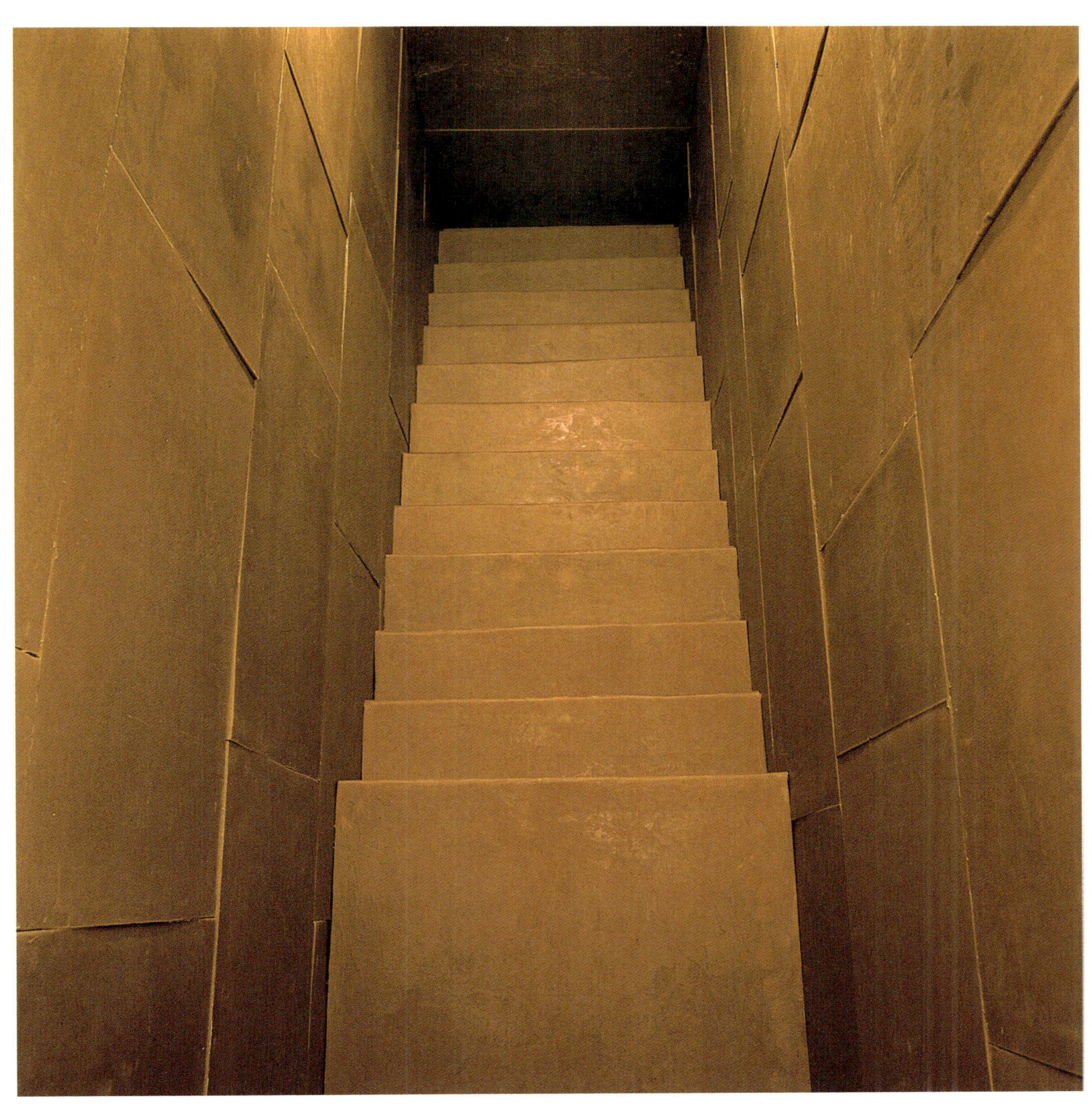

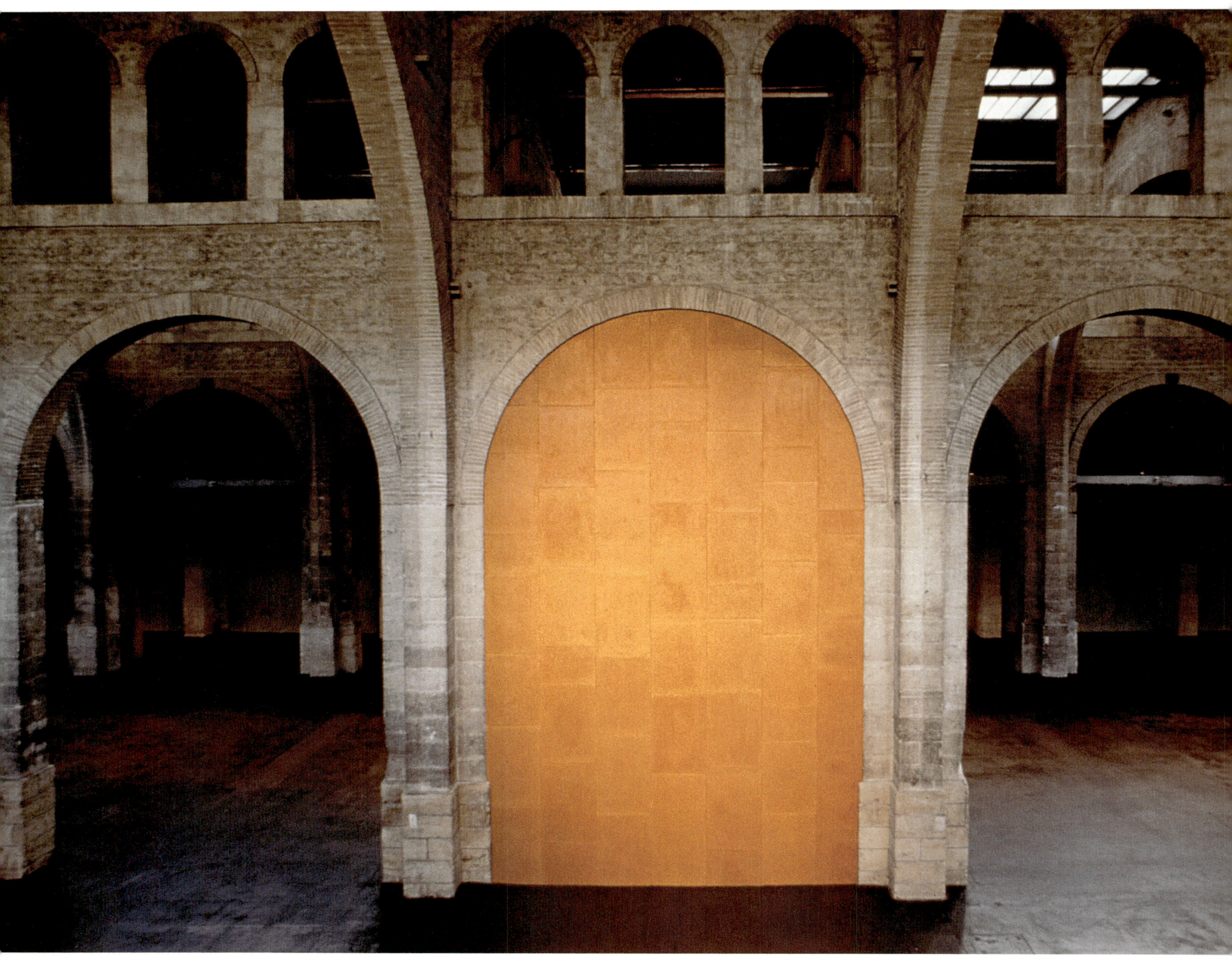

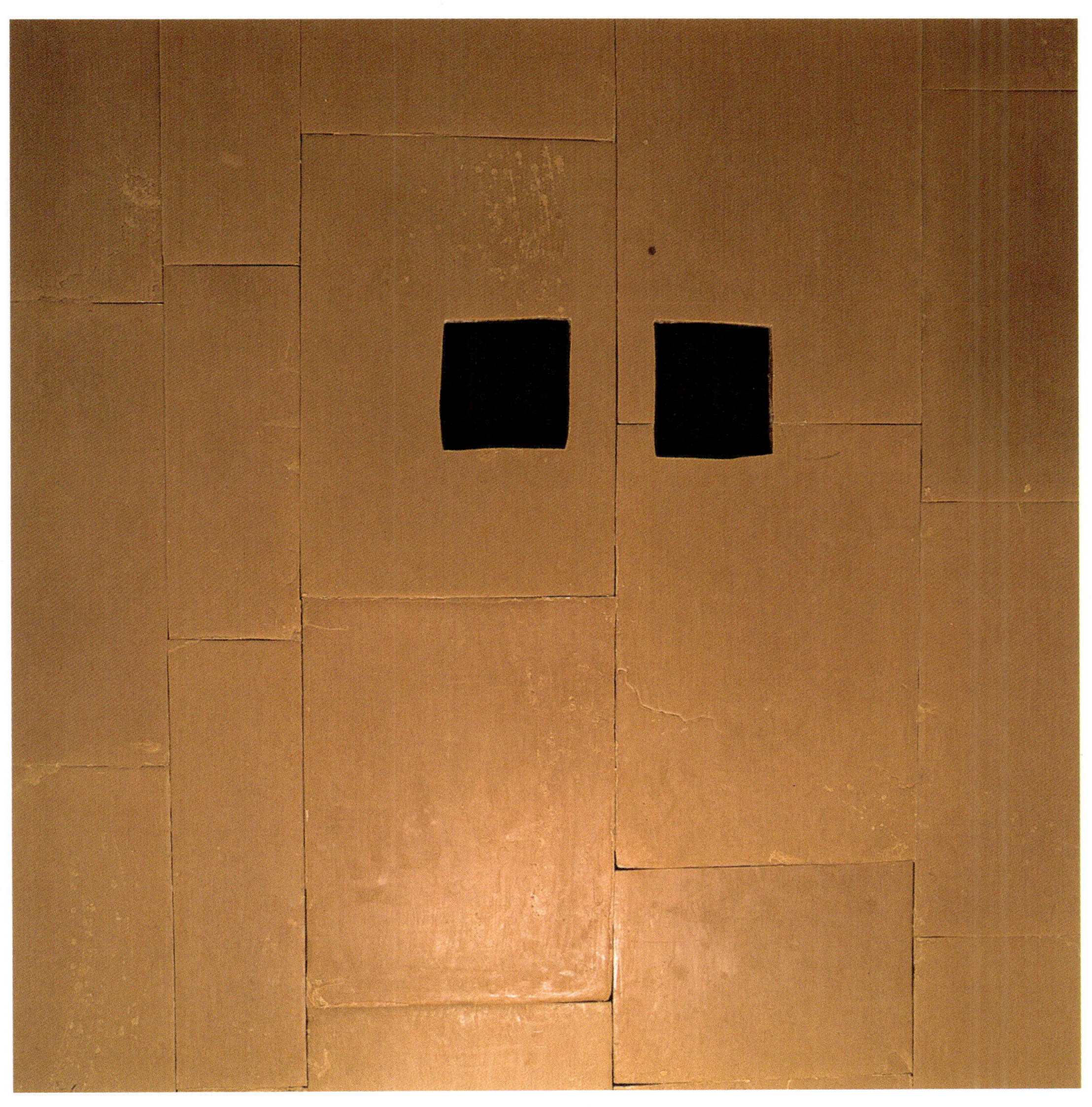

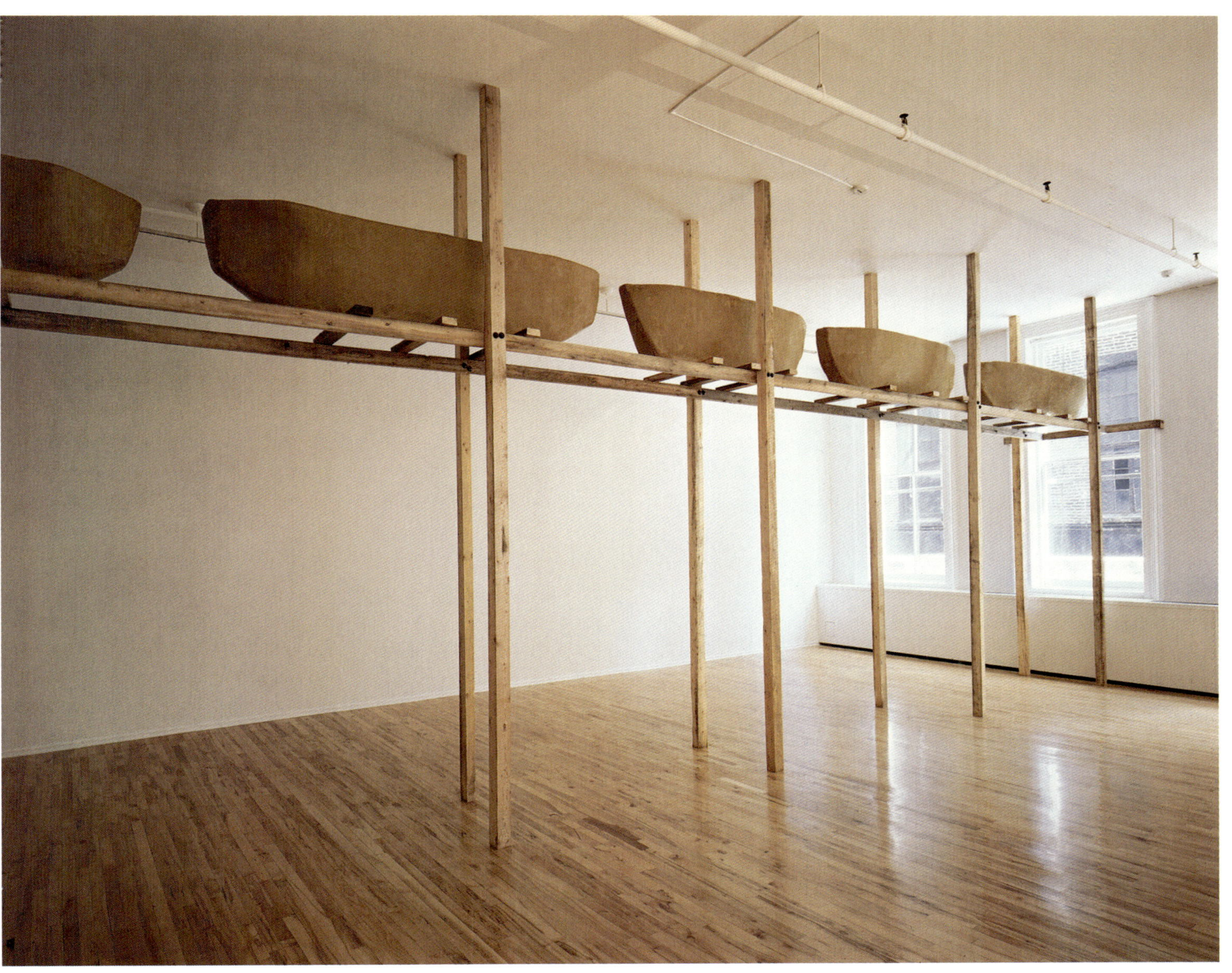

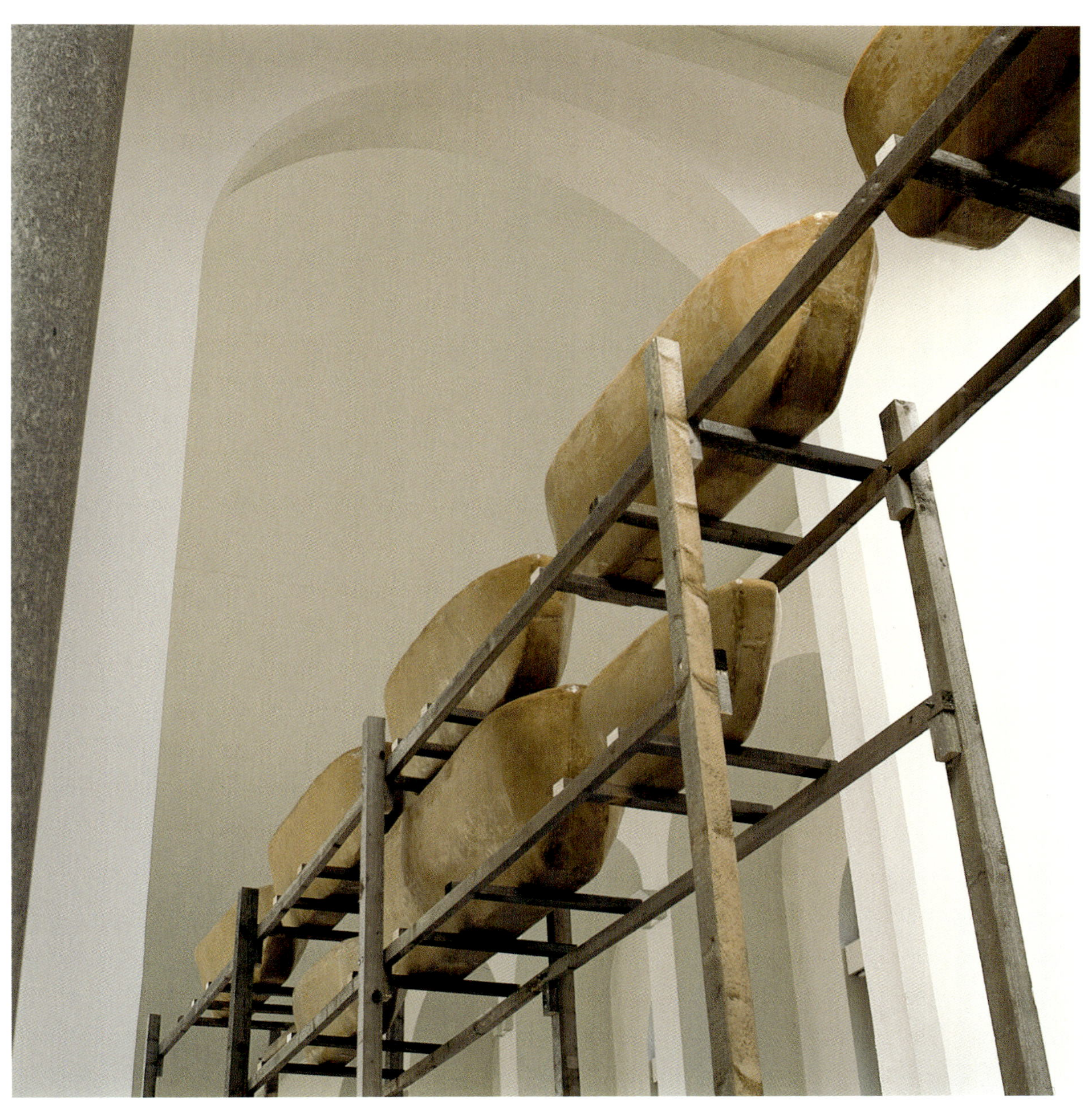

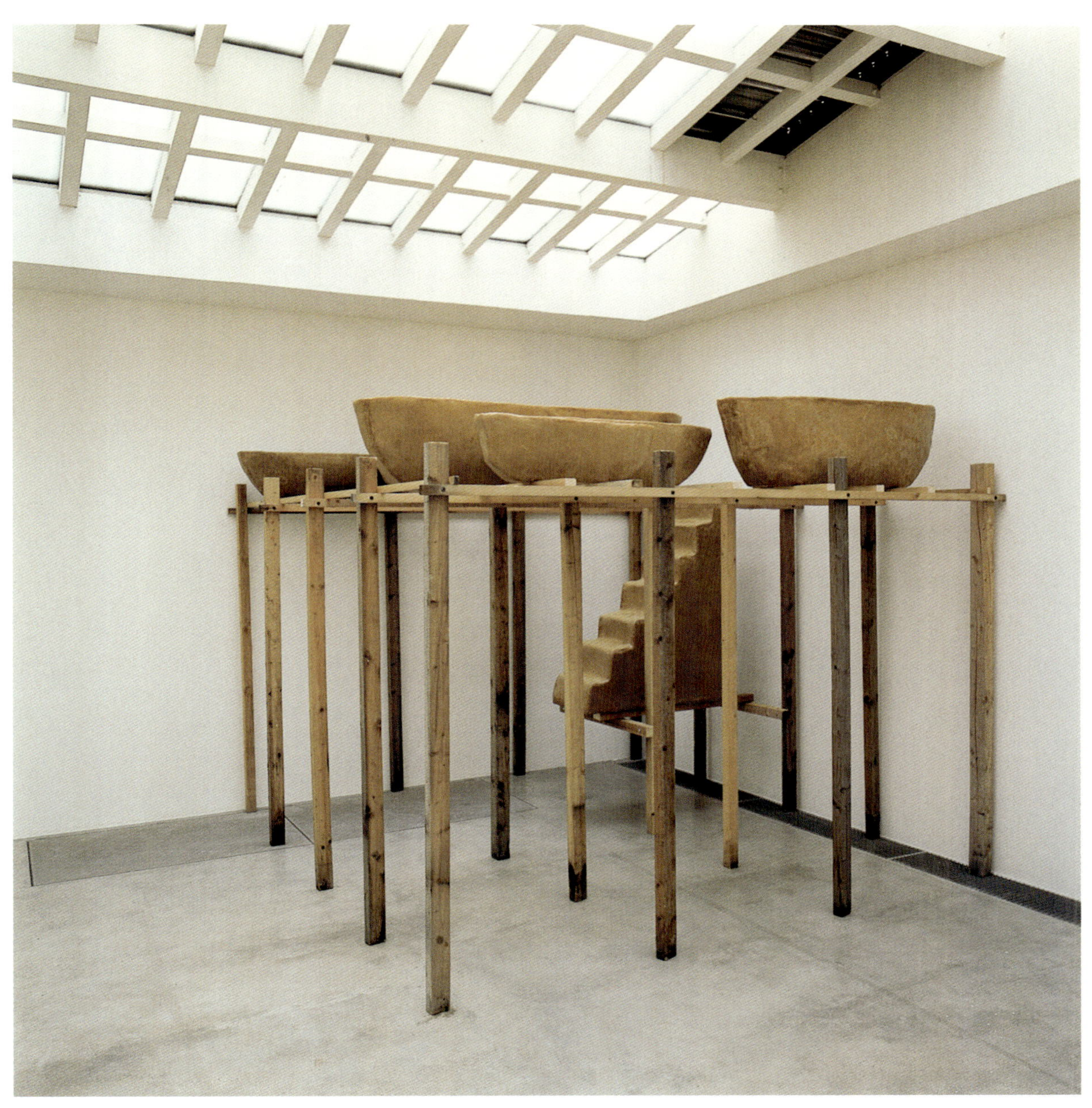

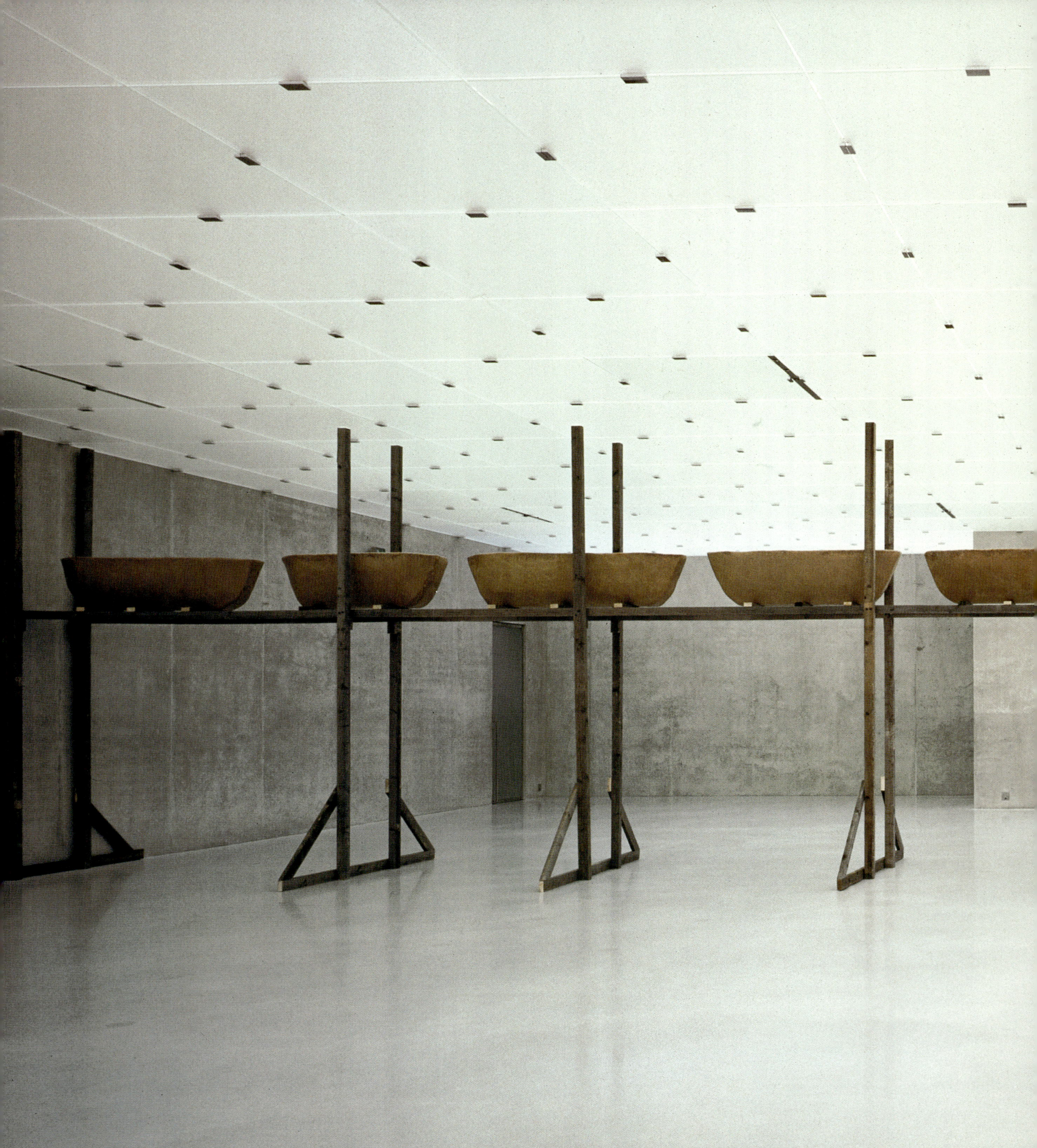

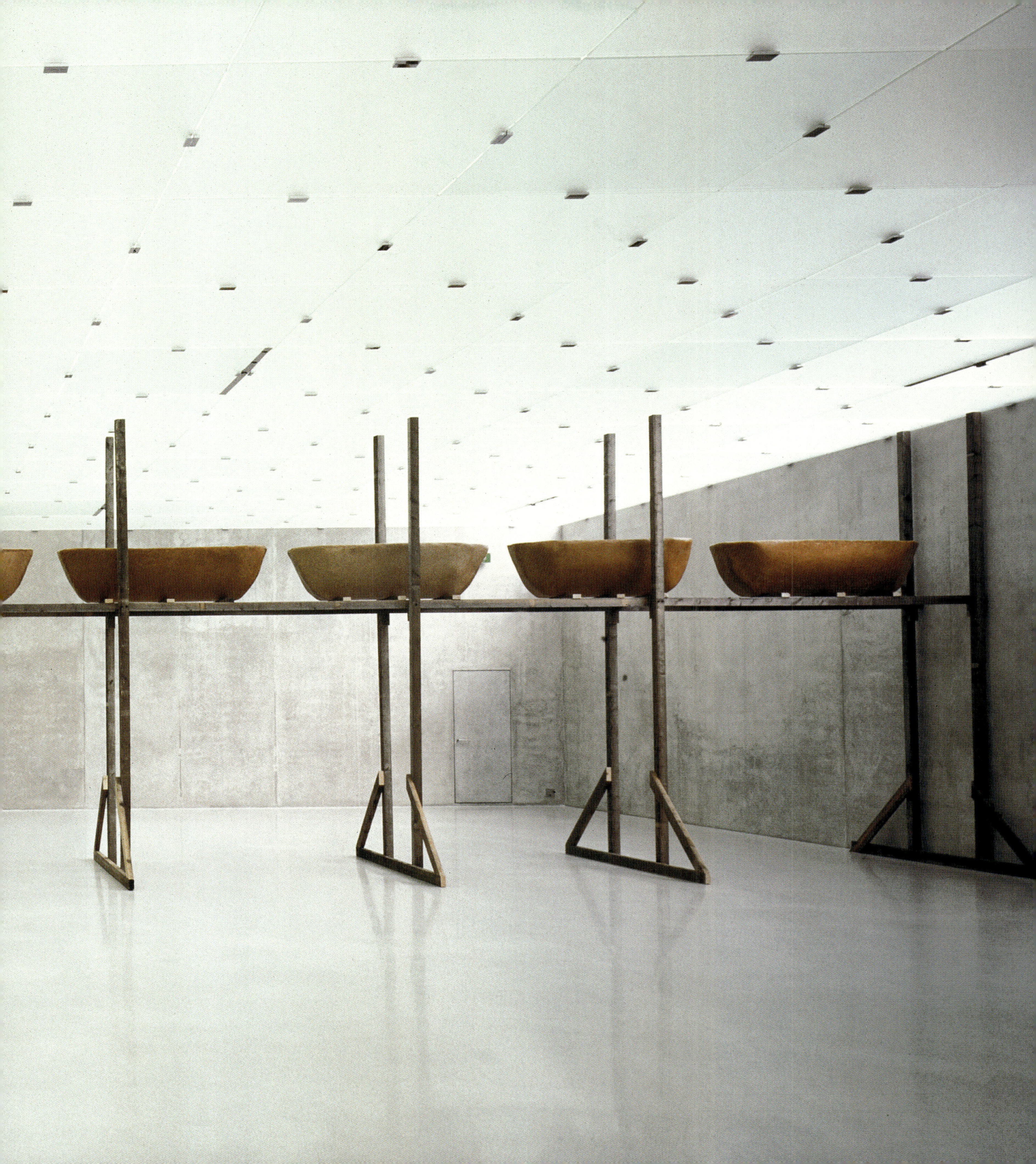

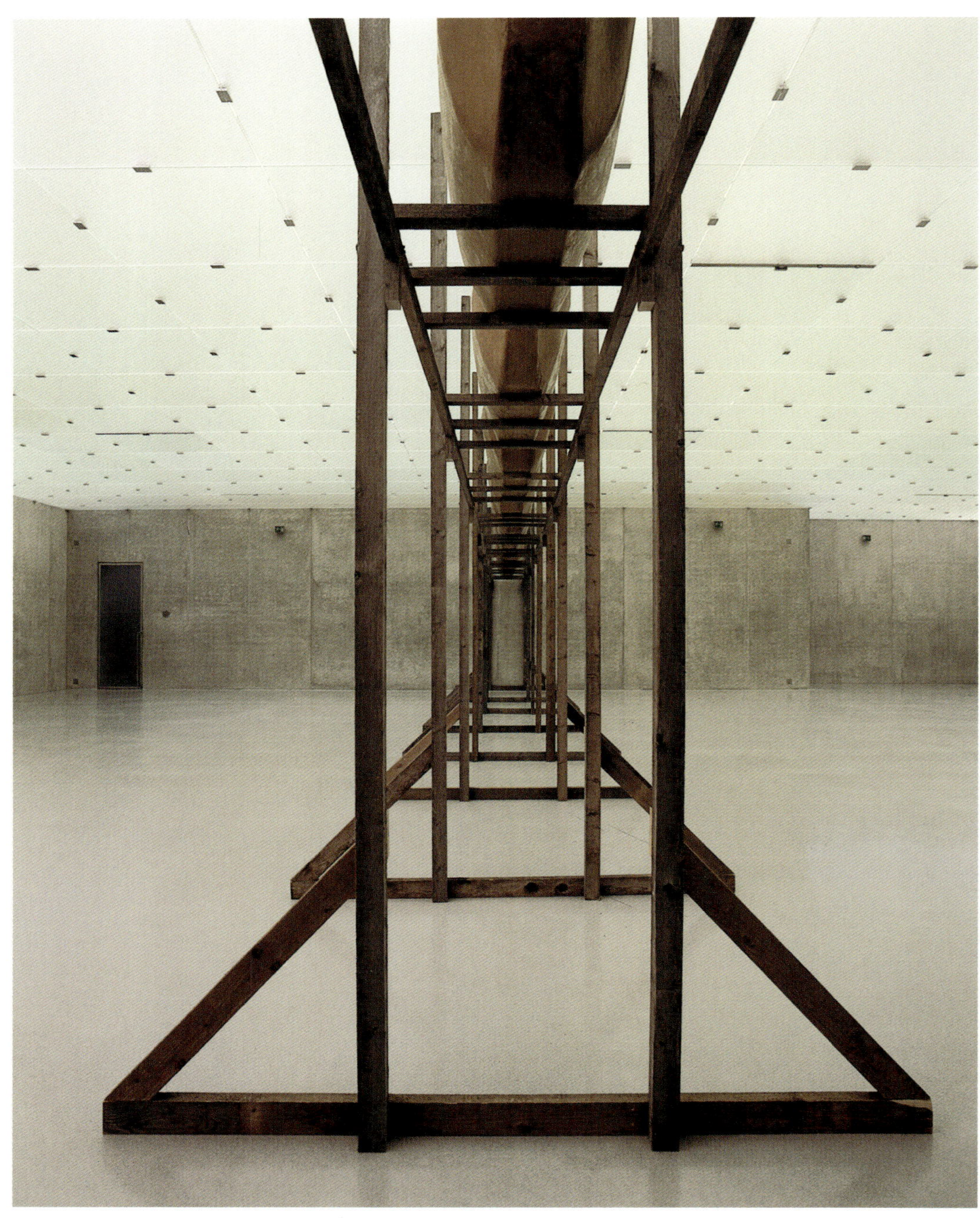

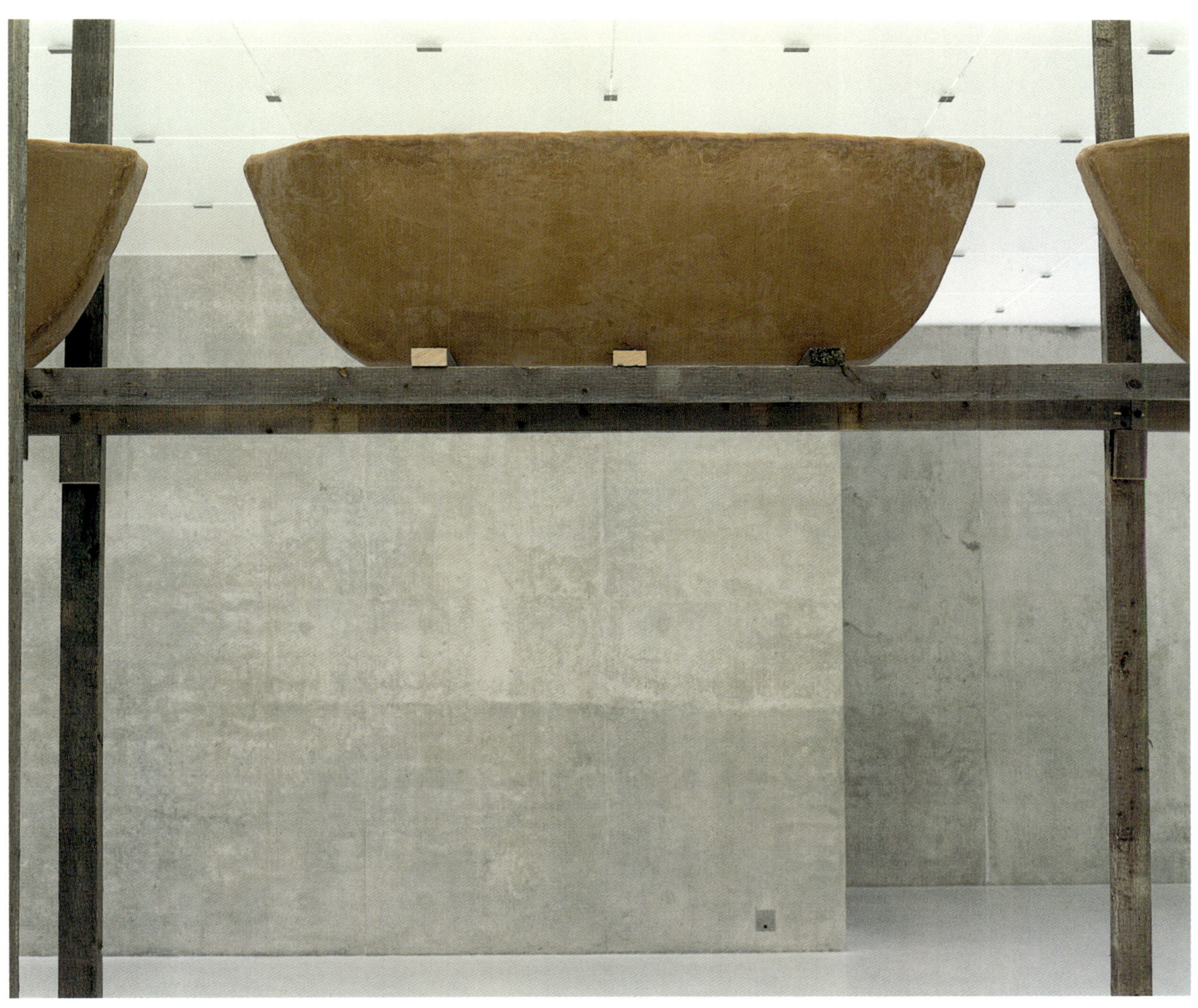

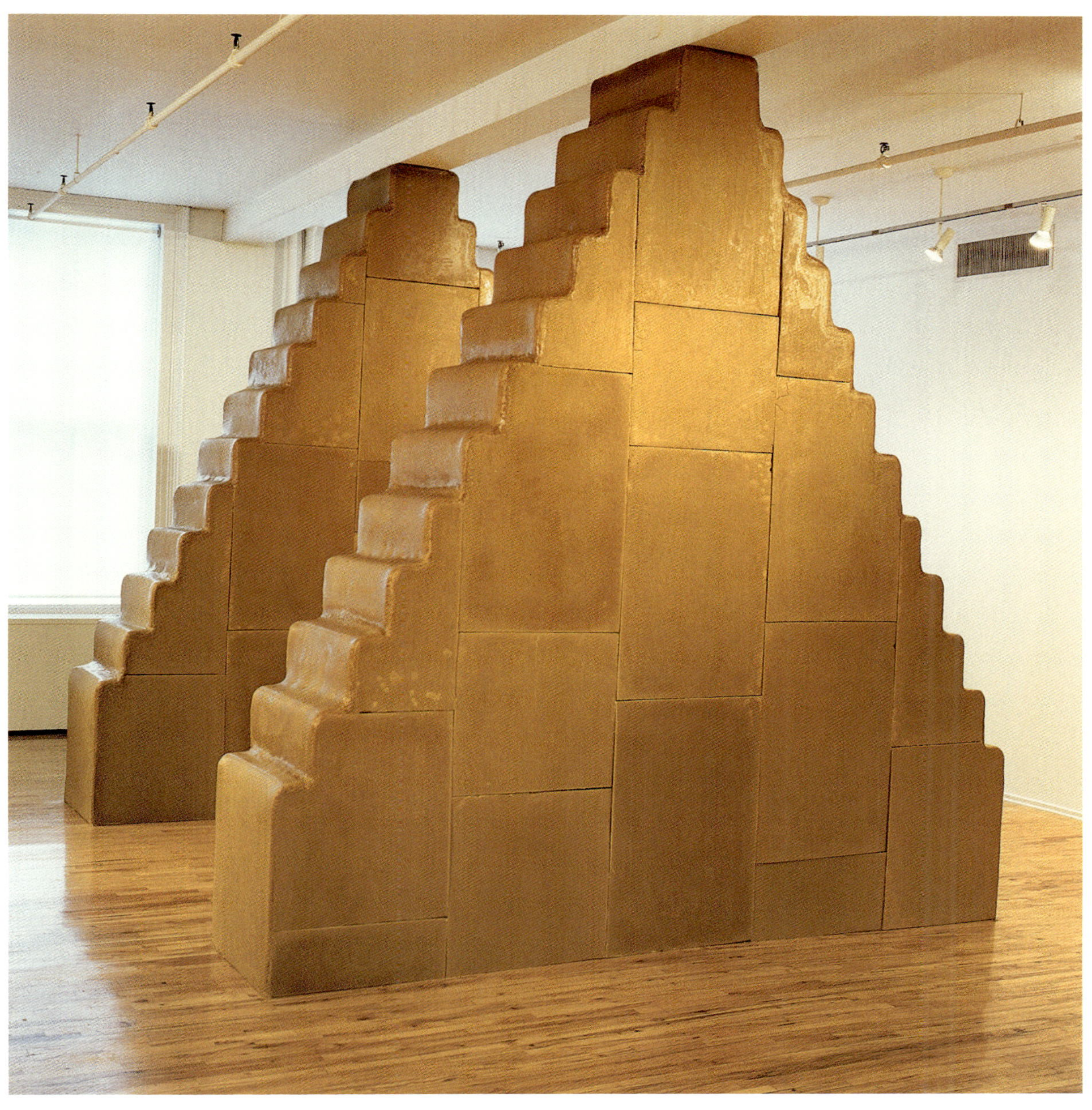

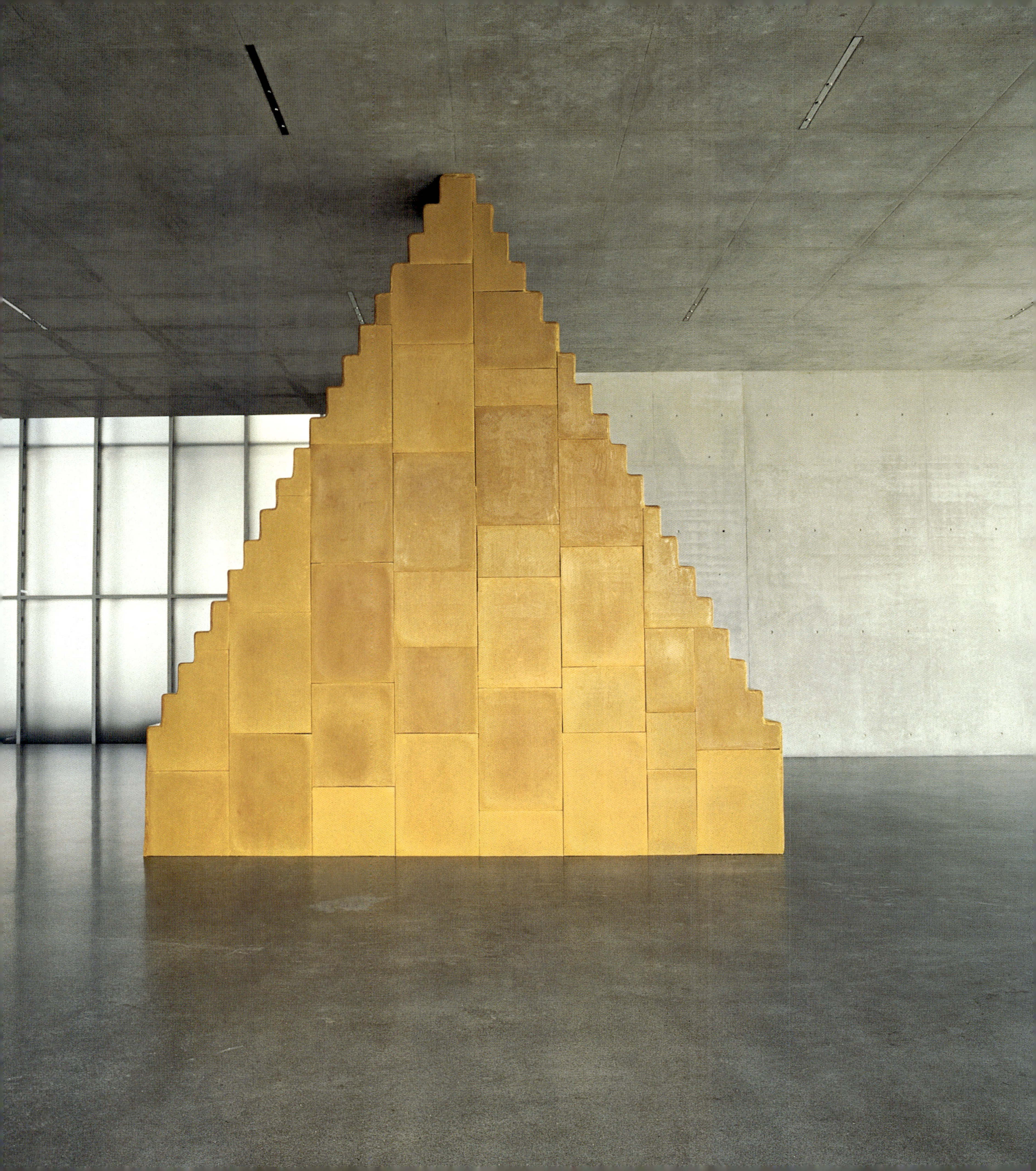

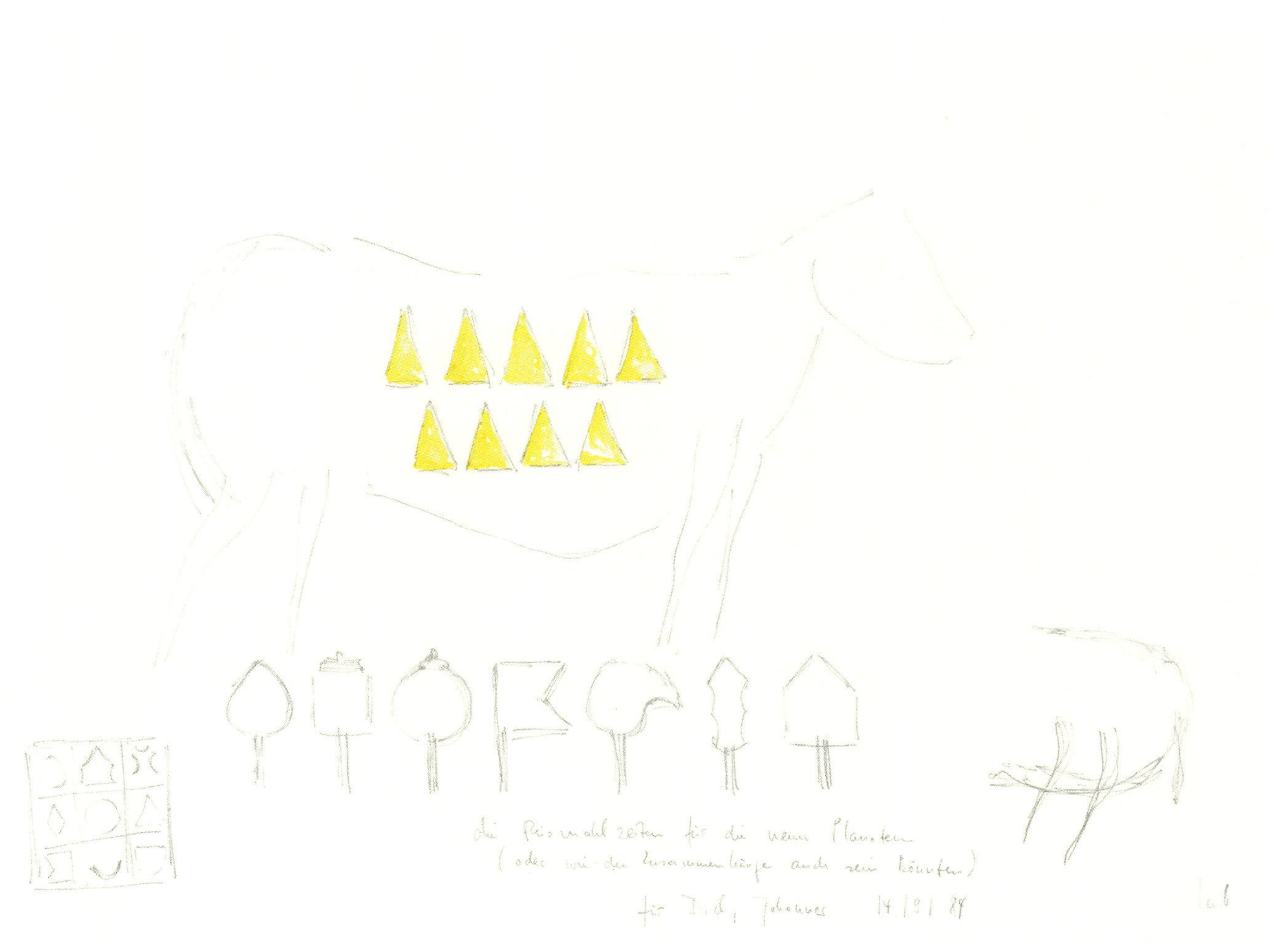

die Reisemahlzeiten für die neuen Planeten
(oder wie die Zusammenhänge auch sein könnten)
für Dich, Johannes   14/9/89

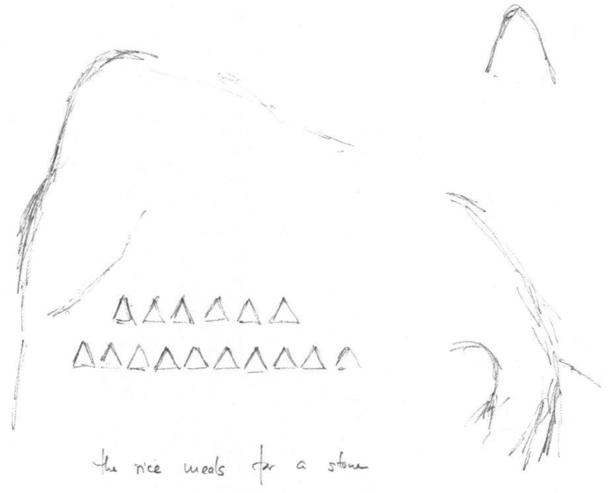

the nice meals for a stone
lab 83

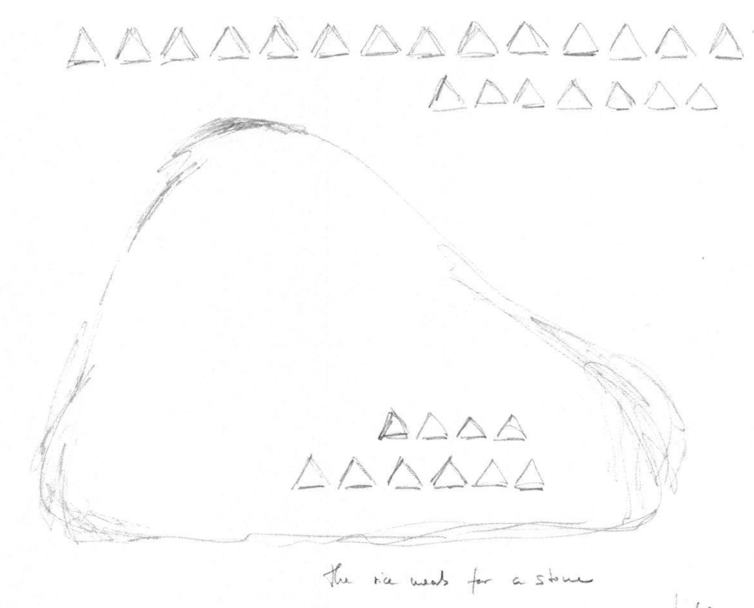

the nice meals for a stone
lab 83

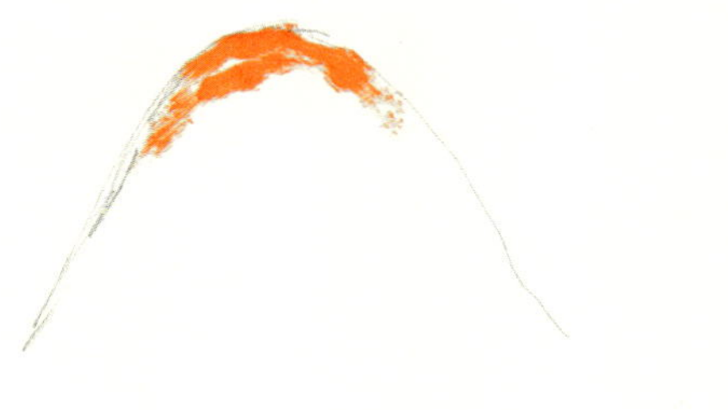
the rice meals for a stone
laib 8

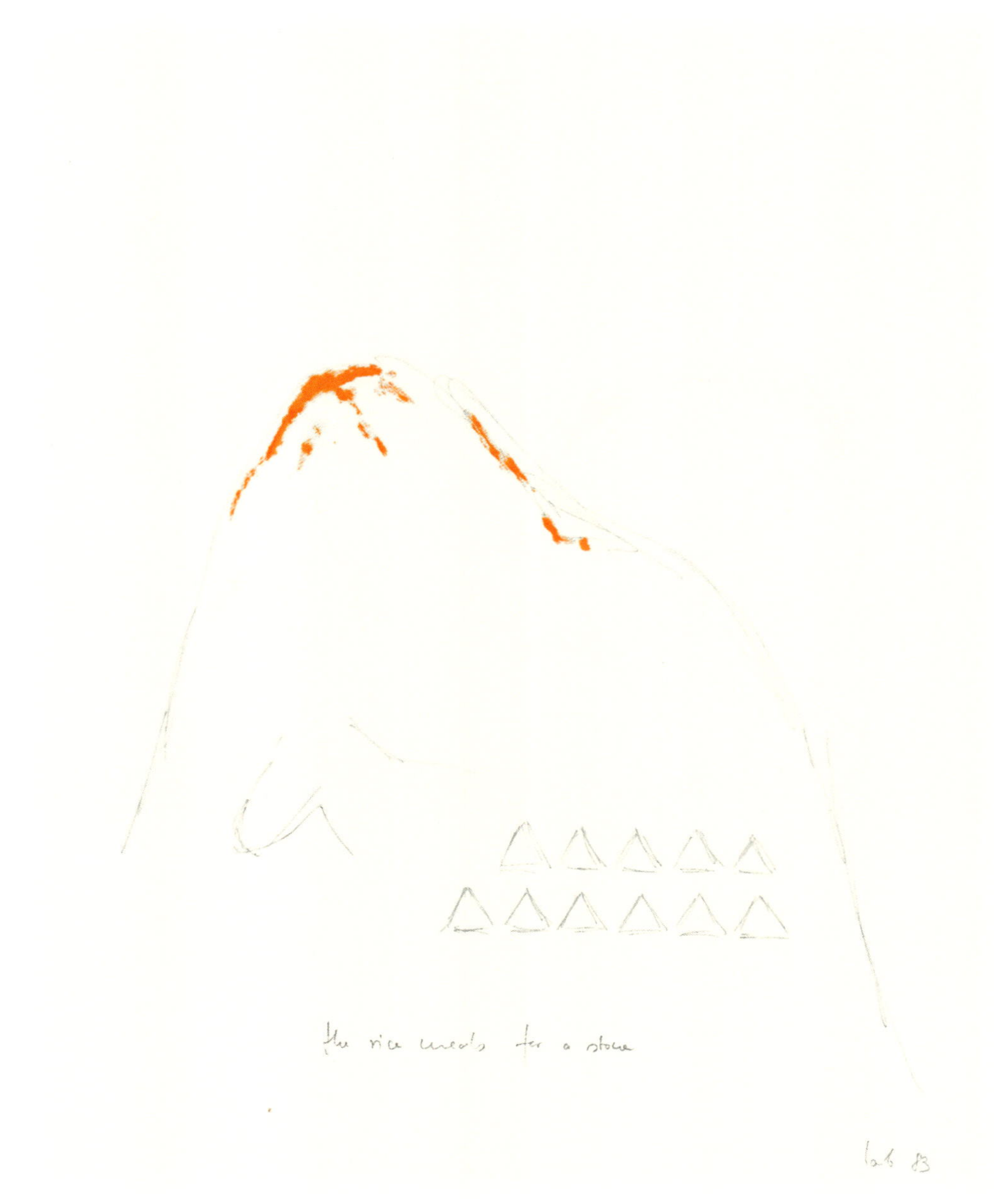

the rice kneels for a stone

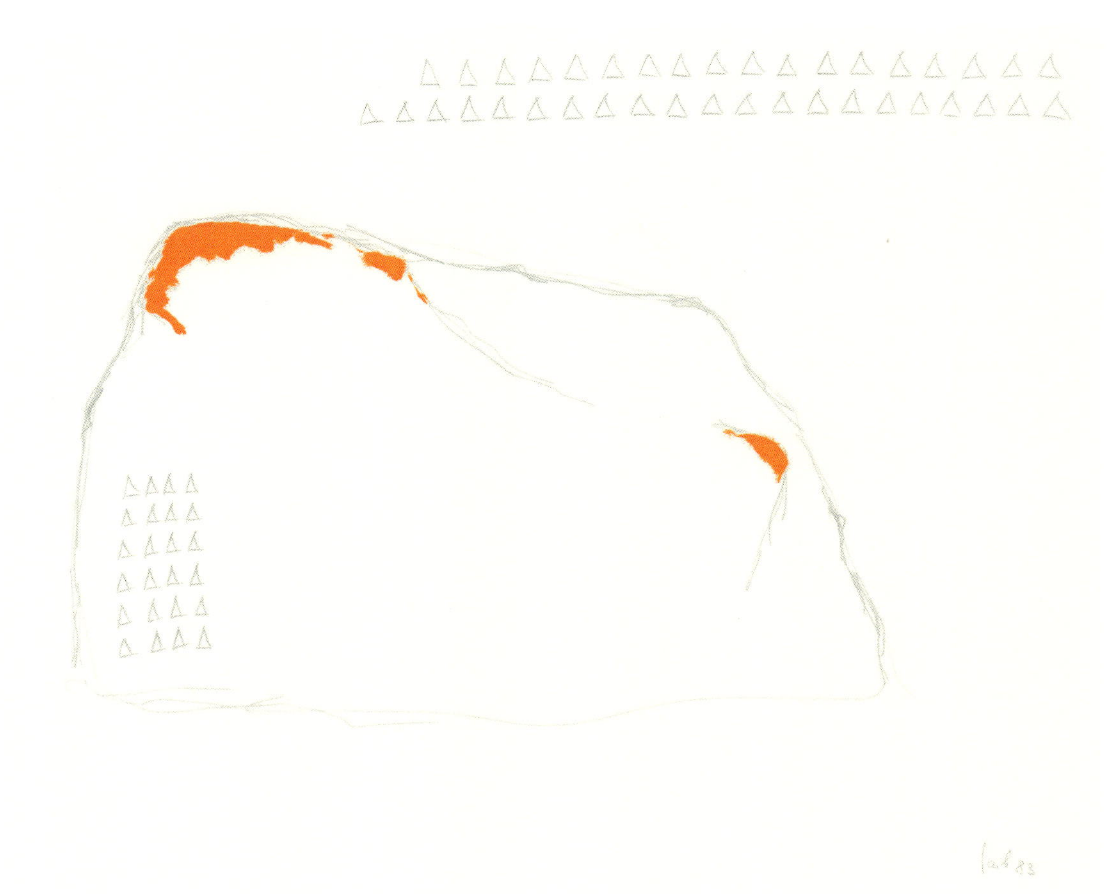

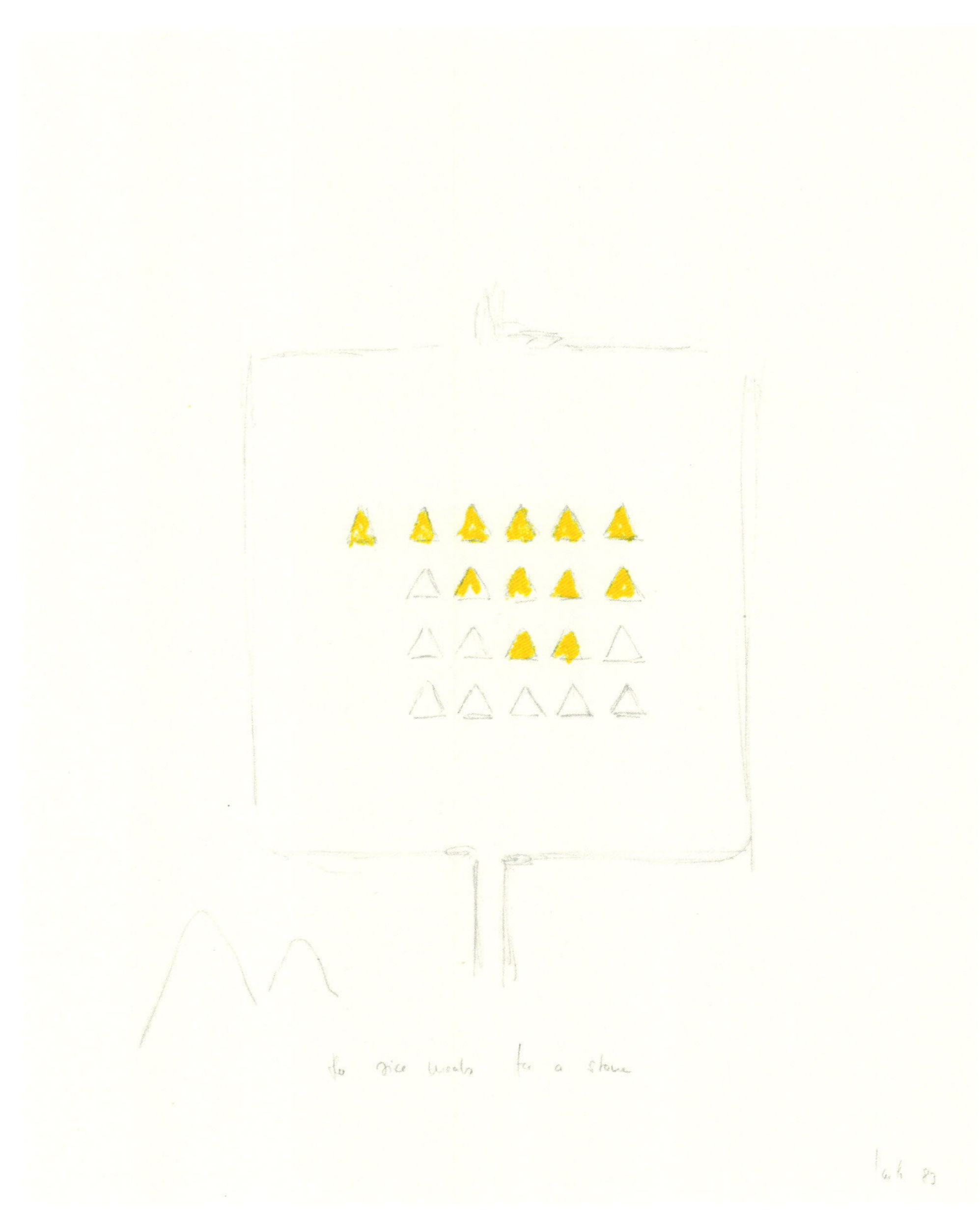
do give words for a stone

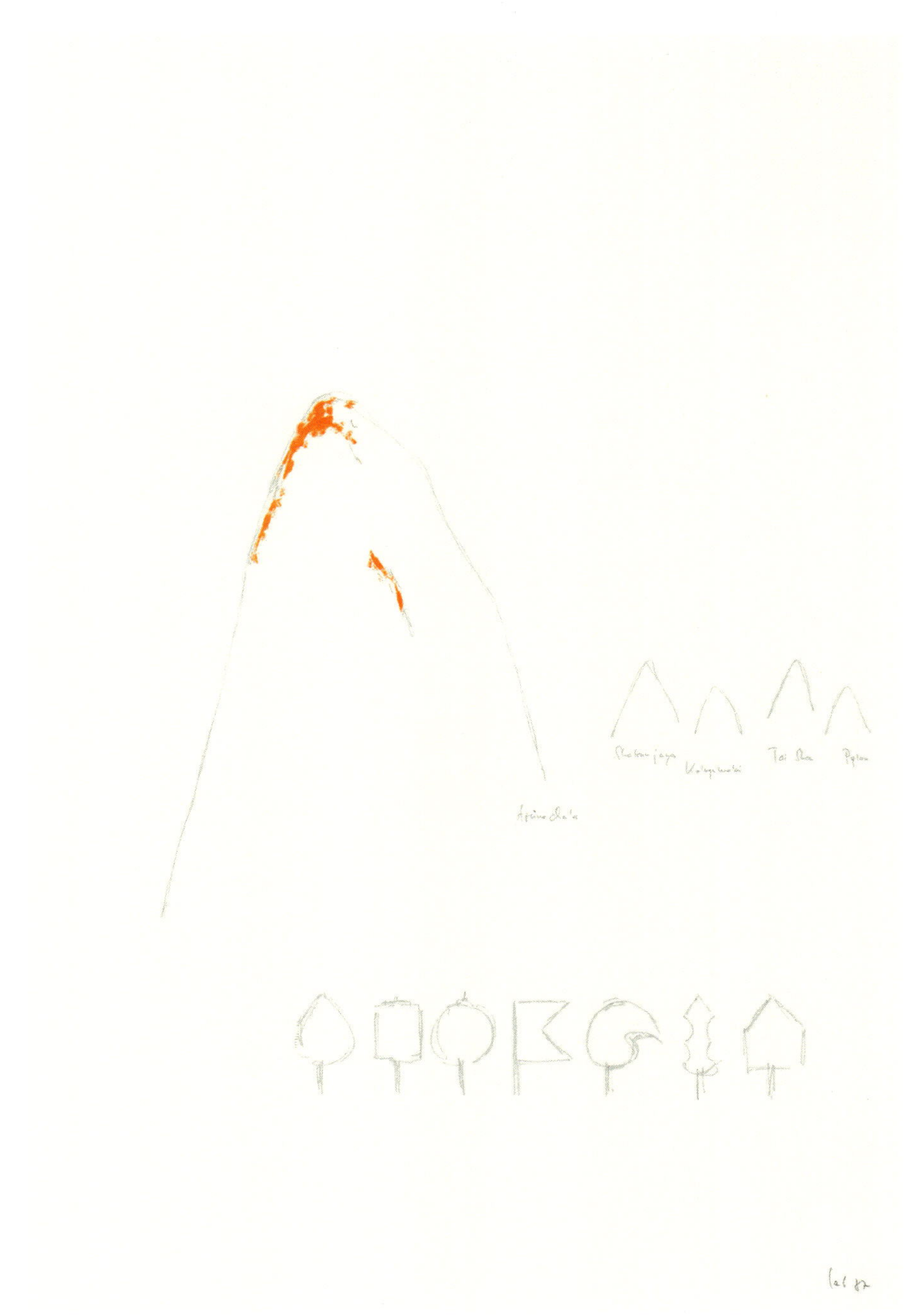

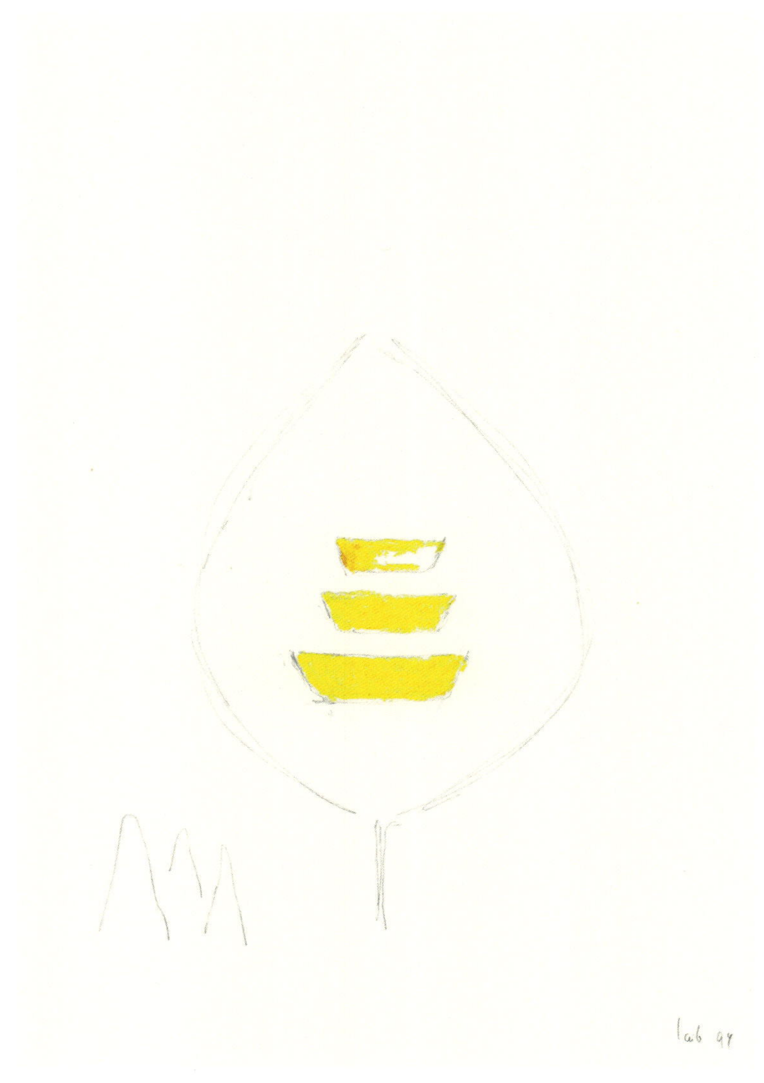
lab 94

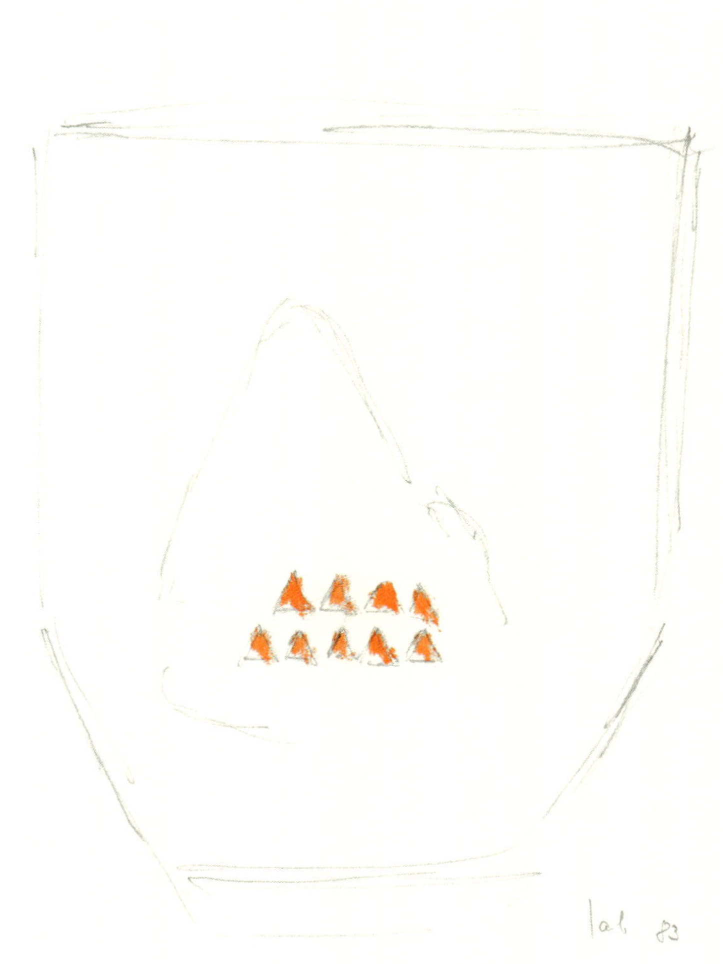

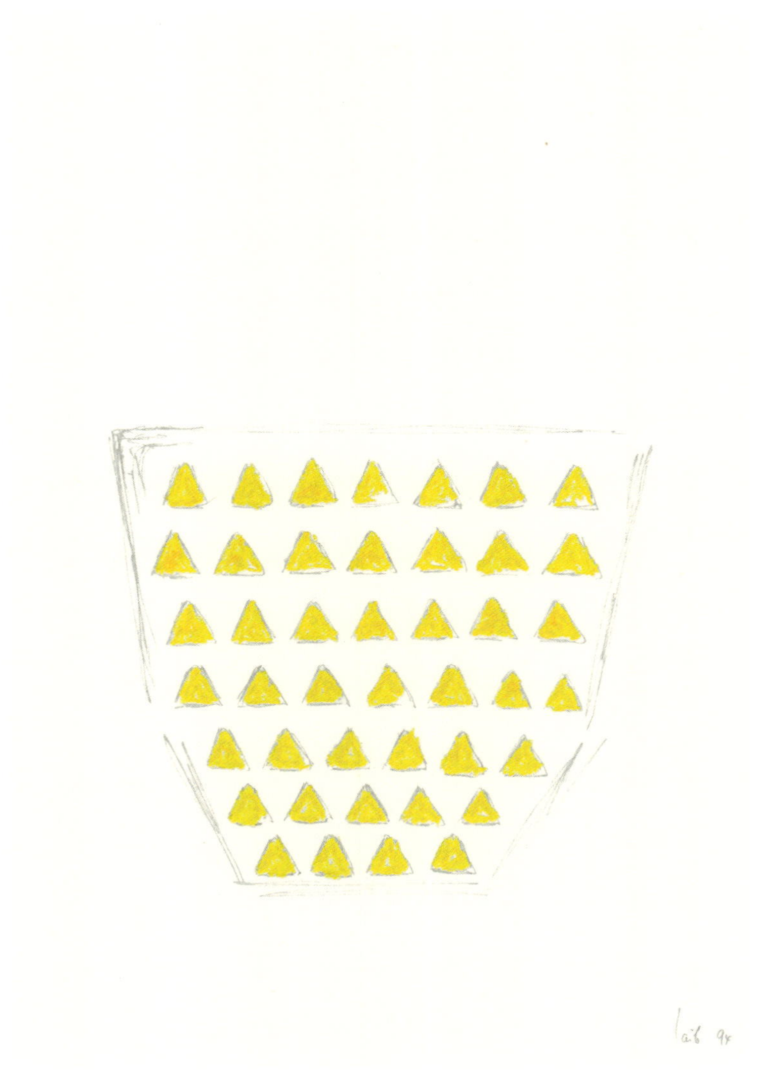

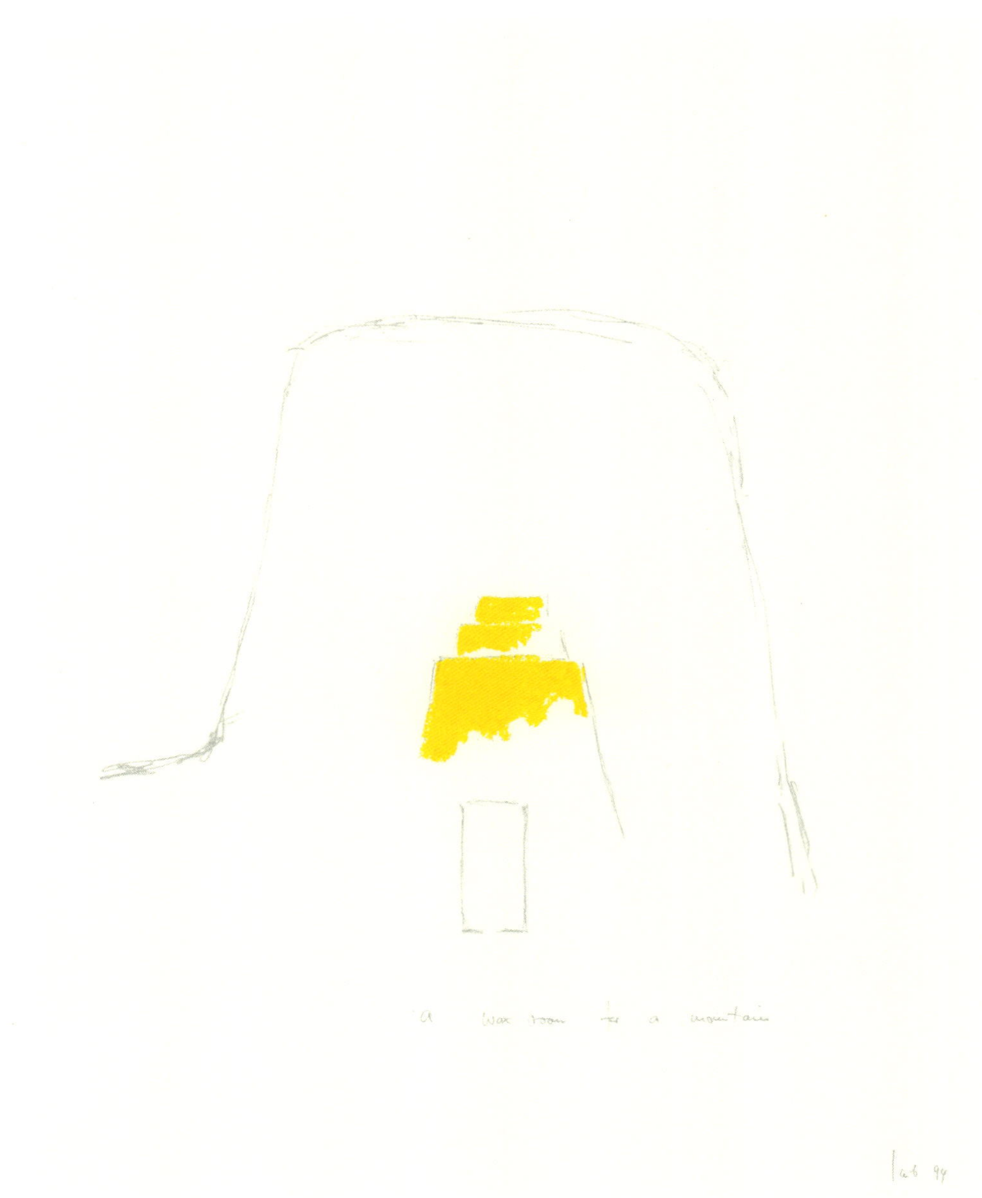

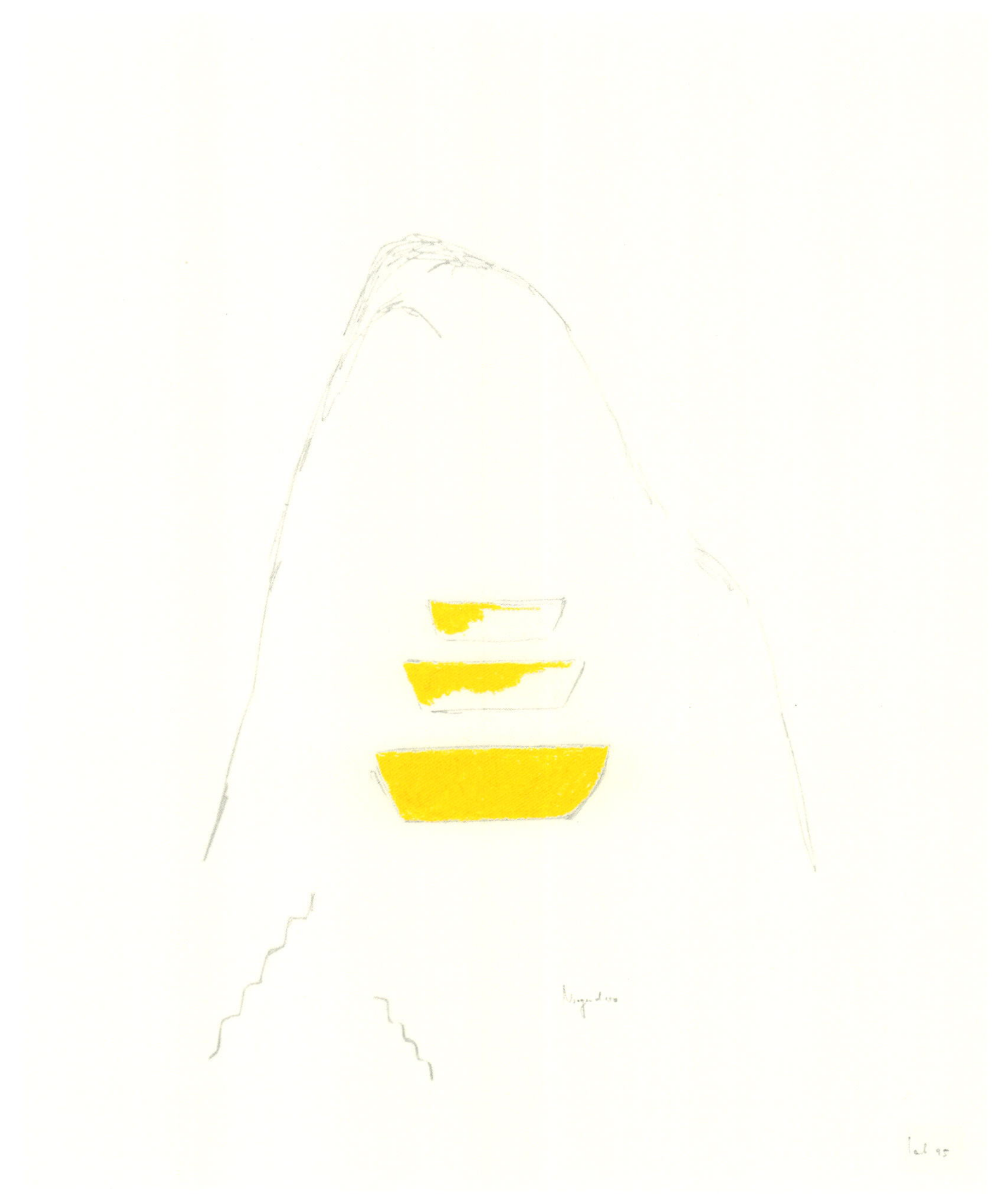

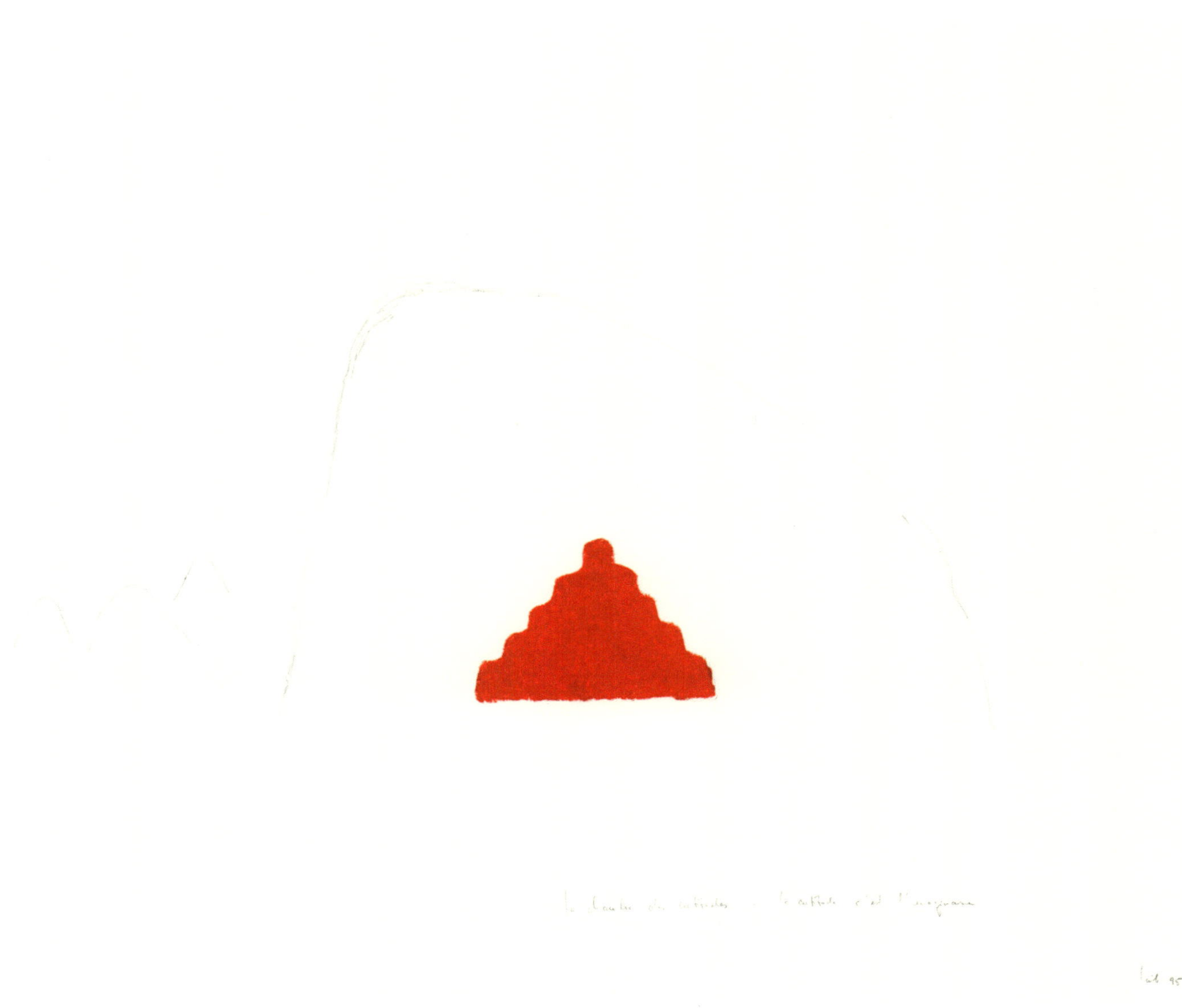

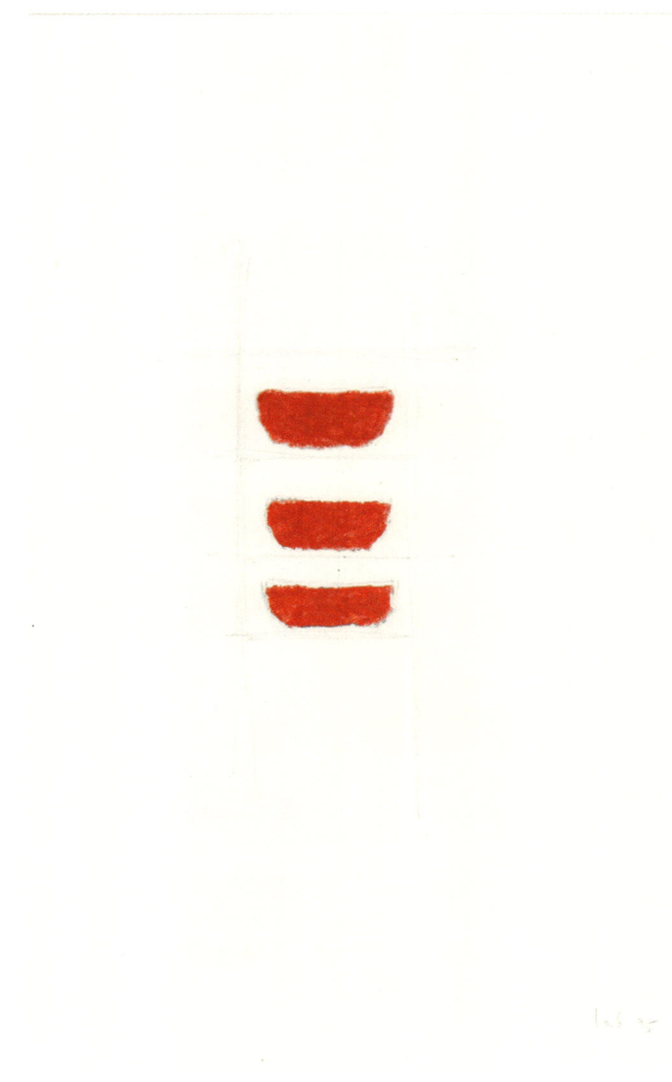

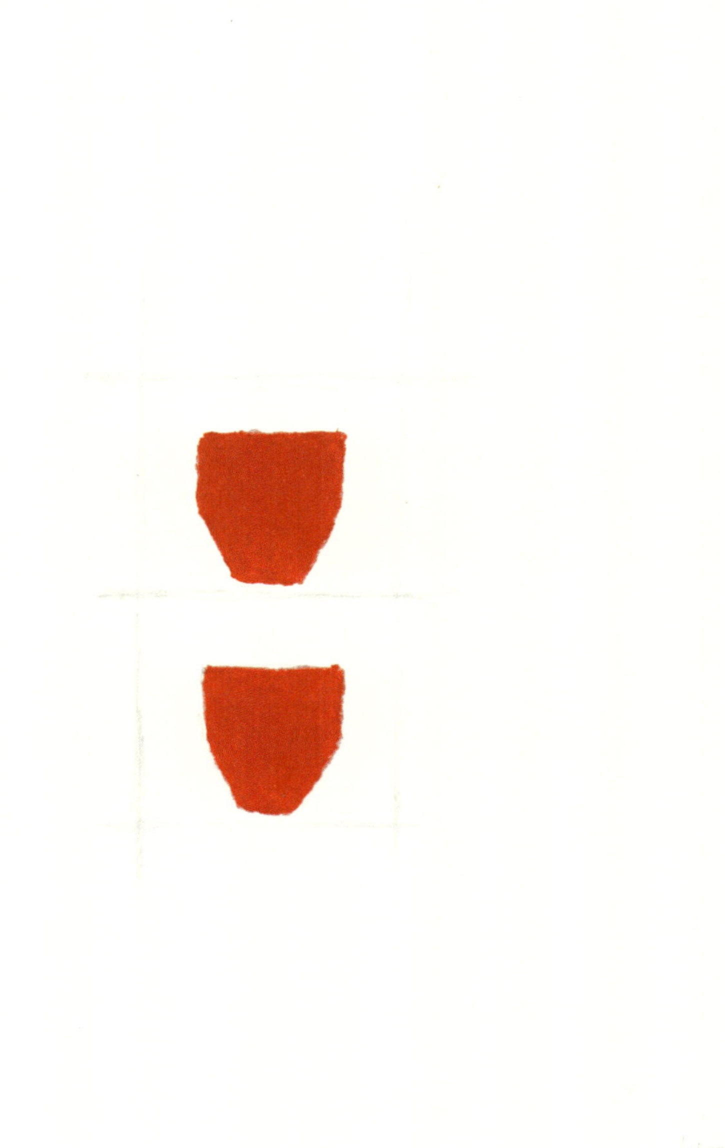

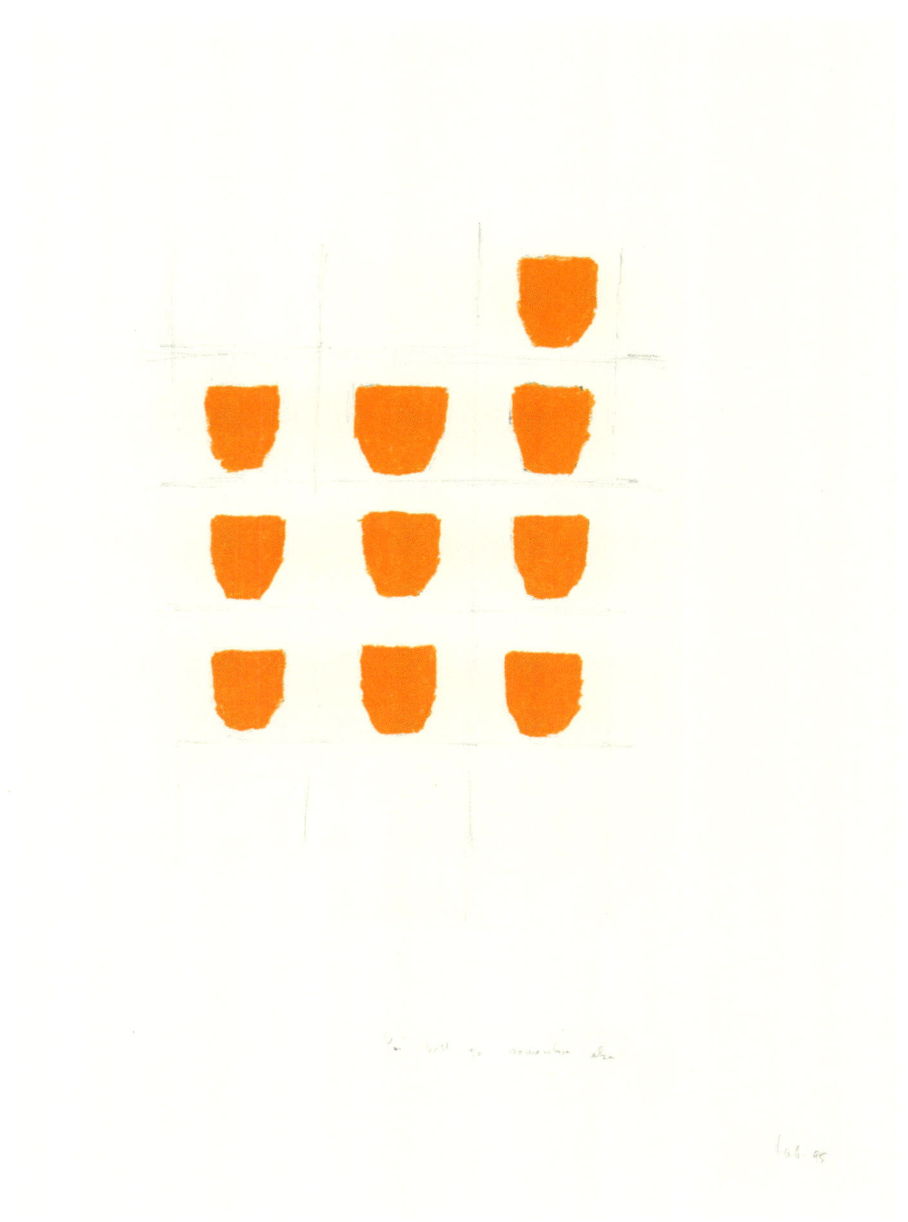

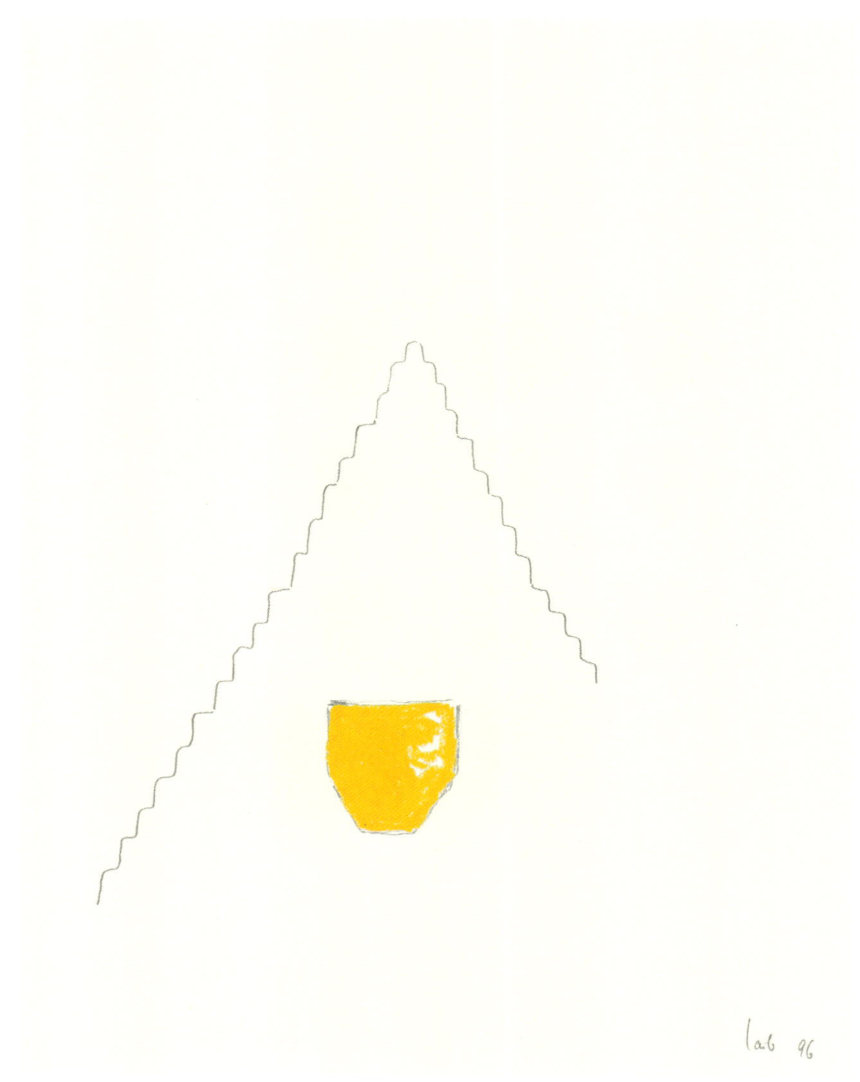

lab 96

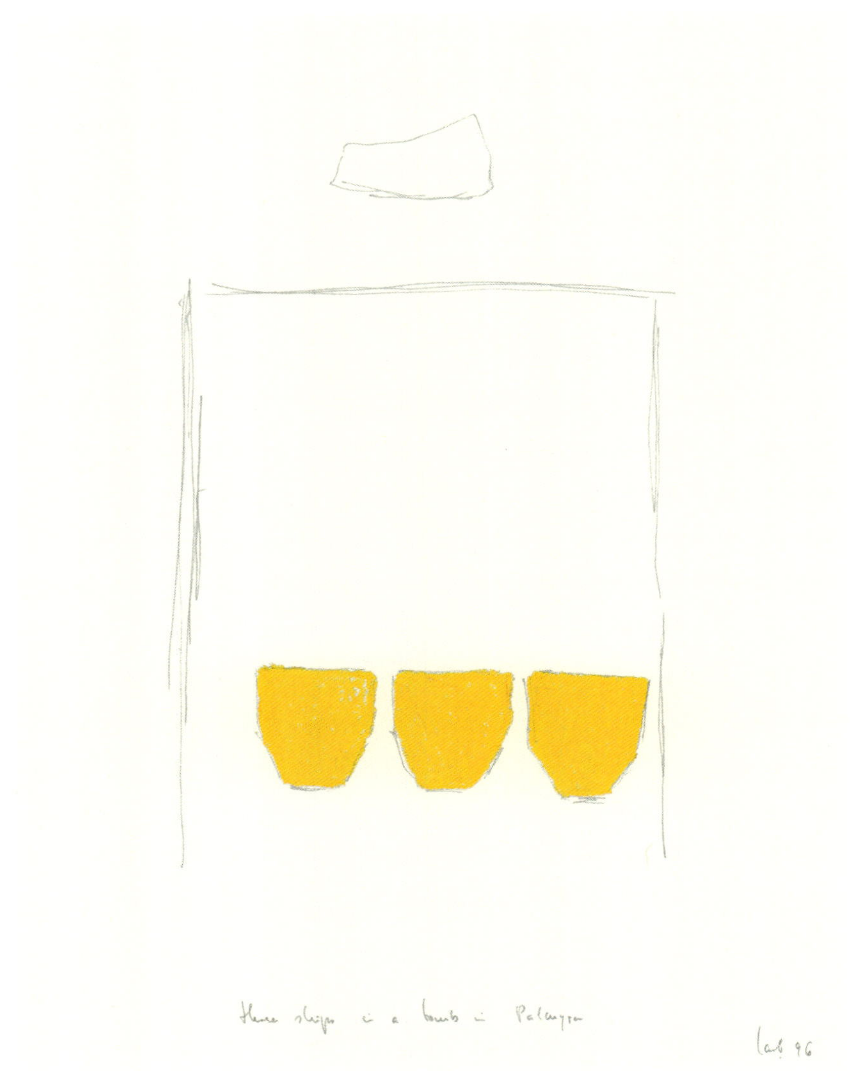

Three ships in a bomb in Palampur
lab 96

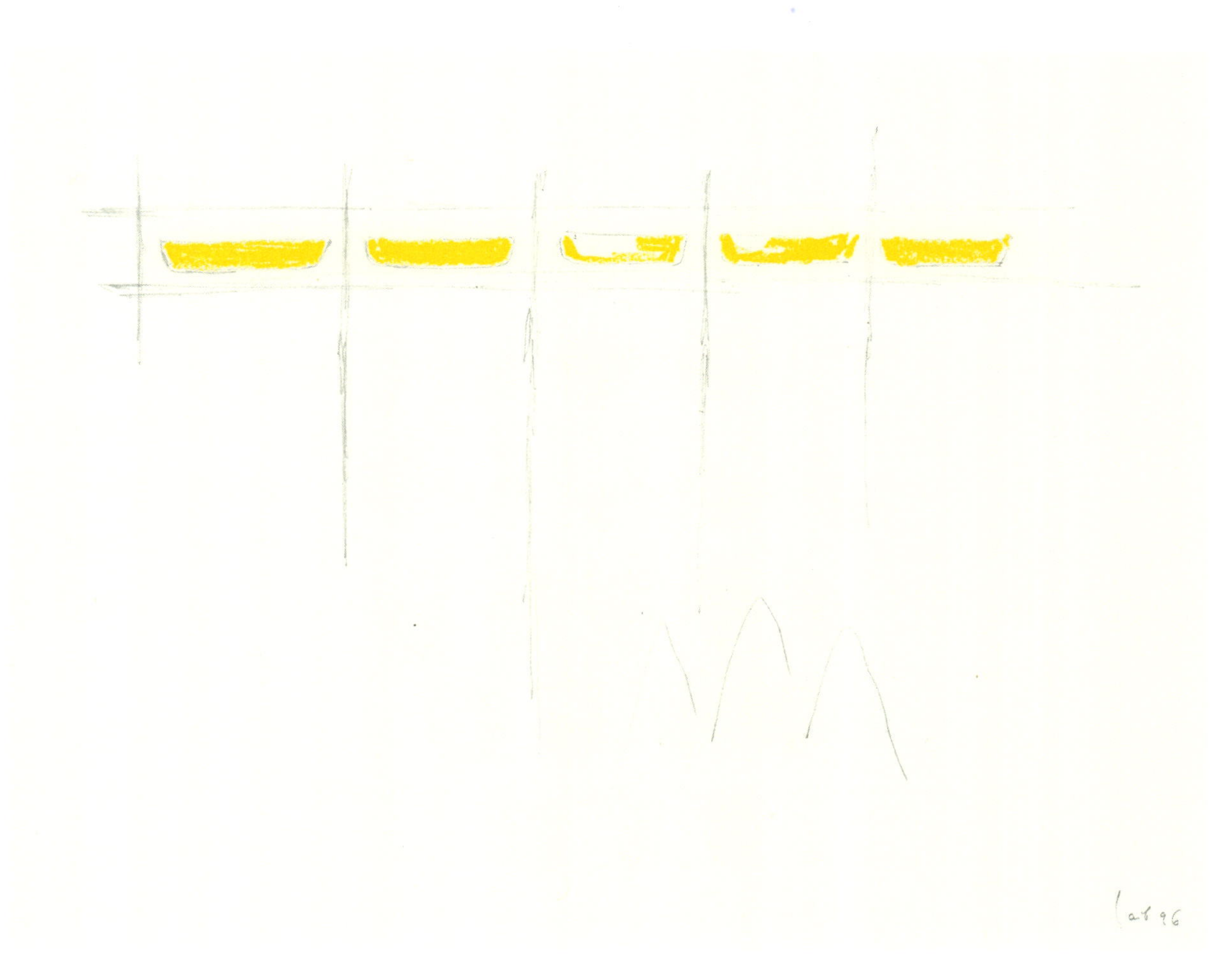

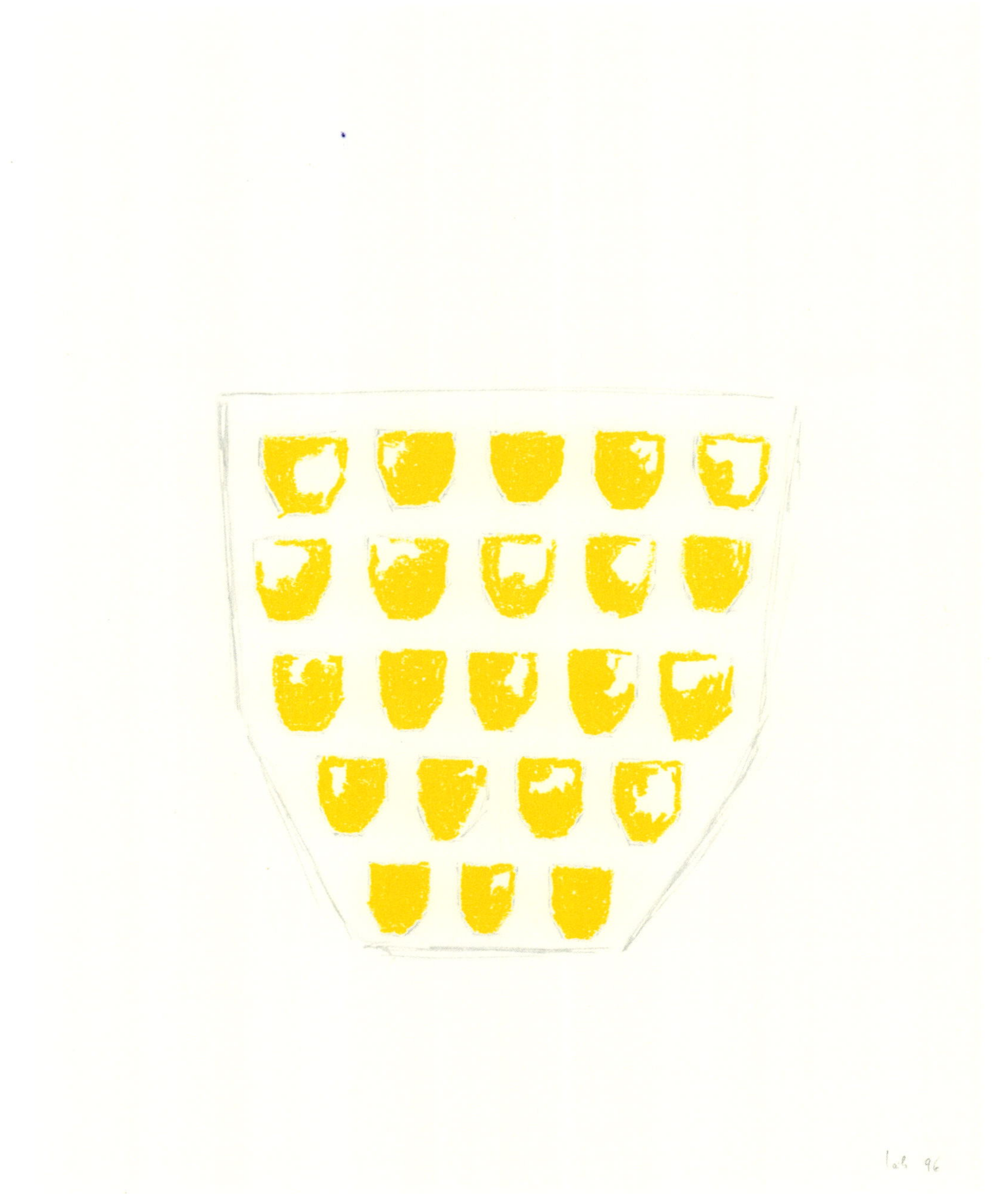

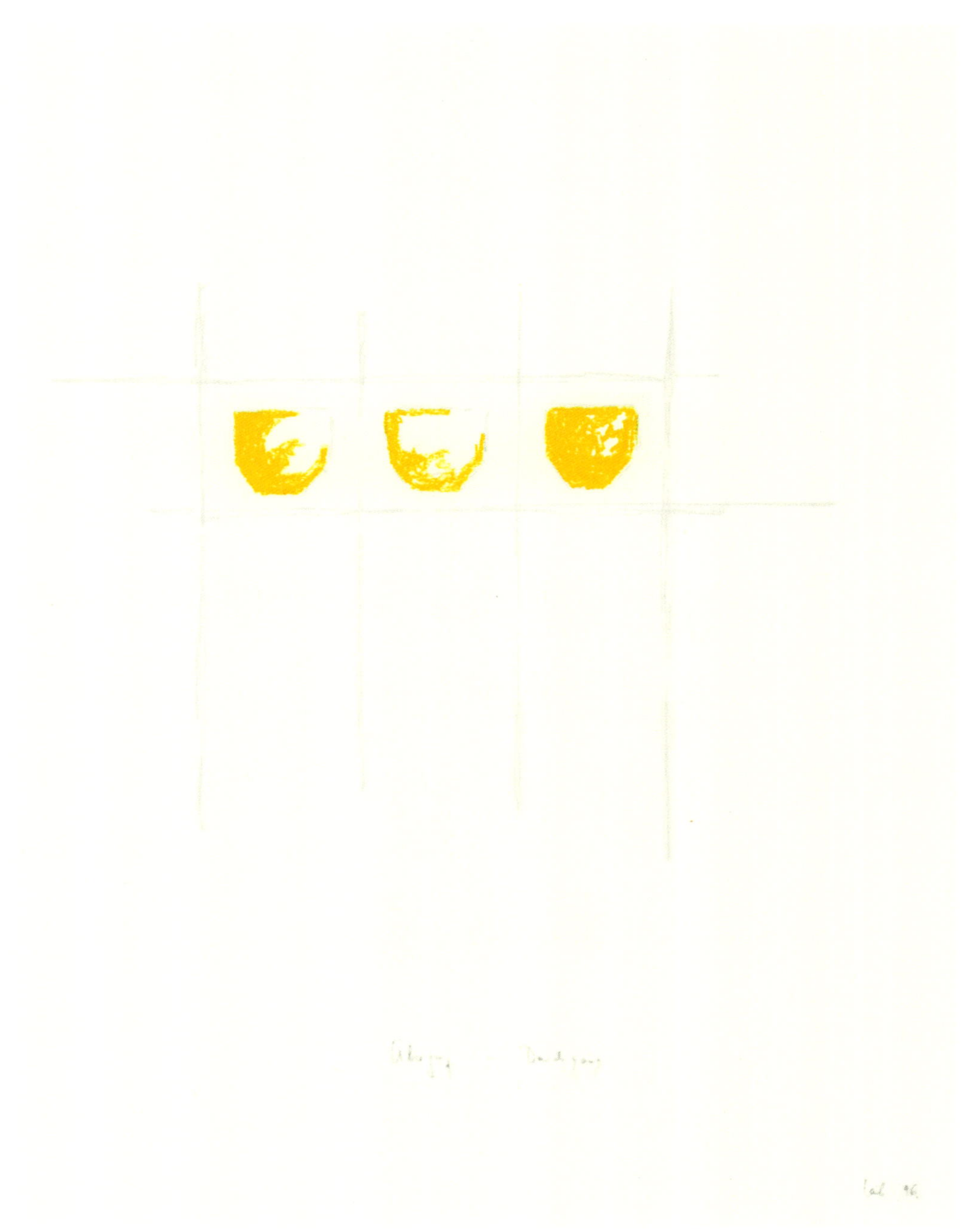

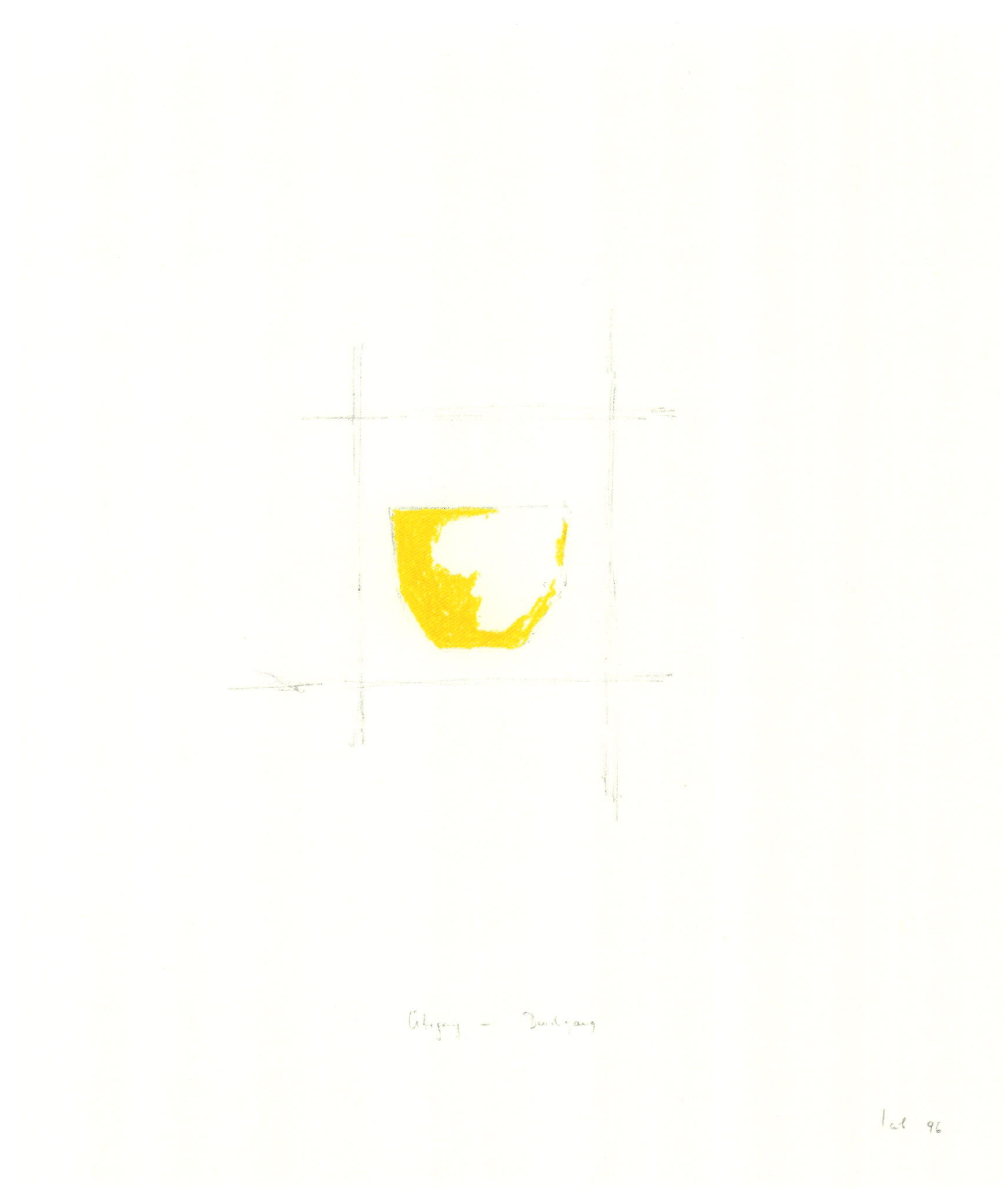

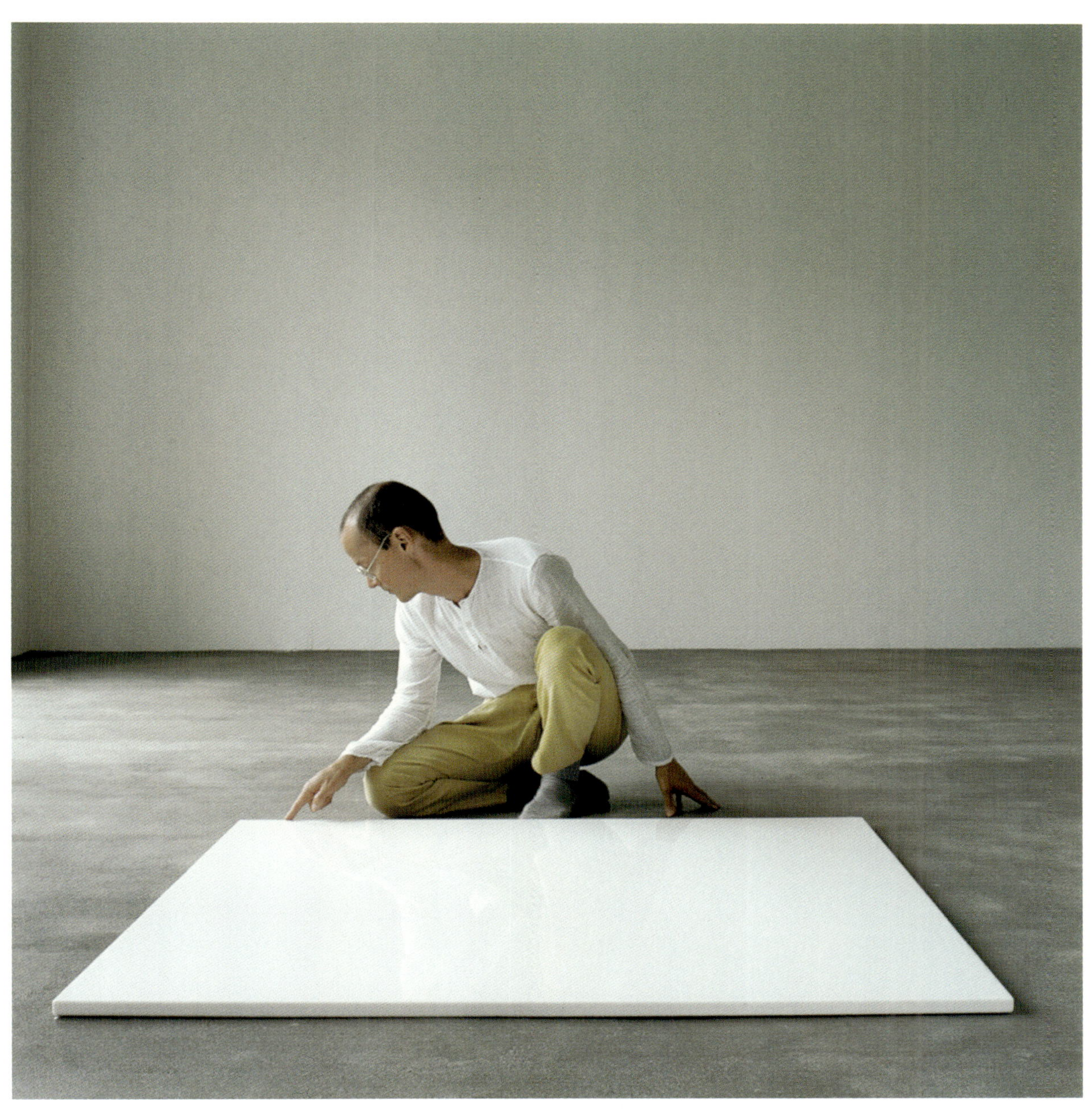

CONVERSATION

WOLFGANG LAIB AND HARALD SZEEMANN

Tegna, Siwtzerland, February 19, 2000

WOLFGANG LAIB: I think we should talk about our longstanding relationship. It has been a very special relationship, something I have never had with another curator, although I have dealt with many curators in my life. It has been more like a relationship I would have with another artist, and it's been like that from the very beginning, since we got to know one another through the first exhibition [*Spuren, Skulpturen und Monumente ihrer präzisen Reise* (*Traces, Sculptures, and Monuments of Their Precise Journey*) at the Kunsthaus Zürich, 1985].

HARALD SZEEMANN: I remember you liked the phrase on the back of the catalogue better than the show's title: "Schwach wie die Monumente und stark wie das Echo" (Weak As the Monuments and Strong As the Echo). It was a group show, and I chose to do a very quiet exhibition with a more sculptural orientation to counterbalance the perpetual showing of "wild" picture painting. I was trying to establish a connection between the exhibition and some of the works in the permanent collection: Brancusi, Medardo Rosso, Giacometti. I wanted to address the concept of the fragility of art, which for me—as I have said repeatedly—is a political statement. I wanted to take the notion of fragility further.

I had previously seen many of your works, and I had seen how they should *not* be shown—as at the Documenta. So I gave you a pure white, triangular room. Then you made the "unclimbable mountains" (*The Five Mountains Not to Climb On*), which became the essence of the exhibition. Those five little piles of dandelion pollen were so fragile, yet so full of form, materialized, yet so light.

From that moment on we made our way together. The exhibition was shown in a changed form in Vienna [*De Sculptura*, at the Messepalast, Wiener Festwochen, 1986]: milkstones and rice houses were added, and the exhibition space was much larger. One thing about group exhibitions that has always interested me is the way in which each work has and retains its own value, but also refers to other works, which results in an entirely different sort of tension in the space. Of course, once the things are placed in the space, the installation might not be perfect, but the impurities—for example, the electrical outlets—are not noticed if the work is in harmony with the space.

After Vienna we went to Düsseldorf [Kunsthalle, 1986]. Of course the title [*SkulpturSein* (*Being Sculpture*)] indicated that the exhibition was intense. It did not include the same group of artists; those who said that it was the same exhibition had not really looked very hard.

From Düsseldorf we went to Berlin [*Zeitlos* at the Hamburger Bahnhof, 1988]. I wanted to cope with that large railway station without architecture. Many of the younger artists did not even want to deal with the problems of a large space—they retreated back into the white cube. But you built your own Casbah, your wonderful beeswax room, which simply played along with the pieces by Serra, Sol LeWitt, James Lee Byars, Beuys, etc.

From Berlin we moved on to Hamburg [*Einleuchten* (*Illumine*) at the Deichtorhallen, 1989], where you made the large beeswax wall.

A year later, we were together again, this time in Tokyo [*LightSeed* at the Watari-um, 1990]. In Japan your pollen works, which were featured on the exhibition poster, became an icon for the show; we felt we had achieved our ambition of bringing "Zen" to Japan.

W L: When I saw the poster, in the cement desert of Tokyo, it was as if it were from another planet, always a very good experience for me. There is not much interest in contemporary art in Japan, but when the Japanese saw the poster and the pollen, something happened. It is incredible what power the pollen has, how deeply into a person it can go, into someone who in his daily life goes only from one place to another in this cement desert. That was especially apparent during this exhibition—and that is what I imagine and understand the function of art to be.

H S: Then we did a one-man exhibition in Ascona [Museo Communale, Switzerland, 1992]. You discovered a new material while visiting here in Ticino, a granite you used as a base for your elevated beeswax houses and beeswax stairs, your granite-wax configurations.

W L: Those were the first granite slabs I ever used for a big installation and the first small staircase out of beeswax.

Yesterday I reread the booklet published for that exhibition, and in it—I had forgotten this—you write that you had asked me for an interview, but that I had said I could not do it, that I felt helpless with words. Later, I wrote you a longer letter, which you also cite in the booklet. You had done a Mondrian exhibition a few years before, which I had seen. It was the first time I had come in close contact with Monte Verità [Mountain of Truth], and I must say for me it was a crucial development in my relationship with you. I still believe, as I wrote you then, that I could never live on Monte Verità, but the connection between it and Mondrian is incredible. You also wrote that Monte Verità has always oriented itself toward the past, and that is of course very disturbing for an artist. All the theories and experiments then become questionable; for an artist like Mondrian or myself, or for someone like you, it is all about the future, and of future designs, and of visions and utopias, which, even if they are not real and will never be realized, exist nevertheless. A utopia—that is what it is all about.

HS: When I think of the Bordeaux exhibition [*GAS, Grandiose Ambitieux, Silencieux* at the capcMusée d'art contemporain, 1993], I always think of a particular slide taken from above, where one sees so incredibly well how large the spaces are between the works, and also how easily a sixty-by-eighty centimeter pollen work can fill a space twenty meters high.

WL: The pollen seen from above, from a distance—something that is seldom possible in a museum—is very special. Even if the space is not particularly good, like the Centre Pompidou, if you have the distance, the detachment, another world is created.

HS: The pollen works are modest in appearance, but they can open up vast dimensions. Of course, in Bordeaux, there was once again the problem of the guards and the pollen. The protection of such very sensitive materials is always problematic.

WL: I want to ask you something. In the last exhibitions, it has always been the dandelion pollen that has interested you most. Why do you always want to show it? Is it, for you, my principal work?

HS: No, I consider your principal work to be the "unclimbable mountains," *The Five Mountains Not to Climb On.*

WL: I would agree, but I have not always thought so. In the beginning, it was probably the milkstones that contained practically all that I find important in this world. But in the "unclimbable mountains" everything is concentrated. All my dreams, all that I find earth-shattering is somehow in there. And since the experience I had with you in 1985—of showing the "mountains" for the first time, and of seeing your fascination with this work—it has become a principal work for me. But why is the dandelion pollen so decisive for you?

HS: Because the dandelion pollen, despite its very small size, has the greatest aura, and its statement is so succinct that it cannot be compared with anything else. It is truly a floor work, as we saw in Venice—it floated as never before in that small room. The floating in Venice was sensational. *The Five Mountains Not to Climb*

On are perceived by many as small; not everyone has our insight and can see something large in something small.

W L: In such group exhibitions there are of course artists who are absolute opposites; I find that to be very good, very explosive. It is in such shows, however, that a utopian vision becomes so important. The more vulgar the artists are on one side, the greater the need for a vision on the other side. Some people say that a utopian vision is naive, particularly at the beginning of the new century, but I do find it to be incredibly important in such exhibitions.

Recently, as you know, I have made some very big works, bigger than I had the confidence to make earlier. Before, I also would have said that something monumental was the opposite of what I wanted. Then I made, for example, the large beeswax ziggurats; at first glance they are monumental, also sculptural. In several exhibitions, however, I contrasted them with a pollen mountain—and I often thought of the Zurich exhibition, and the title. Because despite the various sizes, the seven-centimeter-high pollen mountain has the same size as a beeswax ziggurat measuring six meters. That is the decisive factor for me; that is why it was important that I not only make rectangles on the floor. Suddenly, there could also be a house form, or a house form on a wall—entirely different forms. It was no longer a question of floor sculptures. But whether it was a seven-centimeter-high pollen mountain or a six-meter-high beeswax ziggurat, it was always the same for me, always exactly the same as the "mountains." They deal with the same things.

We have talked about exhibitions almost exclusively. As I see it, for you the exhibition is the final objective. For me, it is the art, for instance, the milkstone or the five unclimbable mountains. The art has an existence completely independent from the exhibitions, which exist only to allow the works to be seen by many people. Of course, I have always had this almost naive belief that a pollen piece, or a milkstone, contains a message that could change the world, and to do that the work must be seen.

H S: Exhibitions are the temporary realization of something that I want to be perceived on a level beyond what is visible.

W L: Why does it not bother you that exhibitions are temporary?

H S: If I were Ludwig II, I would conserve many exhibitions, but generally I've always accepted the temporary nature of exhibitions. Then they don't weigh on me either.

WL: It's the intensity of the temporary. Once the thing's permanent, it becomes the dusty castle of a French king. On the other hand, things do happen that are so important, so world-moving that sometimes it can be a pity to take an exhibition down after six weeks. Don't you think so? There are of course opportunities to do things that will be permanent—I'm thinking of my wax room in the Pyrenees.

HS: What's so great about exhibitions is that—when you work together with an artist—everything has an existence, a life, before it is owned. Once it becomes a property, other rules take over. It makes me sad, when I try to make something temporary as beautiful as possible, and then it becomes property, a footnote to art history.

WL: Yes, that is certainly true. But then when you look at things that are five thousand, a thousand, or ten thousand years old—Giotto's chapel in Padua, a cave painting, or the Pyramids—you know that it would have been a pity if their existence had been "temporary." That leads me to questions of time and timelessness. You called the exhibition in Berlin *Zeitlos* [*Timeless*]; I still believe that as an artist one can elude time. The pollen works could be made a hundred years from now, or they could have been made a hundred years ago.

HS: Yes, they have a timeless quality.

WL: I found it to be so very important that the title of the exhibition was *Zeitlos*, which said for once that "zeitlos" exists, as well as "zeitgeist" [spirit of the time].

HS: Of course it was meant to be somewhat polemic, after the *Zeitgeist* exhibition at the Walter Martin Gropius-Bau in 1982, which was very limited, including painting only.

WL: Do you think, as I do, that art can exist outside of time?

HS: Yes, basically you and your work always exist outside of time, except when you are making the installation. You and the work are in the present again during those six months, but in the end, when it is finished, the work is timeless.

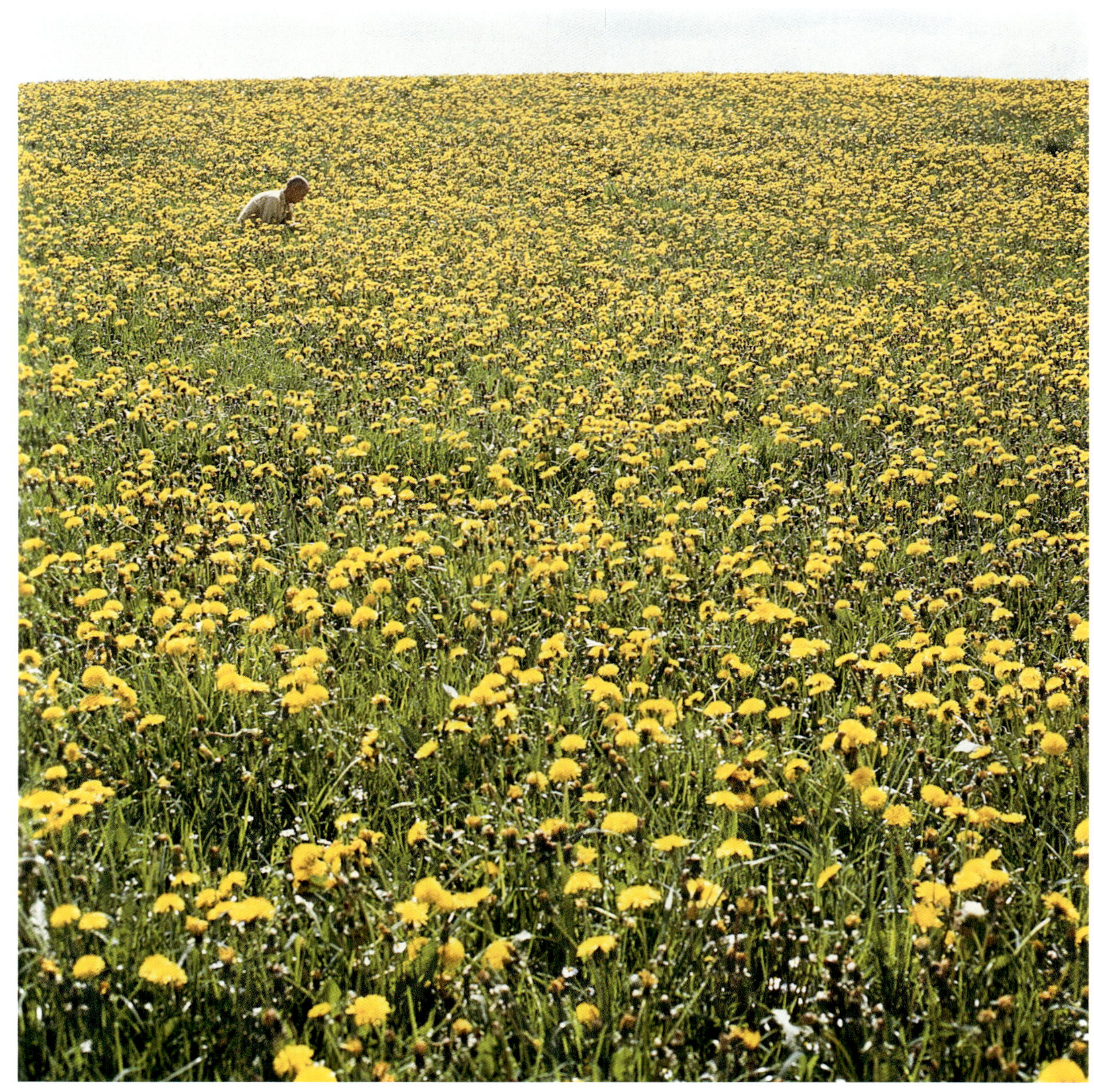

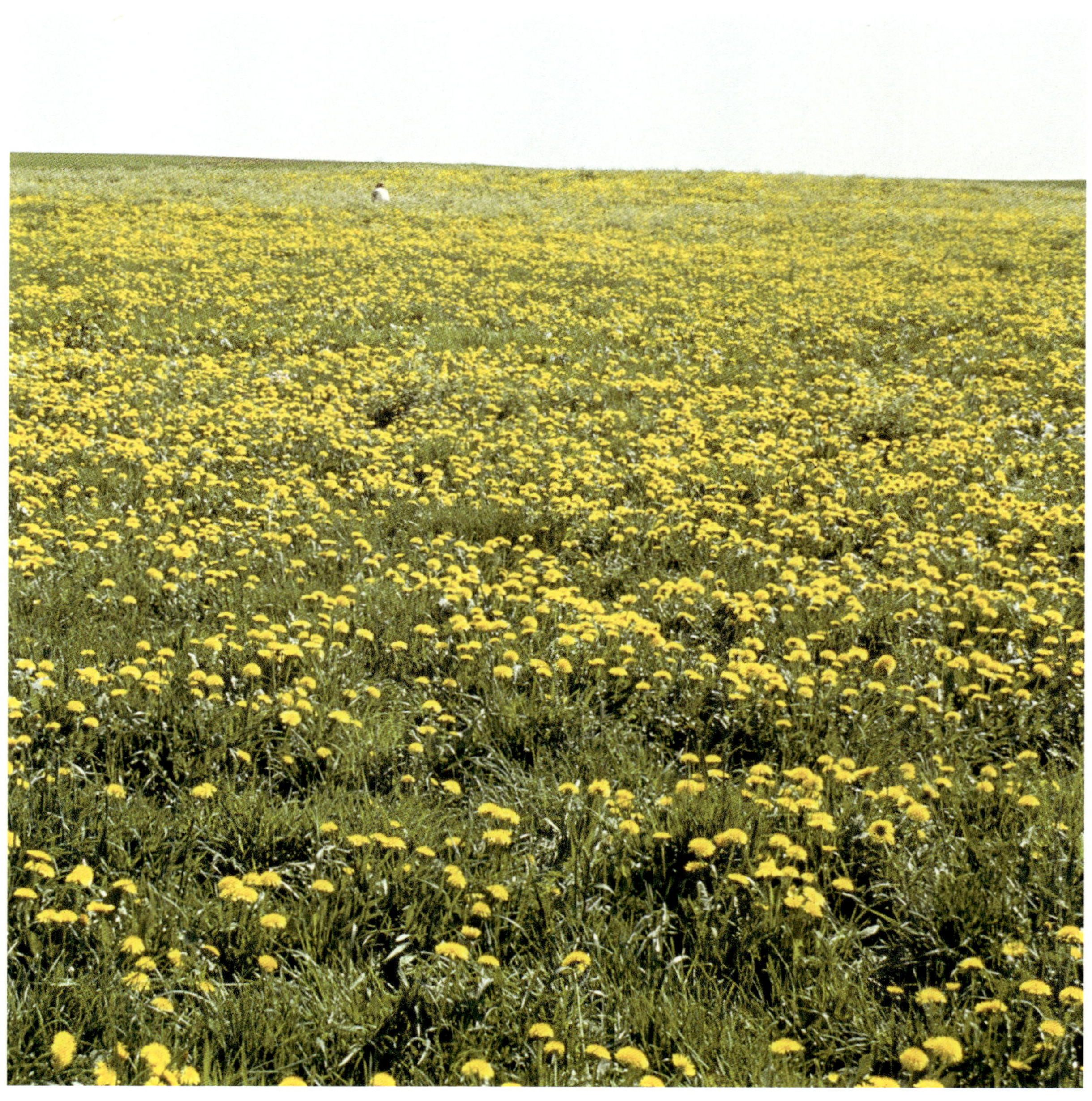

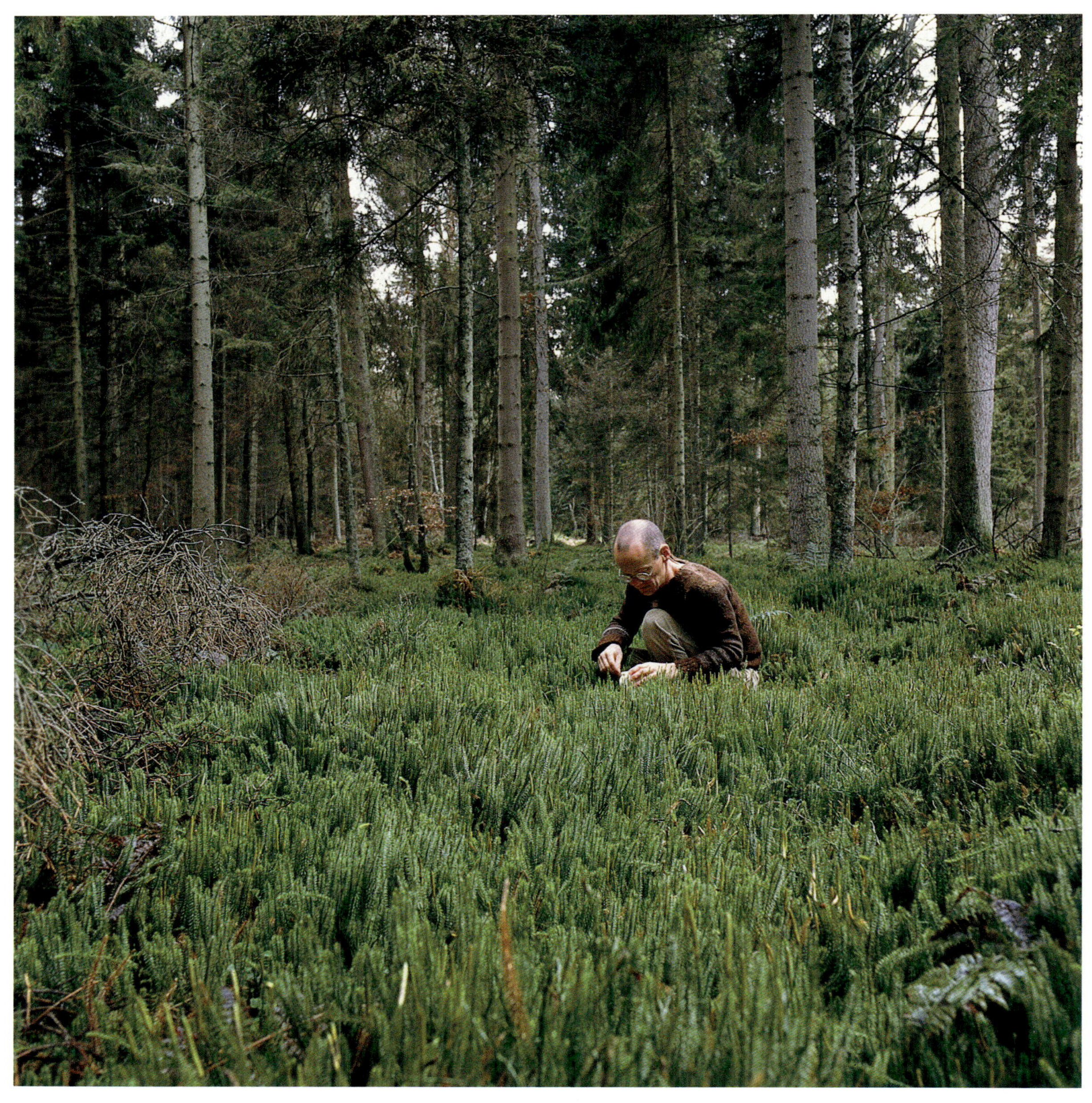

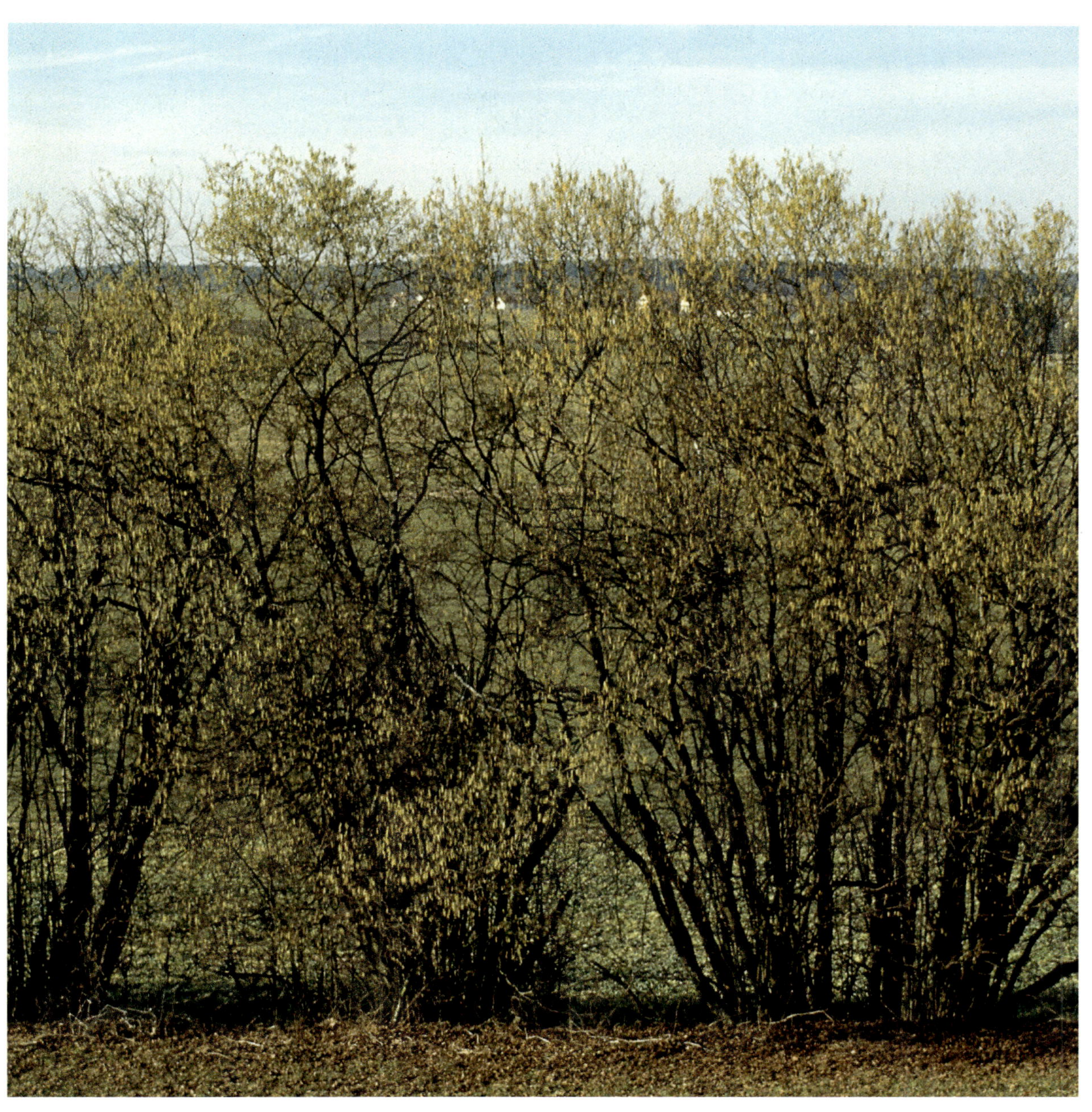

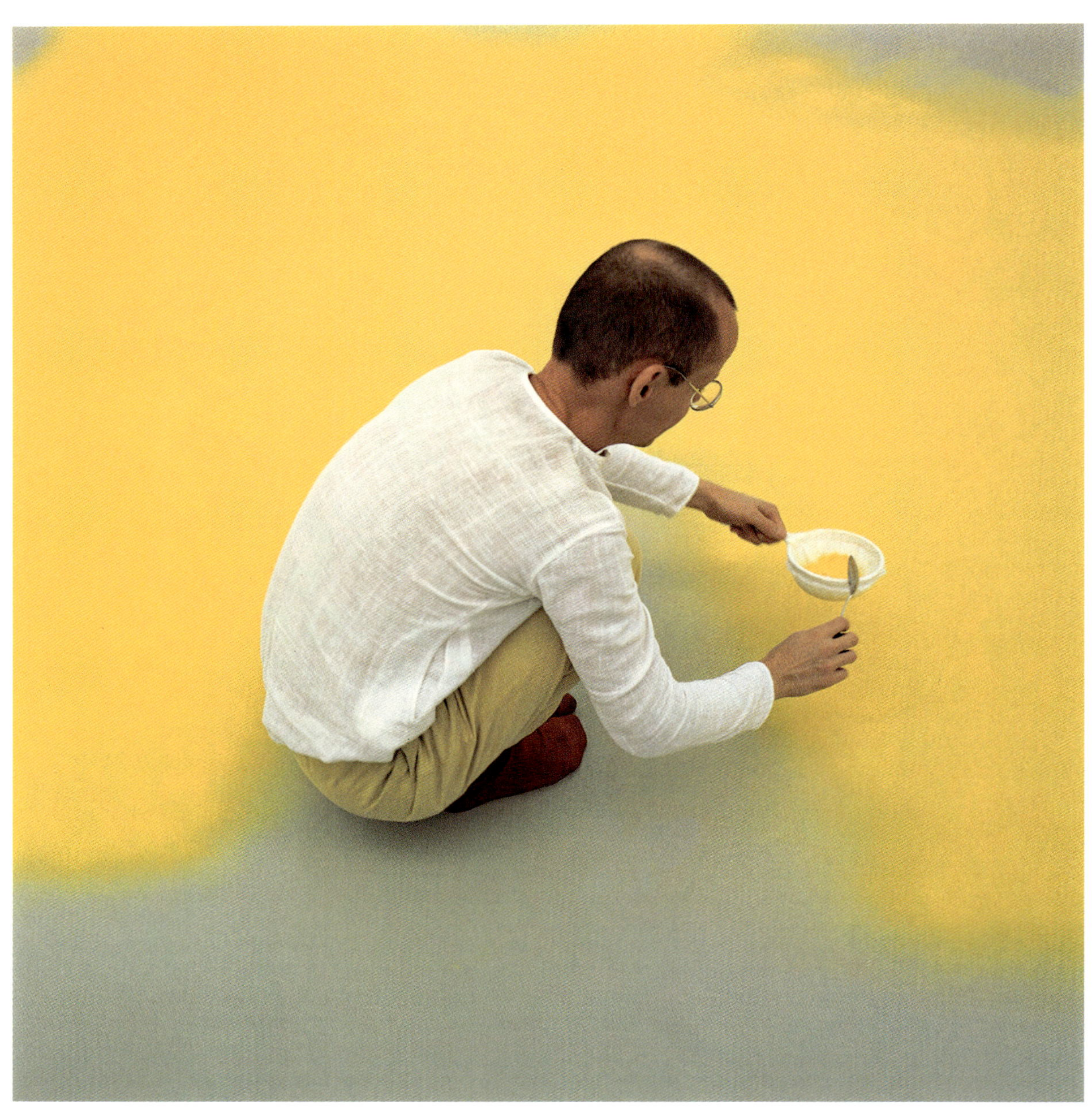

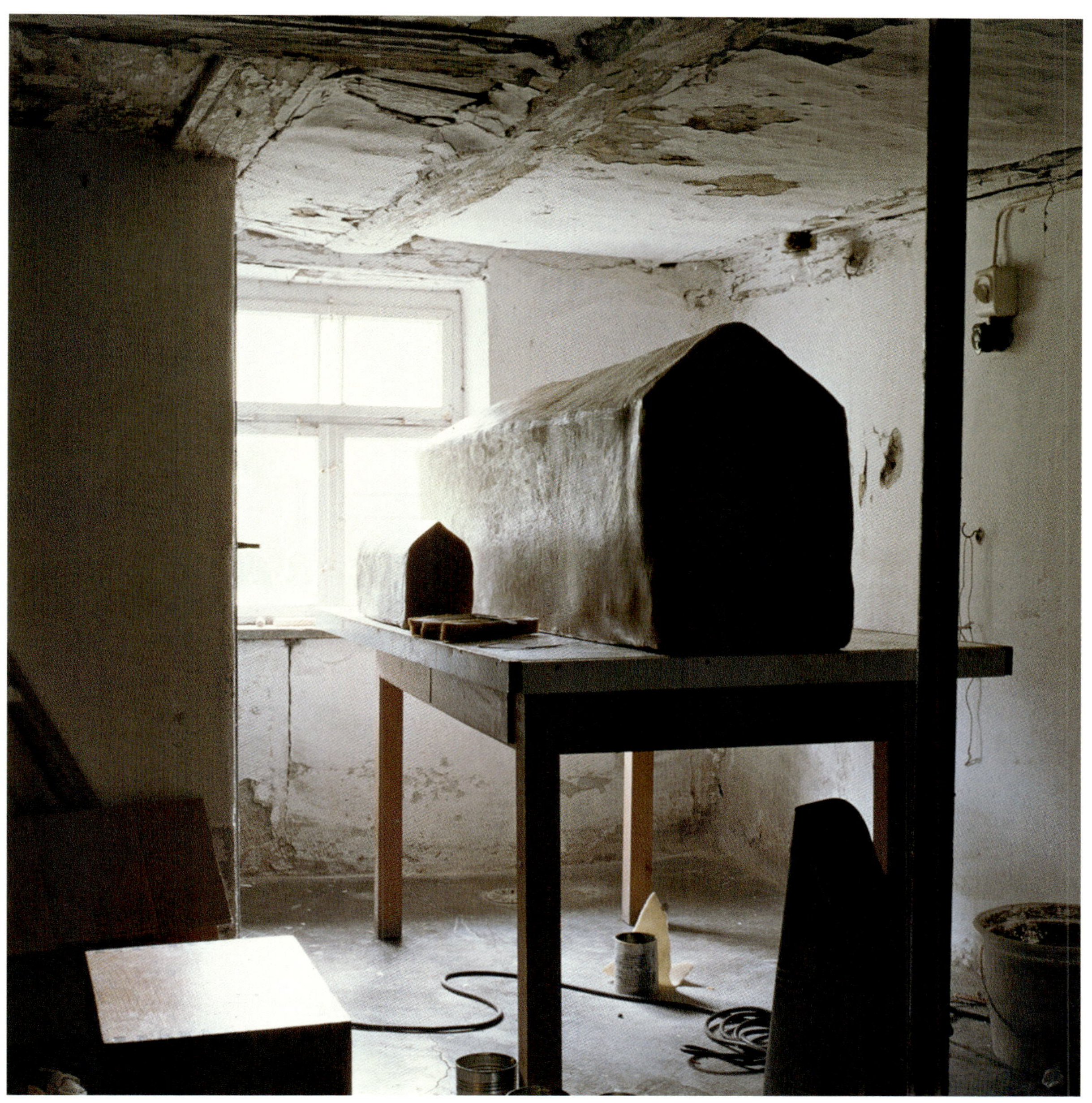

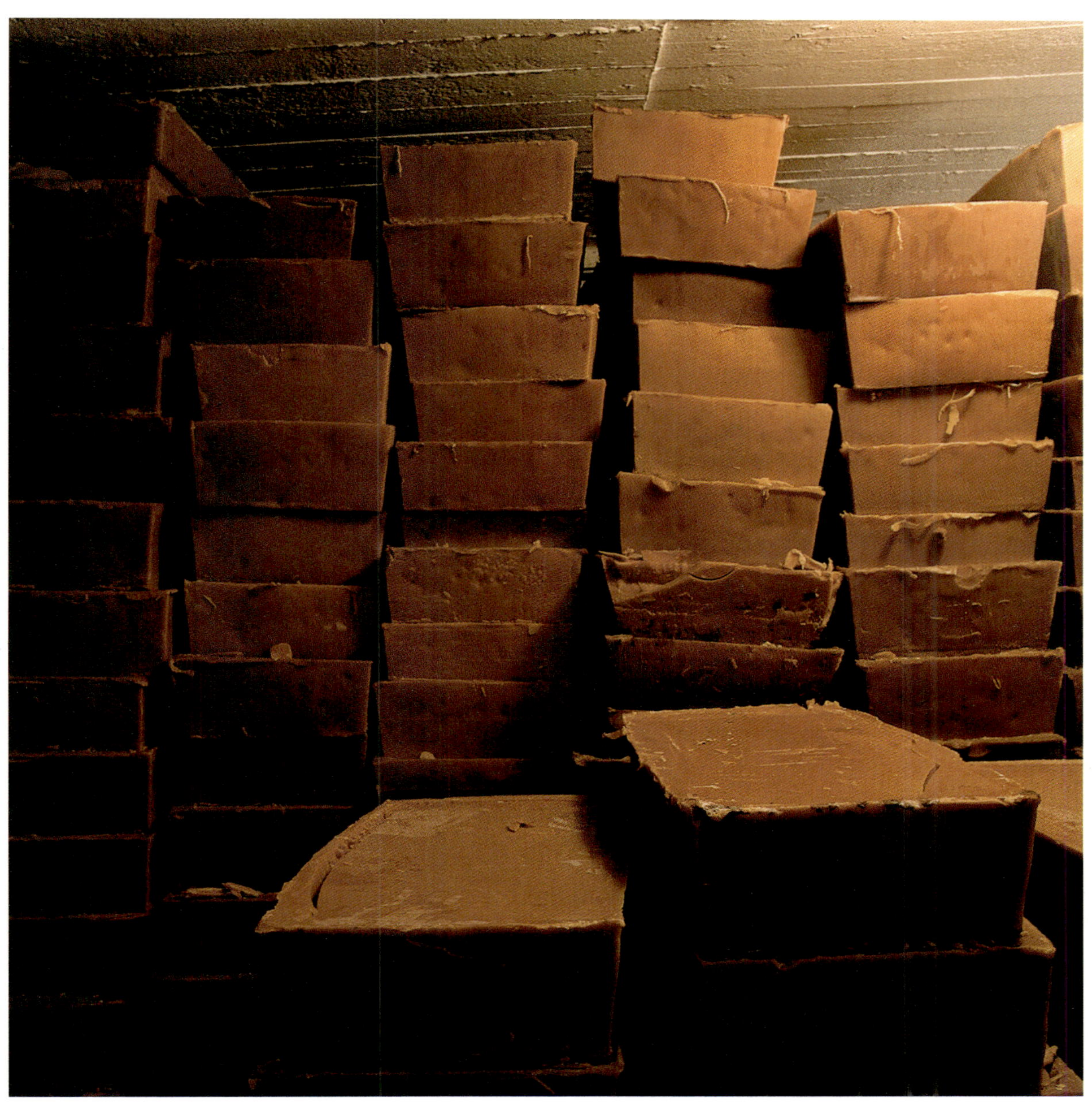

CHRONOLOGY

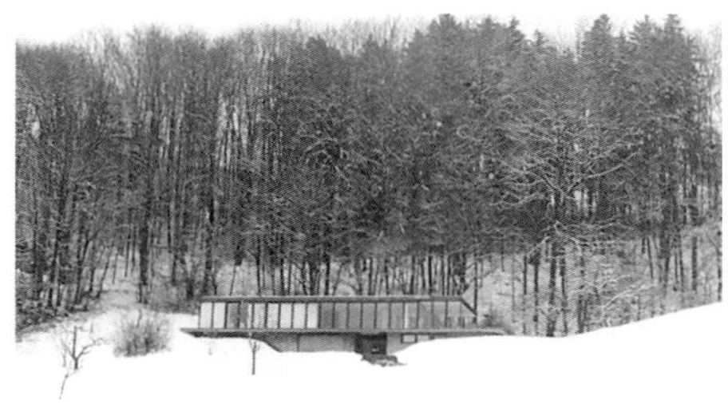

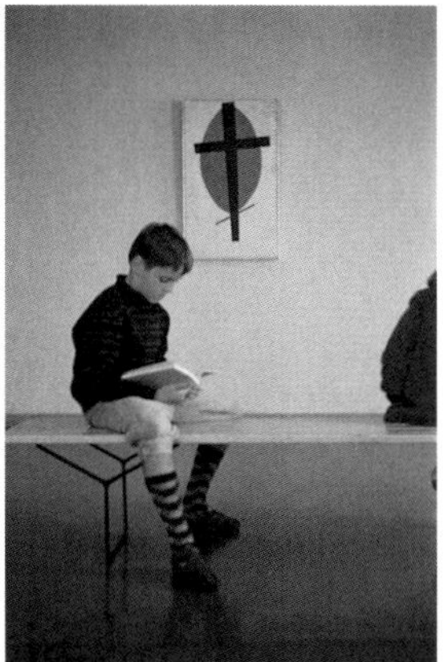

1950
Wolfgang Laib is born in the small town of Metzingen, in southern Germany, on March 25, to Lydia Stübler and Gustav Laib, a doctor. He is the first child of two. (His sister, Eva, will be born in 1952.)

1950–62
Laib grows up in Metzingen. His parents live in the house of his grand-mother, who owns a textile shop in the market square. She is a member of the Pietist community, a strict, devout, South German Protestant movement that strongly influences the family's daily life.

1958
Laib's father opens up his own practice as an orthopedist in Biberach, a small medieval town near Lake Constance. Together with a young Swiss architect from the Hochschule für Gestaltung, Ulm (a school that continues the prin-ciples of the Bauhaus), he begins to build a house outside a nearby village. This simple glass house, set in totally natural surroundings, will have a strong impact on the family's thinking and way of life.

1962
In the autumn, the family moves into the new house.

The family starts to develop what will become a long-term friendship with Jakob Bräckle, a landscape painter resident in Biberach. An intense exchange of thoughts and ideas will evolve between Bräckle and Laib over the years; and until Bräckle's death, in 1987, a few weeks before his ninetieth birthday, he will remain Laib's only friend in the area. In fact he instills an interest in art in the entire family, con-vincing them that art is of ultimate importance. His strikingly modest way of life and his interest in Chinese phi-losophy (especially that of Lao-tzu) will be very influential for Laib.

Bräckle is a friend of the architect Hugo Häring, who has kept all of the paintings by Kasimir Malevich that the Russian artist left behind when he returned home, after a stay in Germany. The paintings are rolled up and stored under Häring's bed, and he and Bräckle sometimes unroll them and enjoy them. They are finally bought by the Stedelijk Museum, Amsterdam, but before they leave for the Netherlands, they are shown in Ulm in a large exhibition.

Laib's father begins to make white paintings himself, and to explore

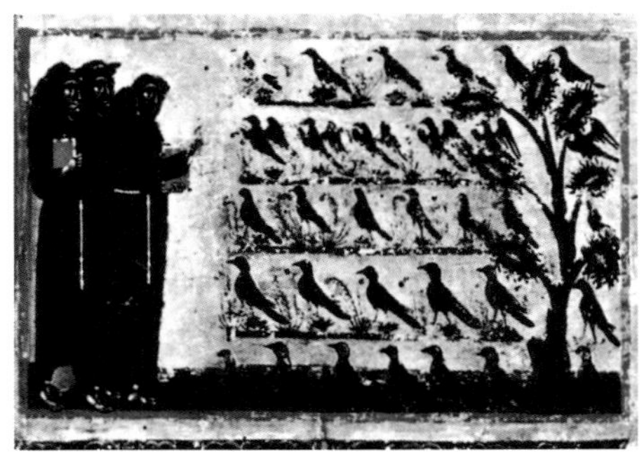

sculptural forms. Also at this time the family begins to travel throughout Europe and eventually eastward. They visit major sites of medieval European art, including Romanesque churches and, several times, the town of Assisi, enduringly associated with Saint Francis. The art of the Middle Ages, the reliquaries preserved in Catholic churches, and above all the figure of Saint Francis will become important influences on Laib.

1965

One of the family's journeys is to Turkey, where Laib visits Konya, site of a former monastery at the tomb of the Sufi poet and mystic Jalal-ud-din Rumi. This site too will be a major source of inspiration for him. The family also observes the simple living spaces of Turkish villages, often featuring empty unfurnished rooms. Under the influence of this experience, the Laibs remove the furniture from the glass house; they sit, eat, and sleep on the floor. The only things left in the house, which is surrounded by meadows and forests, are a few art objects.

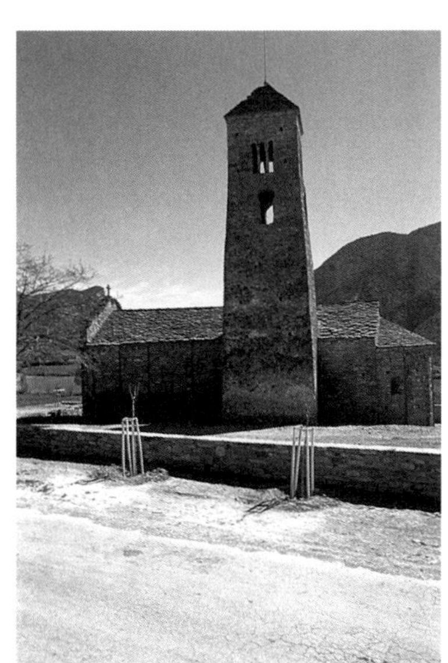

Over the next few years Laib will travel with his family to Asia and the Near East—to Iran and Afghanistan, to Mesopotamia, and then to India. He studies, visits exhibitions, looks at whatever art is within his reach. In Paris he discovers the studio of Constantin Brancusi, which has just been rebuilt in the Musée d'Art Moderne de la Ville de Paris. Over the coming decades it will remain Laib's favorite place in the city. Only two years later he will travel to Tirgu Jiu, Romania, to see Brancusi's *Endless Column, Table of Silence,* and *Gate of the Kiss.*

1968

Laib begins to meet other artists for the first time. He has high expectations of these meetings, but is severely disappointed, for he encounters only mediocre artists living out a bohemian lifestyle. Unable to imagine learning from such people, Laib decides not to go to art school but to study medicine, in Tübingen. To this goal too he brings high expectations, cherishing every possible ideal about medicine, and about the goal of healing and helping other people; but here too he is disappointed, realizing very quickly that as a discipline medicine remains within the limits of the natural sciences, confining itself to the study of the material body. Lonely at the university, he begins to attend lectures in many different fields: philosophy, psychology, psychiatry, archaeology, art history, and Oriental philosophies.

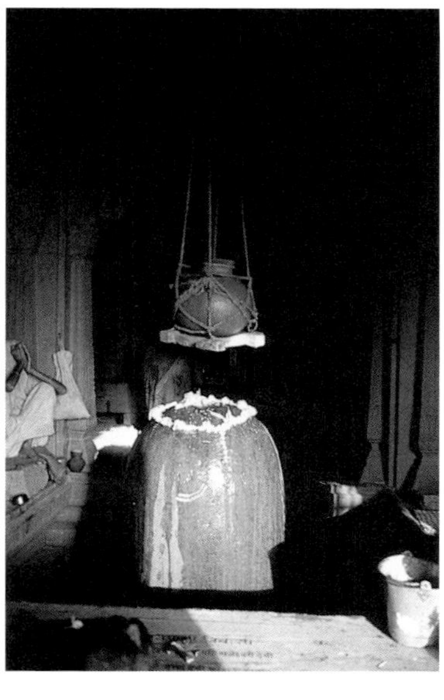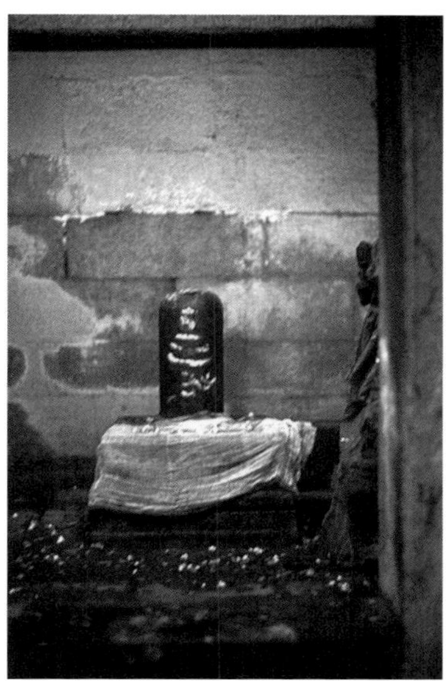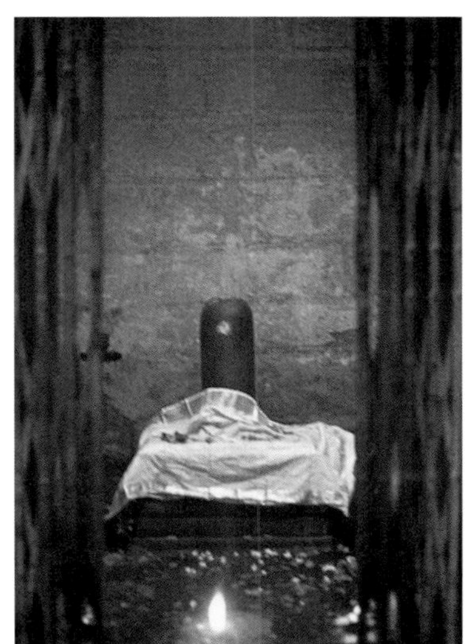

In addition to his medical studies, Laib begins to take courses in Indian language and culture, studying Sanskrit, Hindi, and Tamil.

1972
Laib's father has taken his family on several long trips to India, and he is deeply impressed by the country's poverty. In about 1970 he had started a project to support and develop a whole village near Madurai, in South India, working through Gandhigram, a center of Gandhian thought in the region. Spending every summer since 1970 in South India, the family comes in contact with Indian village life, which influences Laib strongly. In 1972, Laib spends six months in India working on his medical thesis, which he titles "The Hygiene of Drinking Water in Rural Areas of South India." On returning to Germany, however, he does not go back to medical school but starts working with hammer and chisel on a dark boulder that he finds in the countryside near his home and shapes into an egg—a Brahmaṇḍa. The job takes months, and ends when Laib gives the surface a fine polished finish. The close of the year is nearing, and Laib has not yet returned to medical school. After finishing this first sculpture, and as a result of taking it on, he decides to become an artist. First, however, he will complete his medical studies and finalize the material he has collected for his thesis.

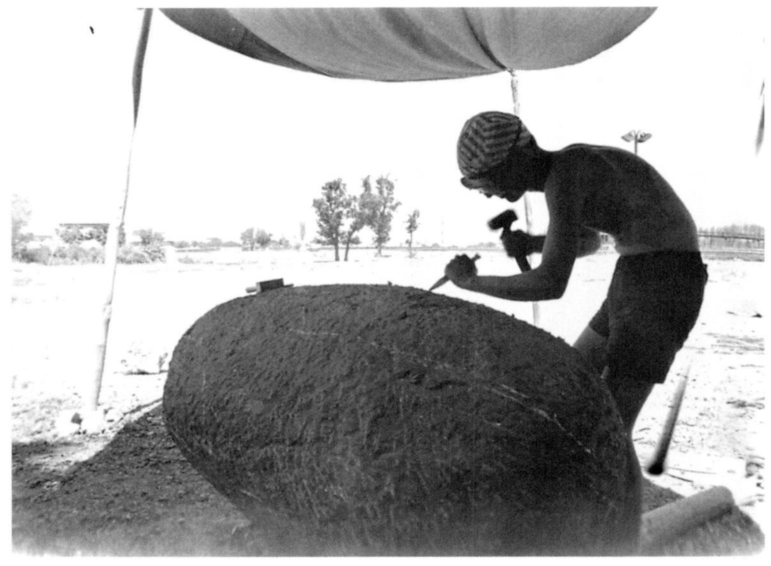

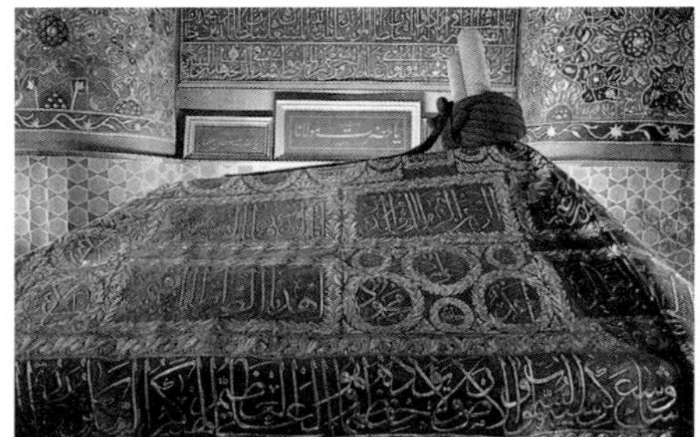

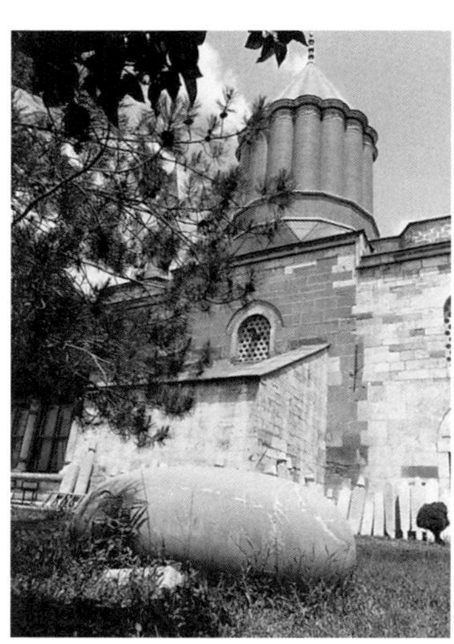

1973
Returning to Konya with his parents, Laib begins work on a second Brahmaṇda as a homage to Jalal-ud-din Rumi on the 700th anniversary of the poet's death. When the stone is finished it is laid near the entrance of the tomb. It soon starts to attract visitors, many of them women who believe it to be a meteorite with the power to grant fertility. The time will come when the authorities in Konya find it necessary to relocate the stone to a less accessible spot.

1973–74
For Laib these are difficult years at the university. Working in hospitals, he comes in contact with the sick and the dying, an experience that deeply affects him. In reaction he starts to read Buddhist and especially Jain scripts intensively. The Jain philosophy of *ahimsa*, or nonviolence—involving a totally different conception of body and soul from the ideas Laib has encountered in his medical studies—becomes important to him. Learning to respect the life of every living being, he becomes a vegetarian. In July 1974 he finishes his examinations and then receives his medical degree. He spends the summer in India. Returning to Biberach, he starts to collect small stones and carve them into eggs, or Brahmaṇdas.

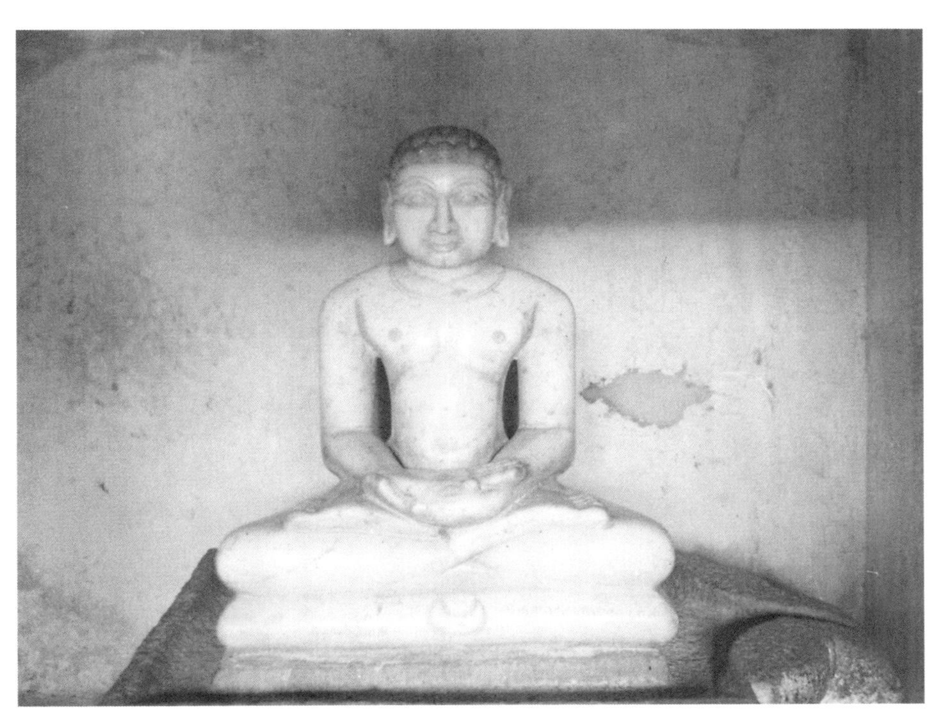

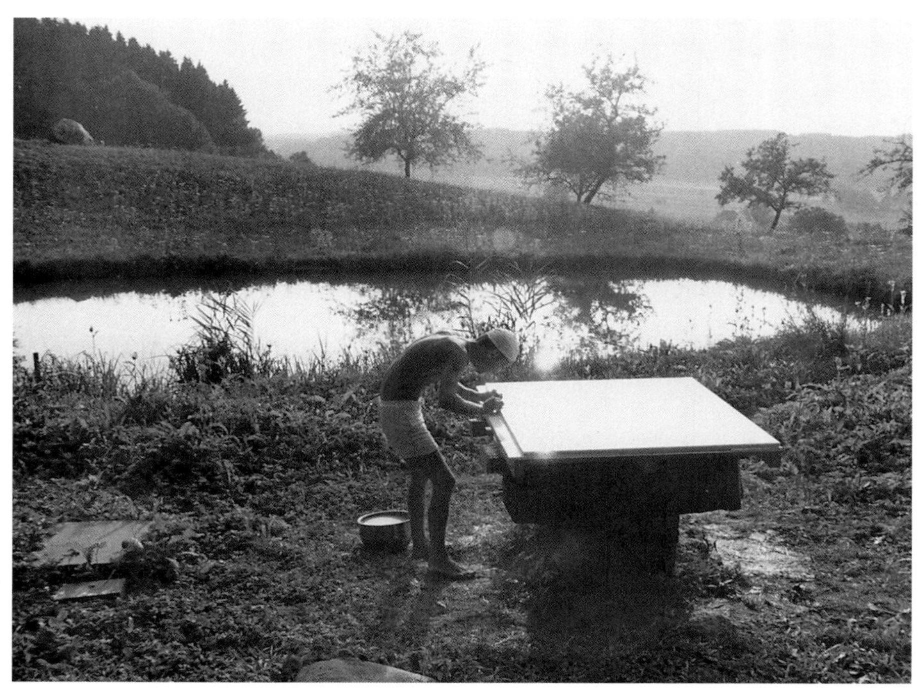

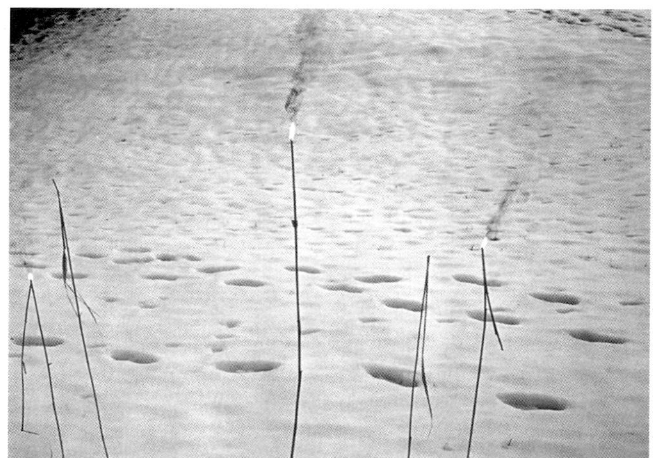

1975
Laib realizes his first milkstone, a direct reply to everything he has seen and experienced in recent years at the university and in the hospitals.

1976
On February 19, Laib celebrates Brancusi's 100th birthday by lighting a row of camphor fires on reeds in a meadow of snow. He has his first exhibition at the Müller-Roth gallery, Stuttgart, and shows six milkstones. A month earlier the same gallery shows three milkstones at the Düsseldorf art fair. The milkstones receive a great deal of attention. A local newspaper features them in a leading article, under the headline "Sackgasse mit Milchsteinen" (Dead End with Milkstones).

1977
In May, Laib begins to collect dandelion pollen in the meadows around his home. Every year from now on, for several months beginning in the spring, he will collect pollen from the flowers and trees around his house and studio: hazelnut, dandelion, buttercup, pine, sorrel, alder, and more.

1978
Along with a selection of milkstones, Laib exhibits works consisting of pollen sifted onto a rectangular piece of glass in four exhibitions: at Salvatore Ala in Milan, Konrad Fischer in Düsseldorf, Rolf Preisig in Basel, and the Kunstraum, Munich.

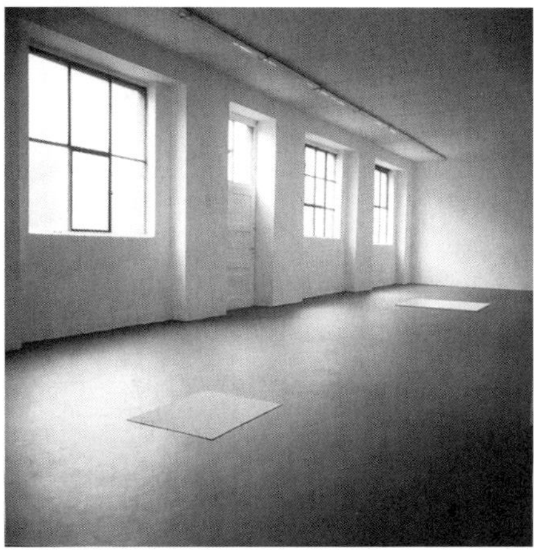

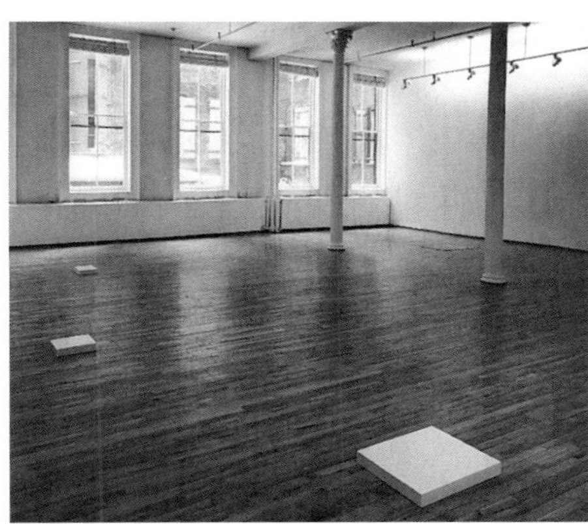

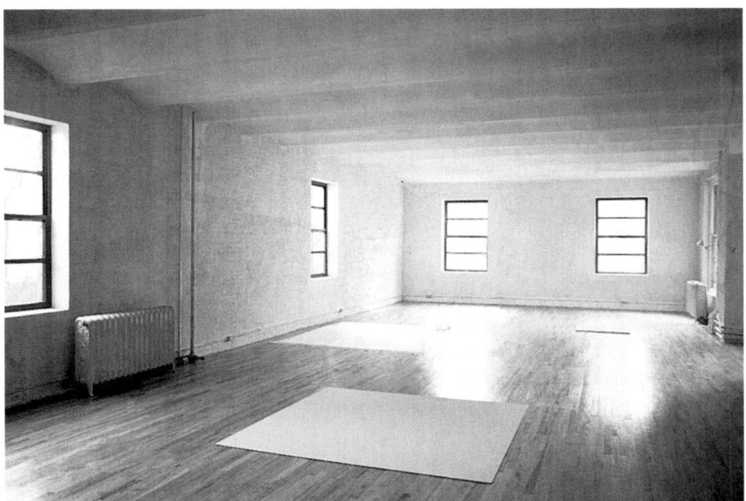

Laib has his first exhibition in
the United States, at the Sperone
Westwater Fischer gallery, New York.
Two large milkstones are destroyed
in transit, so the exhibition comprises
only three small milkstones, a dandelion-pollen work, and a large pine-
pollen work.

1980–81
Laib rents a loft on North Moore Street
in Tribeca, New York, and spends the
winter there. An empty sunlit space, it
contains only a six-inch-high portrait
of Saint Francis, a large pollen piece,
and a white cloth on the floor for sitting. Here Laib finishes several milkstones. During this stay he meets his
future wife: Carolyn Reep, a New
York–based art restorer and conservator
of Asian and ethnographic art objects.
Reep has admired and indeed been
inspired by the work she has seen in
Laib's New York exhibition in 1979. In
1981, Laib has a second exhibition with
Sperone Westwater Fischer, showing
only jars of pollen on the windowsill
in an otherwise empty space. He then
returns to Germany.

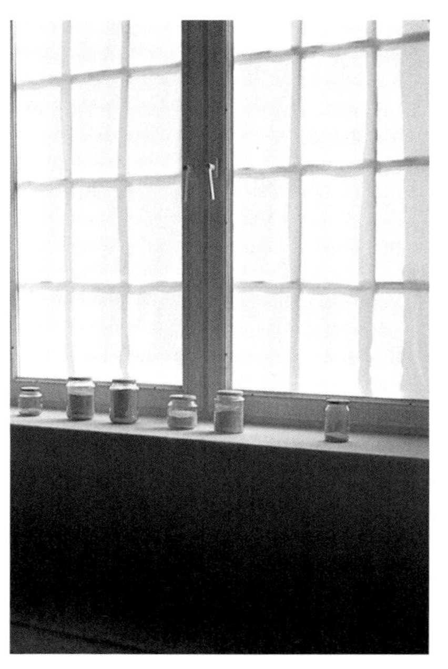

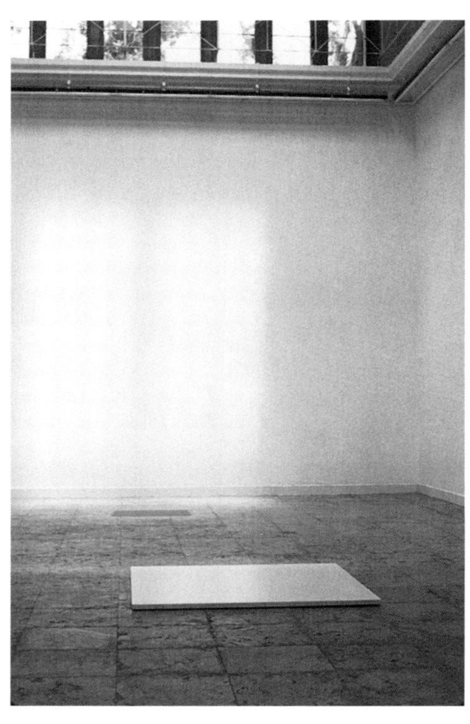

1982
Curator Rudi Fuchs invites Laib to participate in Documenta 7, the international exhibition in Kassel, West Germany, of which Fuchs is this year the director. Here Laib shows a pollen piece on the floor and some pollen jars on the windowsill. Together with Hanne Darboven and Gotthard Graubner, he is also selected to represent Germany in the German Pavilion, curated by Johannes Cladders, at the Venice Biennale; he exhibits his largest milkstone, a work made of dandelion pollen sifted directly onto the floor, and six pollen jars set on a shelf in a corner.

Carolyn Reep visits Laib in Germany for the first time, and spends the summer there. Although not yet ready to live together, they will arrange each year to spend several months together over the next few years, in both New York and Germany.

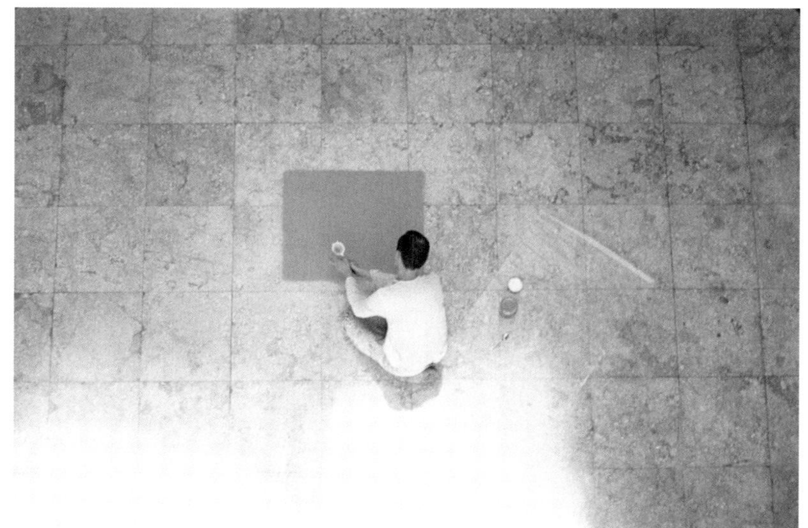

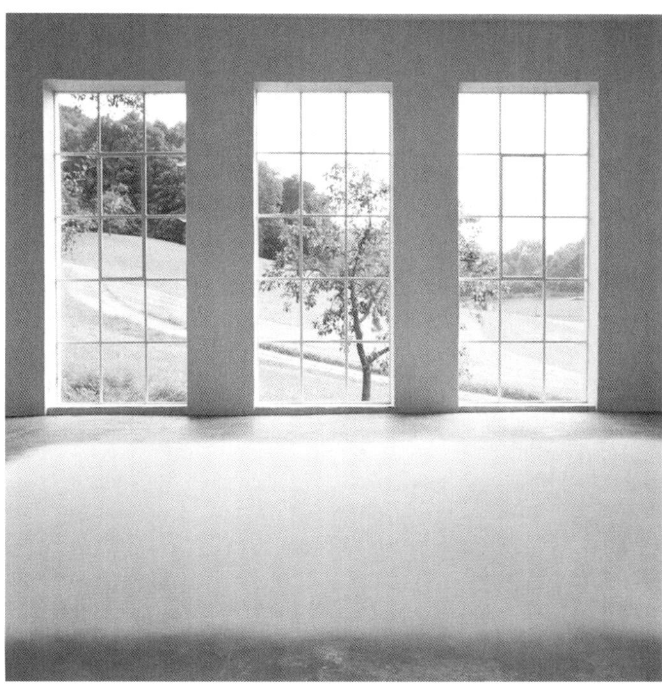

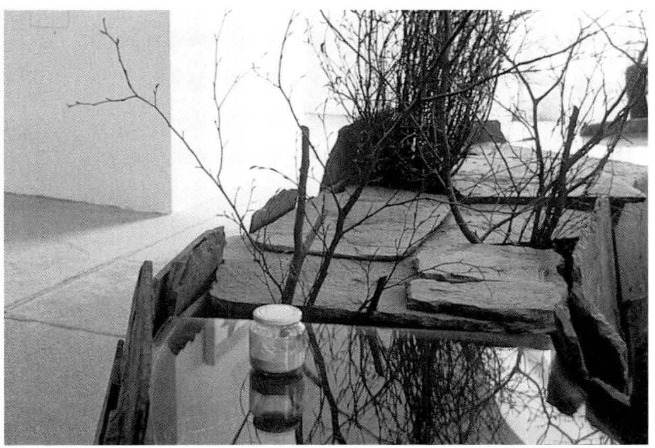

Laib starts work on a nineteenth-century building on the same property as the family's glass house, cleaning it out, installing three floor-to-ceiling windows on its south side, and transforming it into a studio. This simple space—one space, one house—is relatively small but beautifully proportioned. It will function as a work space but also and in fact mostly as a space in which Laib can be alone with one or two of his works. A white cloth is laid on the floor on which to sit in front of a milkstone or a pollen piece. In the other direction, and visible through the windows, lie the meadows and forests where Laib collects his pollen.

On several occasions Laib meets the artist Joseph Beuys, whose work he admires. Although astonished at how close he feels to some of Beuys's ideas, he keeps a careful distance, as he does not want to become Beuys's student. Beuys is very interested in Laib's milkstones and pollen works. Mario and Marisa Merz, with whom Laib has been friends for a number of years, visit him several times. At Documenta in 1982, Mario Merz has exhibited a spiral table, on which he has invited Laib to place a pollen jar.

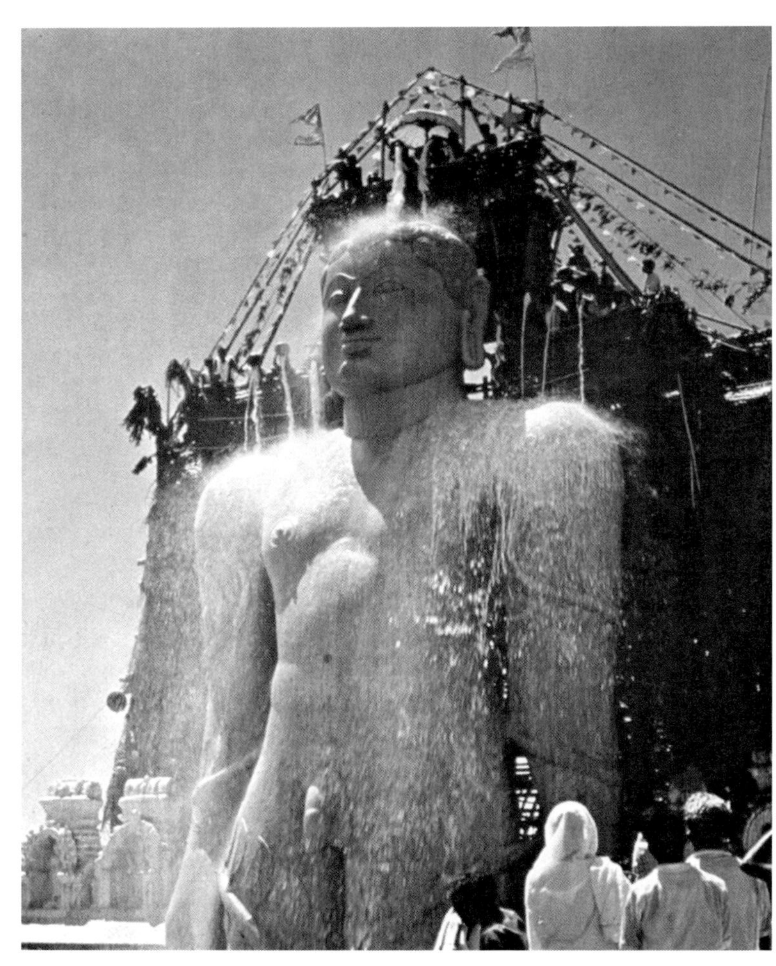

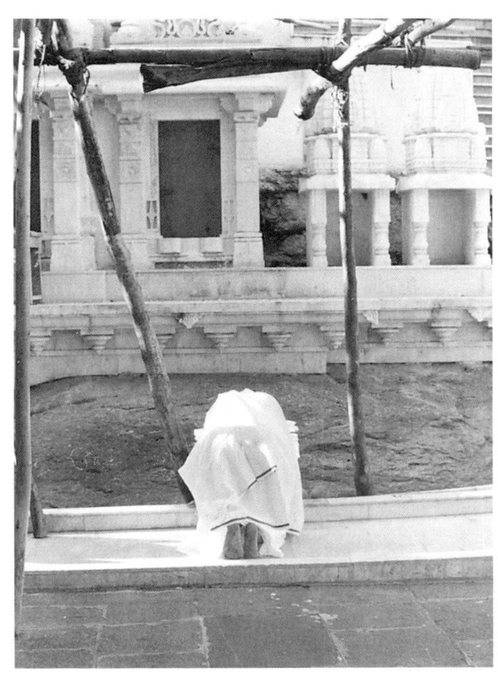

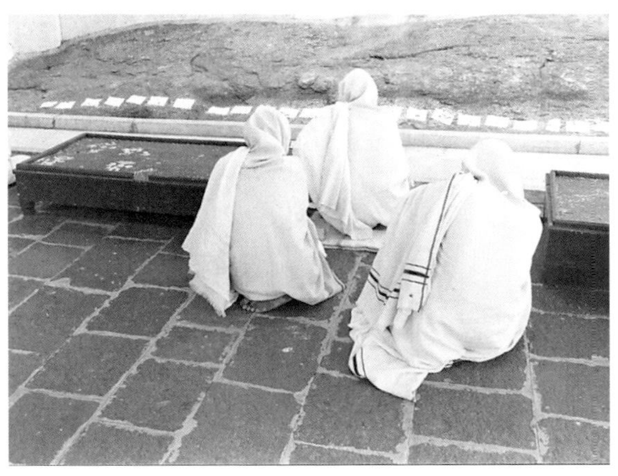

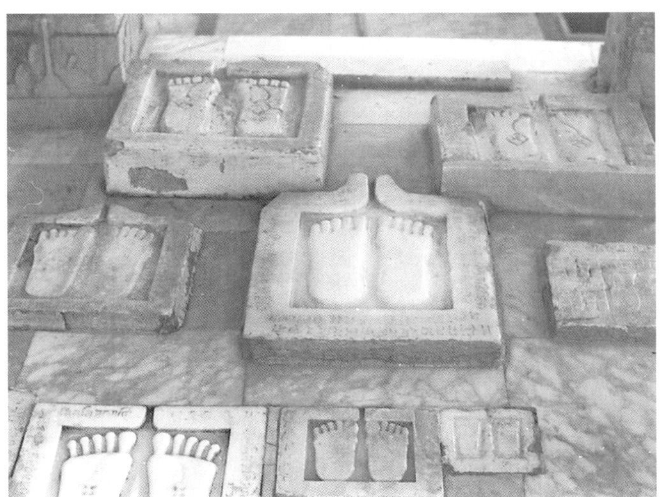

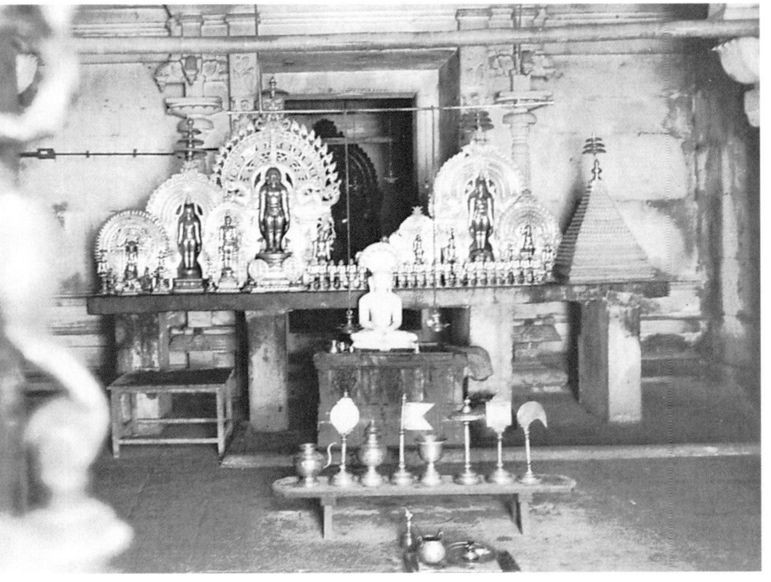

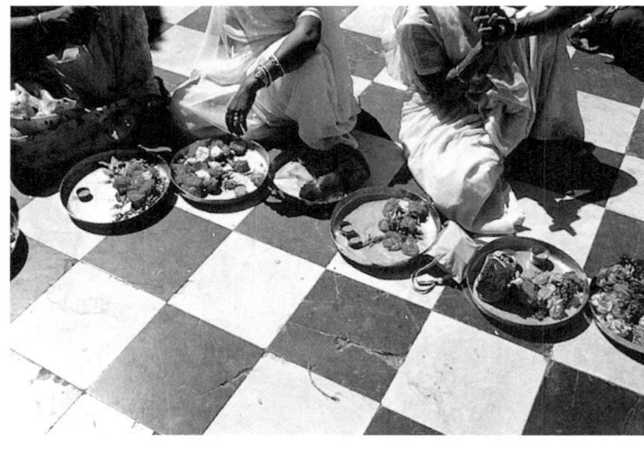

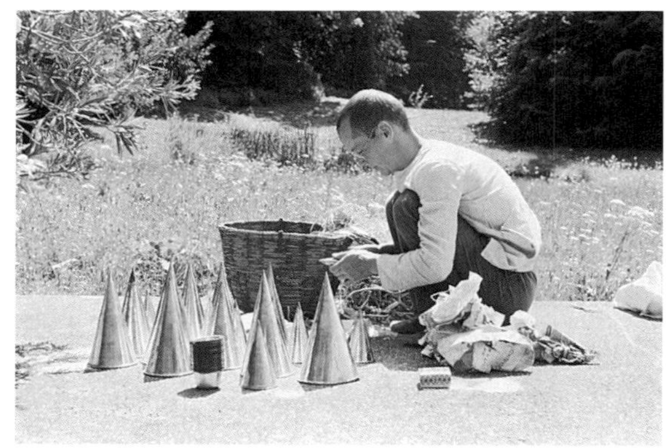

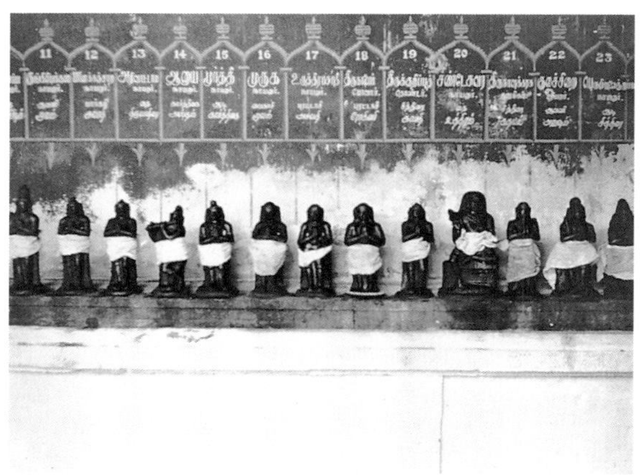

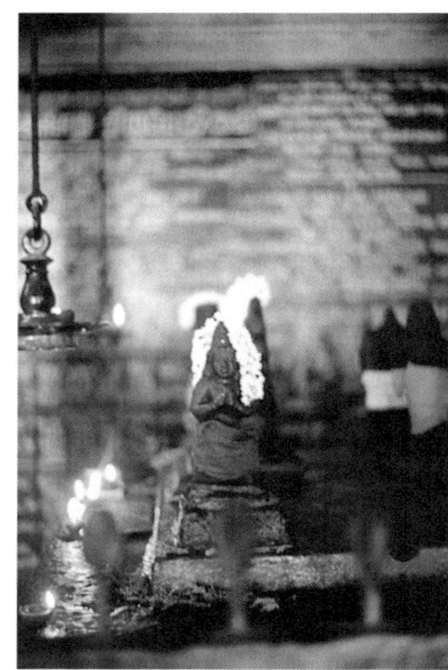

Laib makes a long trip to India, visiting Palitana and Girnar, the holy Jain mountains in the north, then traveling in South India, to Sravana Belgola and other Jain centers. He also visits Sumatra, Hong Kong, and China. On his return from this journey he begins his first works using rice. These include *The Rice Meals for the Nine Planets* and *The Sixty-Three Rice Meals for a Stone,* both of which also include objects in brass—in the former, brass cones that Laib has commissioned in Kumbakonam, South India, in the latter, sixty-three brass plates that he has bought in Palitana, Gujarat. These plates have the shape of the *thali,* the everyday Indian eating plate that is also used by Jain pilgrims to present temple offerings. *The Sixty-Three Rice Meals for a Stone* is shown in the autumn at the Konrad Fischer gallery, Düsseldorf, *The Rice Meals for the Nine Planets* in the exhibition *Kosmische Bilder in der Kunst des 20. Jahrhunderts (Cosmic Images in the Art of the Twentieth Century),* at the Kunsthalle Baden-Baden. Here Laib also shows his first Brahmaṇḍa stone, from 1972.

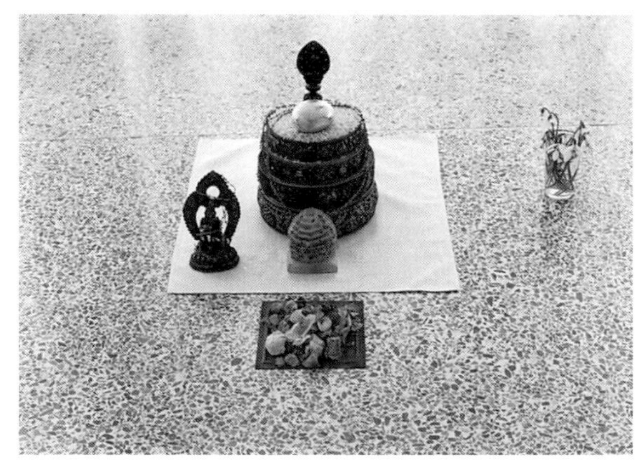

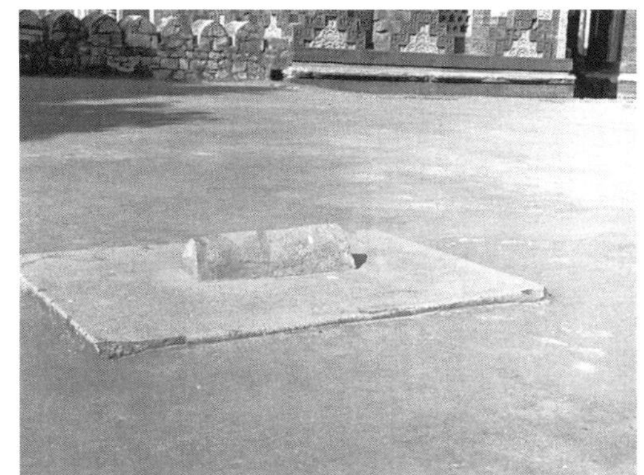

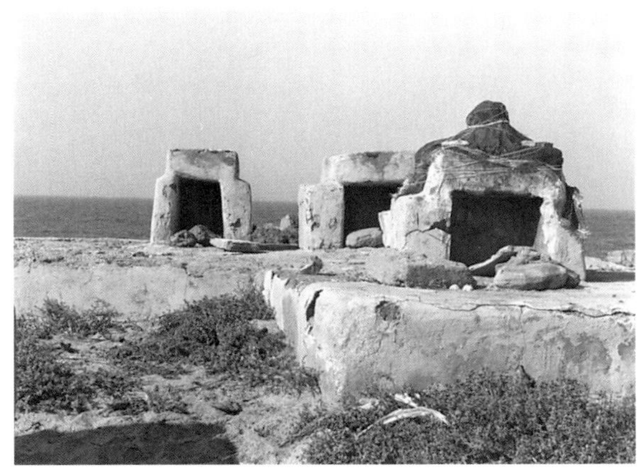

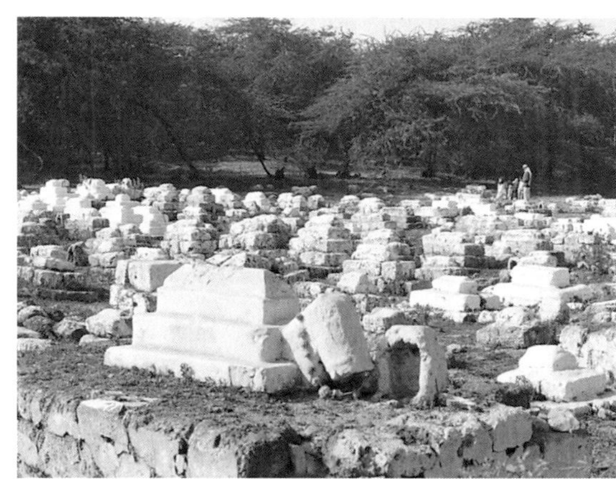

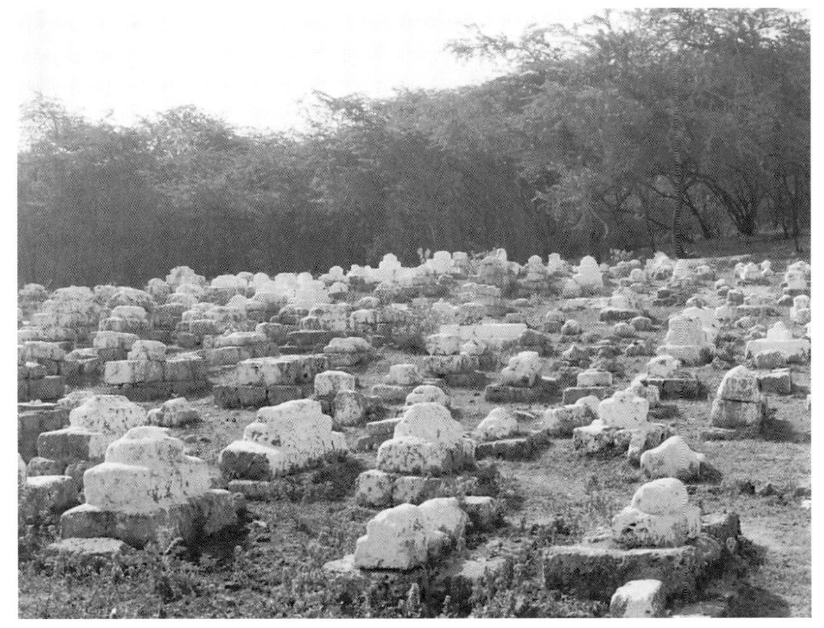

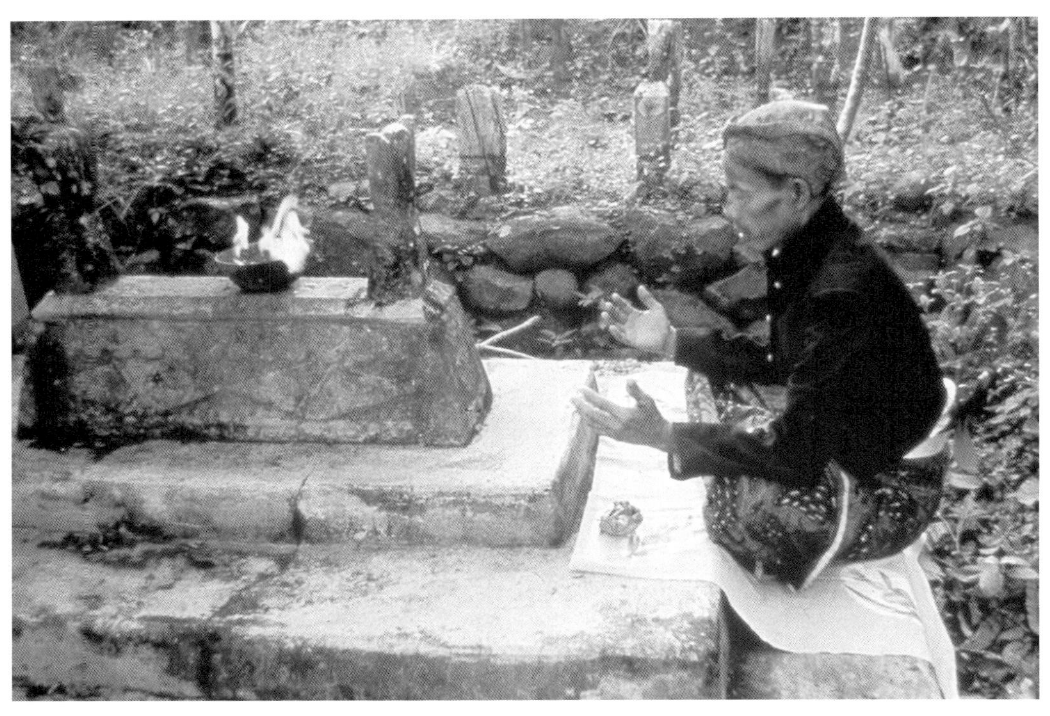

1984
Laib begins his rice houses. The first
are made of wood covered with thin
white metal; they are filled with rice,
and mountains of rice are placed all
around them.

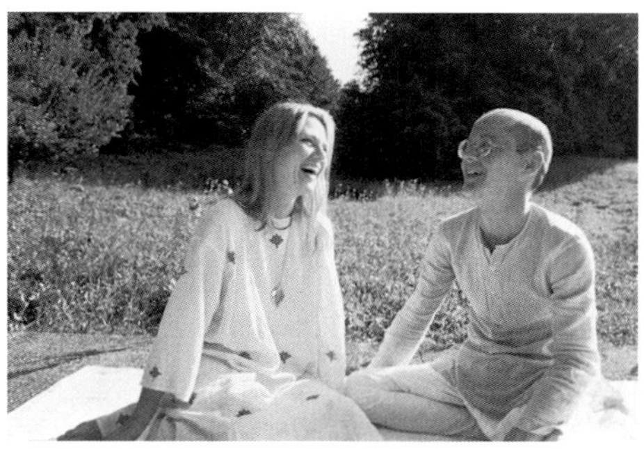

1985
Leaving her New York apartment and
job, Carolyn Reep moves to Germany,
where she and Laib get married.

Having asked Laib to participate
in *Spuren, Skulpturen und Monumente
ihrer präzisen Reise*, a group exhibition
at the Kunsthaus Zürich, the curator
Harald Szeemann visits Laib's studio.
Artist and curator jointly decide that
the work to be shown will be *The Five
Mountains Not to Climb On,* a row of
five pollen "mountains" on the floor
that Laib has realized the previous year.
This work becomes a meeting point for
the two men, who will develop a deep
and enduring friendship. Laib will take
part in many exhibitions curated by
Szeemann all over the world.

1986
A daughter, Chandra Maria Sobeide, is
born to Laib and Carolyn—on January
23, the day Joseph Beuys dies.

Laib realizes the first rice houses
he has made out of solid marble, each
accompanied by mountains of rice
and occasionally also by one of pollen.
He also realizes sealing wax houses,
wooden houses that are filled with rice
and totally covered with sealing wax.

Suzanne Pagé asks Laib to participate in a major one-man exhibition at
the Musée d'Art Moderne de la Ville
de Paris. Harald Szeemann writes the
catalogue essay. Invited by Jean-Louis
Froment to exhibit at the capcMusée

d'art contemporain de Bordeaux, Laib
creates a large hazelnut-pollen work on
the floor—the only piece in the huge
cathedral-like space.

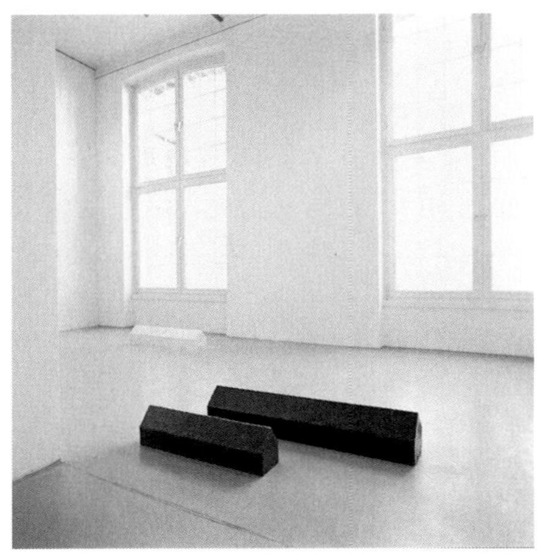

1987
Manfred Schneckenburger asks Laib to take part in Documenta 8, in Kassel; Laib shows three rice houses.

Laib begins to work with beeswax, first making several small pieces, some of them filled with rice.

1988
Laib realizes his first beeswax chamber, *Für einen anderen Körper (For Another Body)*, made for Harald Szeemann's *Zeitlos* exhibition in the Hamburger Bahnhof, Berlin. Later the same year he creates a second beeswax chamber, *Passageway*, for the Carnegie International, Pittsburgh. He also exhibits in New York, Des Moines, and Los Angeles; and to attend these shows, he, Carolyn, and Chandra spend three months in the United States. While here, they visit the deserts of Arizona and New Mexico. These landscapes give Laib the idea of building a beeswax chamber inside a rock in open country.

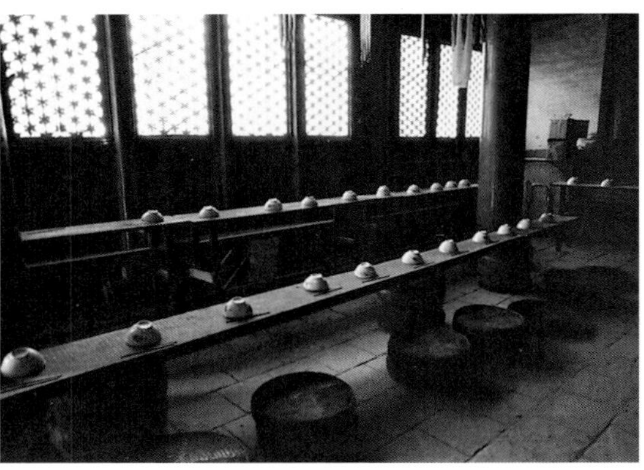

1989
For an exhibition in Tokyo, Laib travels to Japan for the first time. The landscapes and temples make a deep impression on him.

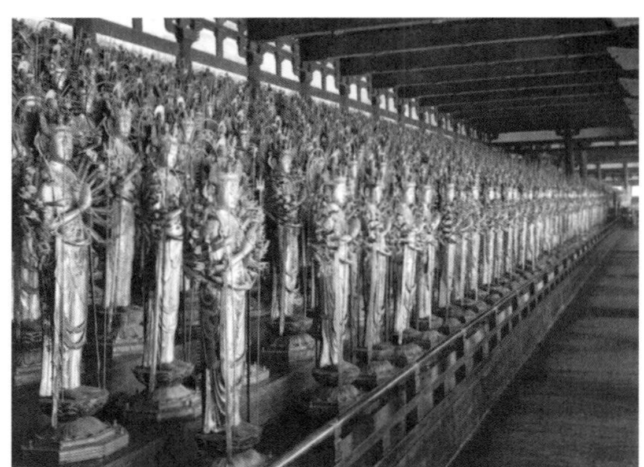

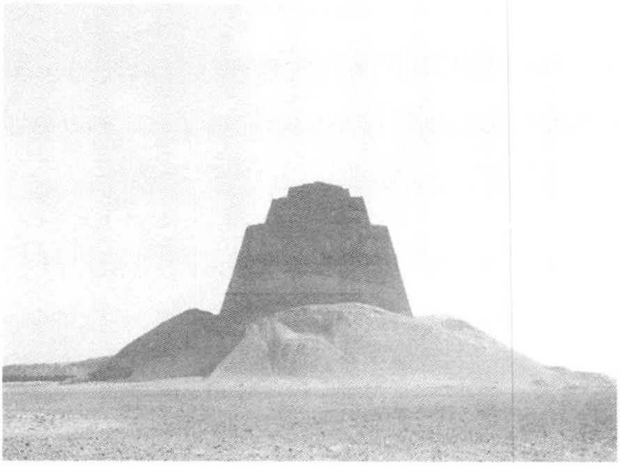

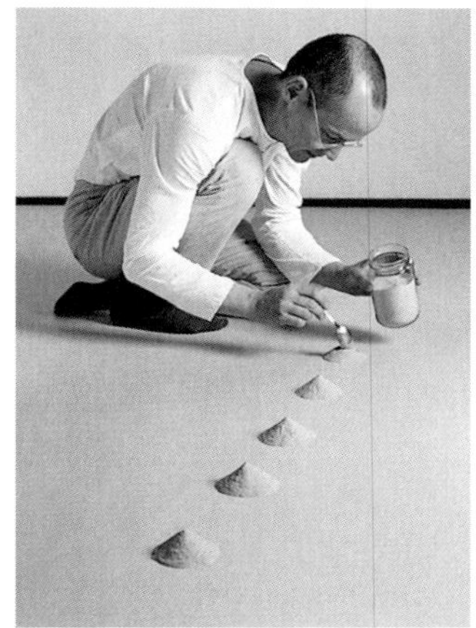

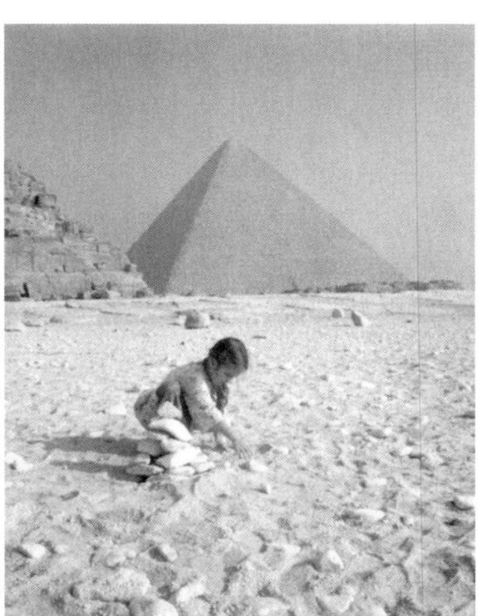

1990

Laib begins to make larger beeswax houses, which he imagines placed high on the wall, or on wooden supports. Revisiting Japan for Harald Szeemann's *LightSeed* exhibition at the Watari-um, Tokyo, he shows pollen works that fascinate the Japanese public.

The family spends the winter in South India, renting a house outside a village near Madurai. Laib works with a printer and box maker in Dindigul to produce a multiple in the form of a box, to contain a slab of beeswax.

1991

Laib for the first time uses gray slabs of granite from quarries in the Maggia valley, Switzerland, that he has discovered while visiting Harald Szeemann in Tegna, a few kilometers away. In future years he will use this granite in major installations to support large beeswax houses or ships.

Laib and his family start to renovate a seventeenth-century house next to his studio, restoring it to its original form and character. The floors are divided into many small rooms, providing spaces effective for working and for storing archives, books, and photographs (there is also a darkroom). The house also provides additional living space for the family's daily activities. One small ground-level room, with a low ceiling and a concrete floor, proves ideal as a wax room: Laib can easily heat it up to 40 degrees centigrade to make the wax malleable enough to shape. Here he can form all the wax pieces he will make in the coming years.

In the fall, on the occasion of an exhibition in Santa Fe, Laib travels extensively in New Mexico, in search of a site for a wax chamber in the landscape. He, Carolyn, and Chandra spend the winter traveling in Egypt and Yemen.

1992

Margit Rowell invites Laib to make a huge pollen piece in the forum of the Centre Georges Pompidou, Paris. A special concrete floor is made for the whole forum.

Harald Szeemann invites Laib to exhibit in a small museum in Ascona, Switzerland, in the foothills of the Monte Verità (Mountain of Truth). They choose pollen mountains as the main works in the exhibition, and a rice house is shown in a house on the Monte Verità. The pollen mountains appear on a poster seen all over the little town. Unfortunately the town's mayor and council are highly bothered by the milkstones and pollen pieces ("We don't want art that you can blow away"), and this is the last exhibition Szeemann is asked to curate in Ascona. The mayor also tries to withhold the return of one large work in the exhibition, to reduce the museum's costs.

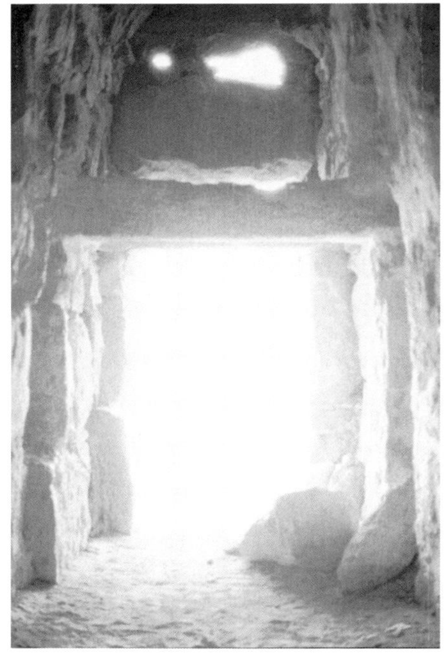

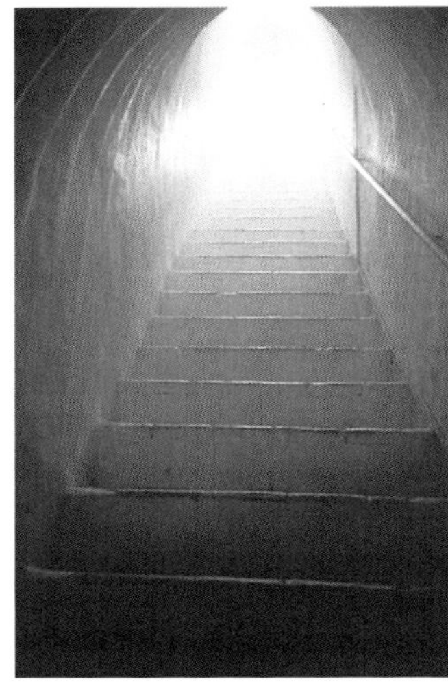

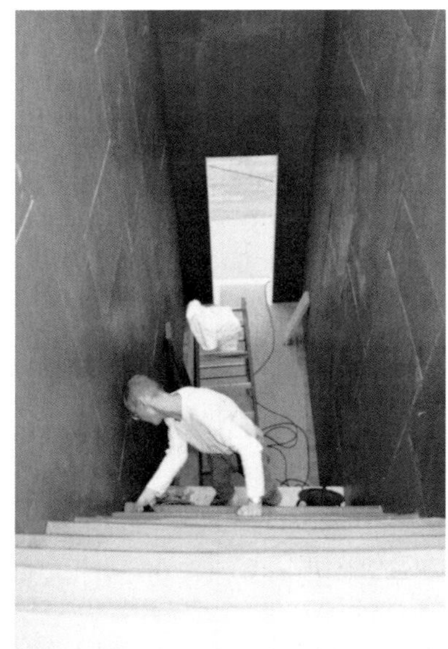

Jean-Louis Froment curates an exhibition in Collioure, a small French town on the Mediterranean, where many French artists spent time in the early twentieth century. Froment invites Laib, Richard Serra, Richard Long, and Lawrence Weiner to participate, and Laib tells the curator about his idea of building a wax chamber in an outdoor rock. Froment is highly intrigued, since he is already interested in the notion of expanding the museum beyond its walls—the museum, he thinks, is everywhere. He suggests looking for a site in the nearby Pyrenees mountains.

The Kunstmuseum Bonn organizes a major Laib exhibition, for which the artist creates a new wax chamber—an enclosed wax stairway with beeswax steps, rising from floor to ceiling. Working with The Museum of Contemporary Art, Los Angeles, where a smaller version of the exhibition will appear at the end of the year, the Kunstmuseum publishes a major monograph. The capcMusée d'art contemporain de Bordeaux organizes a second Laib exhibition in its large space, this time with a work entitled *Passage*, in which one of the building's huge arches is filled from both sides with beeswax. In a long continuous row in a corridor, Laib also shows *The Sixty-Three Rice Meals for a Stone*.

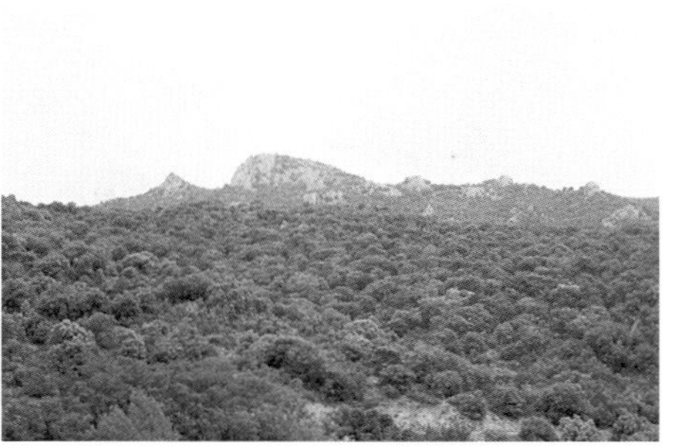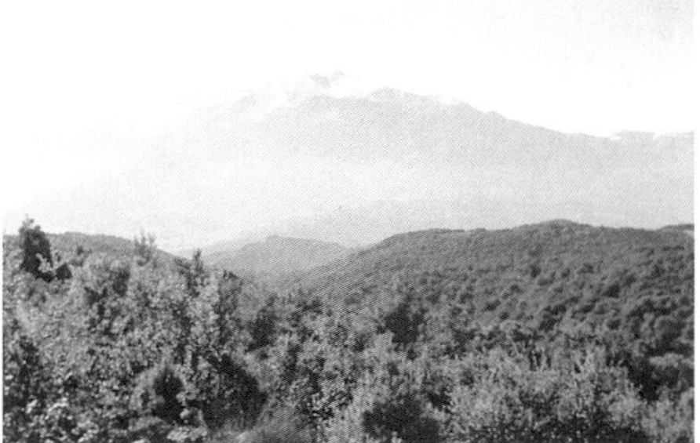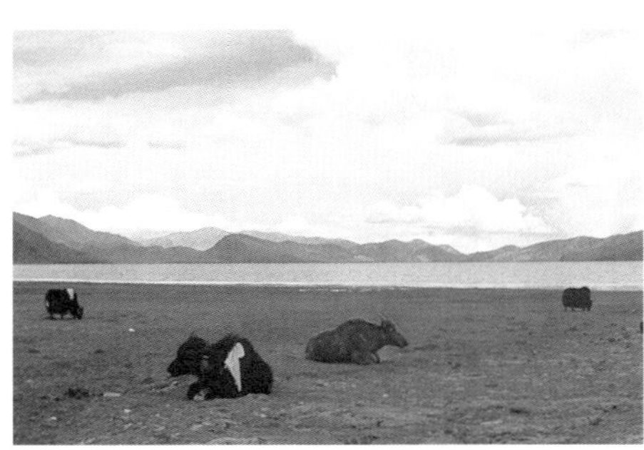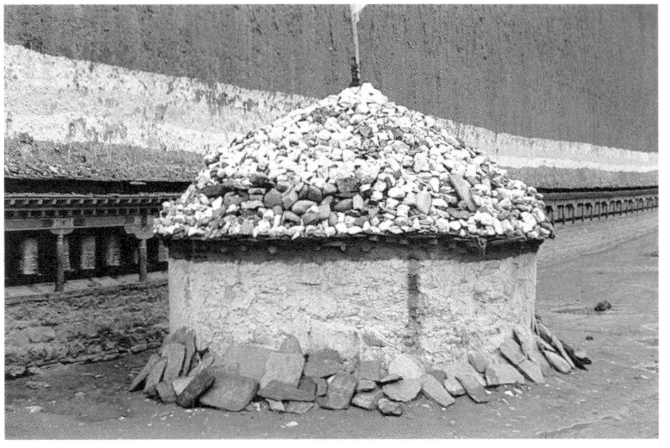

1993
Laib and his family spend the summer
in Burma.

In the fall Laib visits the Pyrenees
for a second time, searching for a site
for his wax chamber. After long and
arduous travels through the mountains,
he selects the area of the Massif du
Canigou, the sacred mountain of the
Catalans, a region with many Romanesque churches and hermitages. The
specific site is the Roc del Maure, a
small granite ridge facing the Massif
du Canigou, and featuring wild Mediterranean vegetation and an extraordinary view.

1994
Working with the Henry Moore
Sculpture Trust, Laib realizes a large
wax chamber containing three elements
that in previous works had always
appeared separately: a chamber, a wall,
and a corridor. One walks down the
forty-foot-long corridor into the chamber, where one finds oneself in front of
a beeswax wall.

The family spends the summer
in Tibet, undertaking a long and stren-
uous journey from Lhasa to Benares.
Laib is fascinated by the remote Tibetan monasteries in their mesalike landscapes, and by the life that is lived
there. On returning to Germany, he
spends many months questioning and
thinking about his experience before
going back to work.

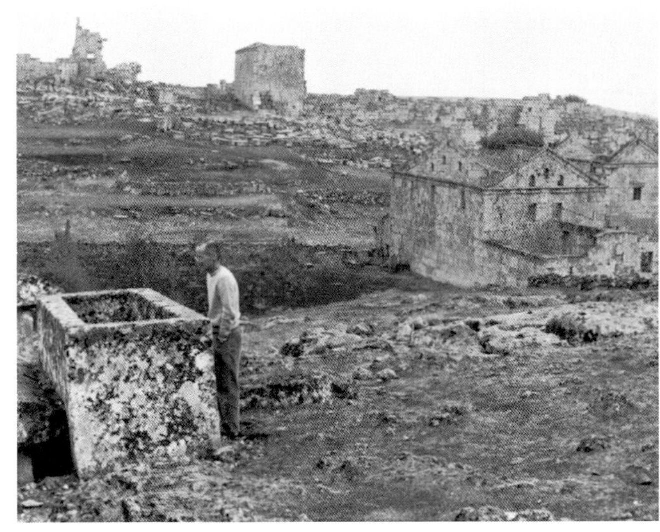

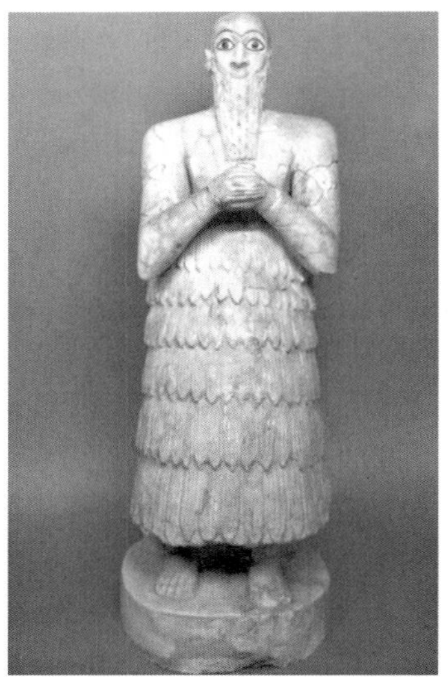

1995
Laib begins to make beeswax ships. These he exhibits with a small beeswax ziggurat form, and installs on granite slabs at the Sprengel Museum, Hannover. A second large installation of six beeswax ships, posed on a wooden construction, is shown at the Sperone Westwater gallery, New York. This installation's title, *You Will Go Somewhere Else*, refers to the wooden constructions that hold sacred books in the Potala, Lhasa.

In the fall, Laib travels in the deserts of Mesopotamia, visiting Mari, whose sculptures have been among his favorite artworks for many years.

1996
For the Konrad Fischer gallery, Düsseldorf, at a time when Fischer is very sick (he will die in November of this year), Laib produces a work entitled *Durchgang—Übergang*: a row of six ships sitting on a scaffolding that traverses a doorway between two spaces. He also makes a second ship installation for the Chantal Crousel gallery, Paris, with the title *Nicht hier (Not Here)*.

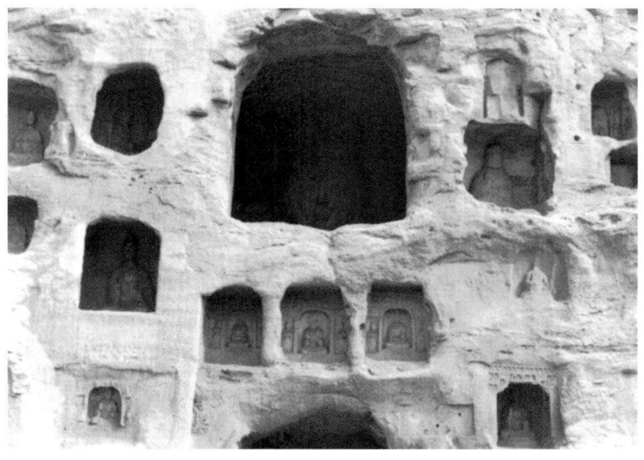

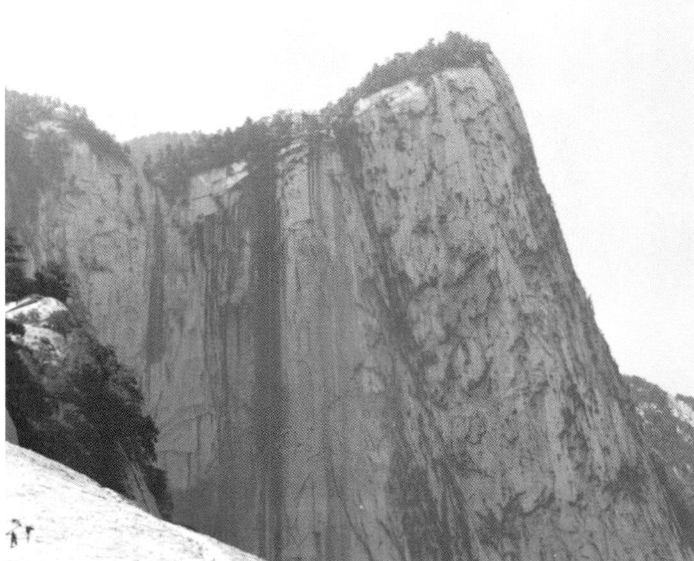

1997
An enlarged version of the ship installation *You Will Go Somewhere Else* is
shown at the Venice Biennale, in the
Arsenale, the city's old shipyard.

The family spends the summer in
China and Korea, where Laib con-
tributes a dandelion-pollen piece to
the Kwangju Biennale. They visit the
sacred mountains of China, and the
coalmine region of Datong, with its
Buddhist caves.

In the fall, Klaus Schrenk, who has
worked on Laib's 1992 exhibition in
the Bonn Kunstmuseum, invites him
to exhibit in the Orangerie of the
Staatliche Kunsthalle, Karlsruhe. The
result is *Ich bin nicht hier (I Am Not
Here)*, an installation of ten ships on a
wooden structure.

1998
The Arts Club of Chicago organizes an
exhibition of several large installations
by Laib, all them having previously
appeared elsewhere.

In the spring, Laib realizes two
beeswax ziggurats standing side-by-
side in the main gallery space of the
Sperone Westwater gallery, New York.
Titled *Nowhere Everywhere,* these are
his first beeswax works to extend from
floor to ceiling.

Laib again spends the summer with
his family in South India.

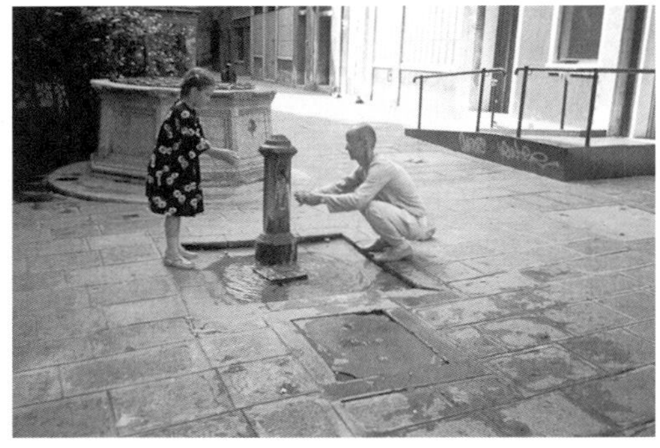

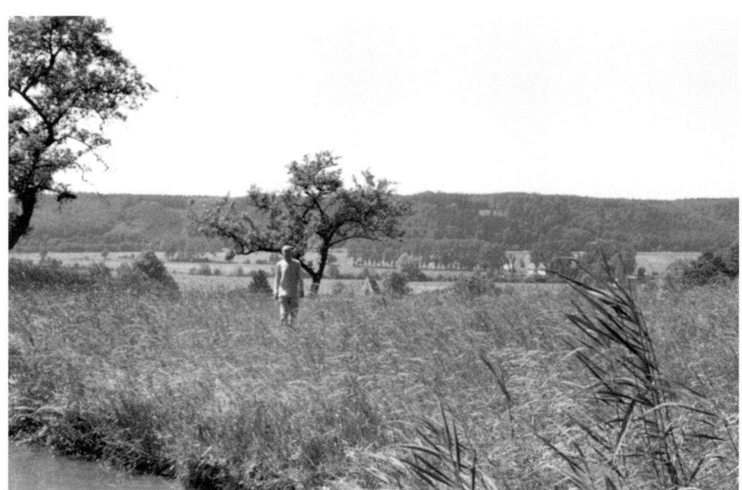

of the Musée d'art contemporain de Nîmes after its postponement due to the leaving of Jean-Louis Froment from his museum in Bordeaux.

Harald Szeemann invites Laib to make a dandelion-pollen piece at the Venice Biennale; the work is destroyed after a month by rain coming in through the roof.

For an exhibition in the Kunsthaus Bregenz, Laib conceives a beeswax ziggurat about twenty feet high. This work appears on the ground floor of the museum; the exhibition continues over four floors with other major installations, ending with a big pine-pollen piece on the top floor. The exhibition creates a unique conjunction with Peter Zumthor's architecture.

At the Belvedere castle, just outside Weimar, Germany, Laib installs *The Five Mountains Not to Climb On* in the cupola and four ships on a wooden construction in the old chapel. Attending a full performance of Goethe's *Faust* in Weimar, he is deeply touched and surprised at how closely the ideas raised in the play correspond to questions within his own realm of thinking.

In the summer he travels to eastern Germany to see the landscapes where Caspar David Friedrich lived and painted. He also visits Berlin, Dessau, and Wörlitz.

In the late autumn, work starts in the Pyrenees. The path up to the Roc del Maure is made.

1999

The Carré d'Art, Musée d'art contemporain de Nîmes, organizes a major Laib exhibition. (The artist has had a long friendship with the museum's director, Guy Tosatto, with whom he worked ten years earlier on an exhibition at the Musée Départemental de Rochechouart.) Now Laib returns to the pursuit of the project in the Pyrenees, this time with the support

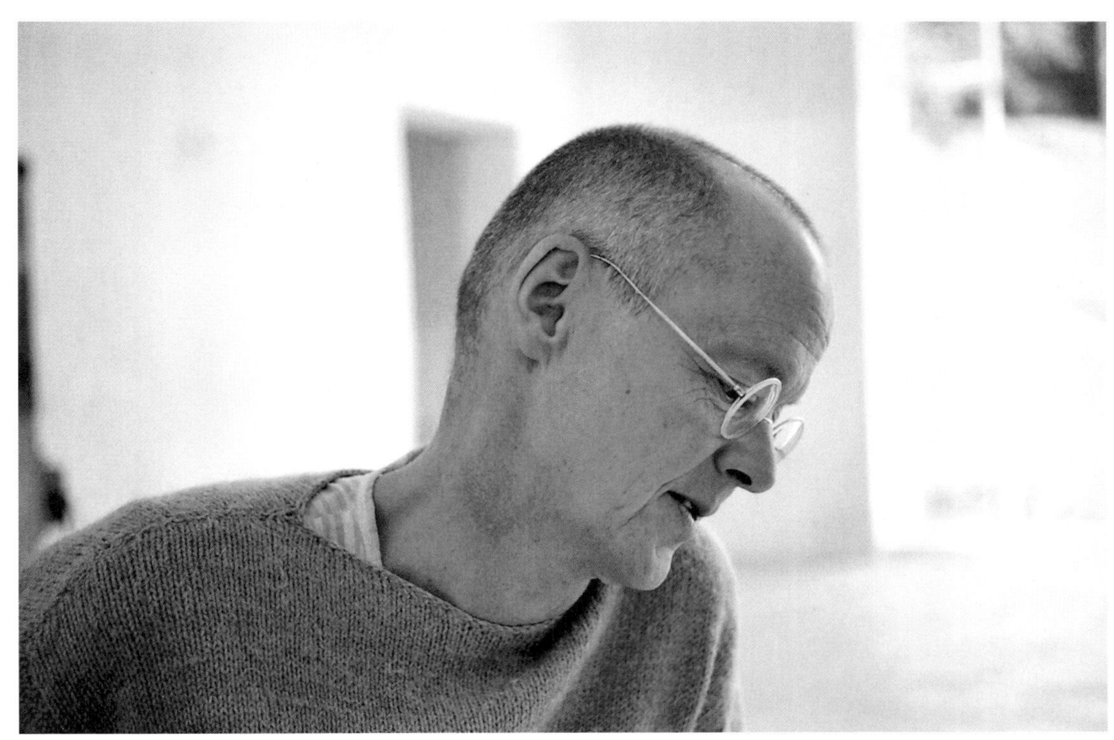

LIST OF ILLUSTRATIONS

Those works with an asterisk (*) are in the exhibition that this catalogue accompanies.
Unless otherwise indicated, all works are by Wolfgang Laib, and are courtesy of the artist.

PAGE 10
Duccio di Buoninsegna, *The Calling of the Apostles Peter and Andrew*, ca. 1255
Tempera on panel
17⅛ x 18⅛ in. (43.5 x 46 cm)
National Gallery of Art, Washington, D.C.; Samuel H. Kress Collection

PAGE 24
Caspar David Friedrich, *The Monk at the Sea*, 1809
Oil on canvas
43¼ x 67½ in. (110 x 171.5 cm)
Staatliche Museen zu Berlin—Preußischer Kulturbesitz Nationalgalerie

PAGE 43
Brahmaṇḍa, 1972
Natural black boulder
26¾ x 26¾ x 47¼ in.
(68 x 68 x 120 cm)
Installation: artist's house

PAGE 45
Brahmaṇḍas, 1972–75*
8 stones
3½ to 7 in. (9 to 18 cm)
Installation: artist's studio

PAGE 46
Laib pouring the milk for *Milkstone*, 1987–89
White marble, milk
¾ x 48 x 51⅛ in. (2 x 122 x 130 cm)
Installation: artist's studio

PAGE 47
Milkstone, 1987–89
White marble, milk
¾ x 48 x 51⅛ in. (2 x 122 x 130 cm)
Related piece, not illustrated:
Milkstone, 1983–87*
White marble, milk
⅞ x 41 x 43 in. (2 x 104 x 109 cm)
The Edward R. Broida Collection

PAGE 49
Milkstone, 1978
White marble, milk
2⅛ x 10 x 11⅛ in.
(5.5 x 25.5 x 28.2 cm)
Private collection

PAGE 50
Pollen from Hazelnut, 1992*
Pollen
138 x 157½ in. (350 x 400 cm)
Installation: Centre Pompidou, Paris, 1992

PAGE 51
Laib sifting pollen from hazelnut
Installation: Centre Pompidou, Paris, 1992

PAGE 53
Pollen from Hazelnut, 1986
Pollen
126 x 141⅞ in. (320 x 360 cm)
Installation: capcMusée d'art contemporain, Bordeaux, 1986

PAGE 54
Laib sifting pollen from dandelion
Installation: Venice Biennale (German Pavilion), 1982

PAGE 55
Pollen from Dandelion, 1990*
Pollen
23⅝ x 31½ in. (60 x 80 cm)
Installation: Gallery Burnett Miller, Los Angeles, 1990

PAGE 57
Pollen from Dandelion, 1988
Pollen
24 x 30 (61 x 76 cm)
Installation: Hamburger Bahnhof, Berlin, 1988

PAGE 59
Pollen from Pine, 1998
90½ x 102⅜ (230 x 260 cm)
Private collection
Installation: Kenji Taki Gallery, Nagoya, 1998

PAGE 79

Right:
Rice House, 1998–99*
Marble, rice
17¾ x 22½ x 69 in.
(45 x 57 x 175 cm)

Left:
Rice House, 1993–94
Marble, rice
12¾ x 16⅜ x 49⅜ in.
(32.5 x 41.5 x 125.5 cm)
Private collection, Switzerland
Installation: Kunsthaus Bregenz,
1999

PAGE 81

Front:
Rice House, 1993*
Sealing wax, wood, rice
8¼ x 7⅞ x 42¾ in.
(21 x 20 x 108.5 cm)

Back:
Rice House, 1989*
Sealing wax, wood, rice
7⅛ x 5½ x 26⅝ in.
(18 x 14 x 67.5 cm)
Installation: artist's studio

PAGE 83
Rice House, 1990*
Sealing wax, wood, rice
8¾ x 17⅜ x 17⅜ in.
(22 x 44 x 44 cm)
Collection Anthony T. Podesta,
Washington, D.C
Installation: artist's studio

PAGE 85
Rice House, 1987
Beeswax, rice
11⅜ x 9⅛ x 27¼ (29 x 23 x 69 cm)
Private collection
Installation: artist's studio

PAGE 87
Untitled, 1988
Beeswax
12¼ x 11⅞ x 28¾ (31 x 30 x 73 cm)
Installation: artist's studio

PAGE 88
*Ein Verschlossenes Haus (A Taciturn
House)*, 1988–90*
Beeswax, wood
(1 beeswax house installed on
the wall)
17¾ x 19⅞ x 63 (45 x 50.5 x 160 cm)
Installation: Museum Abteiberg,
Mönchengladbach, 1988–90
Related piece, not illustrated:
Untitled, 1990–91*
Beeswax, wood
(2 beeswax houses installed on
the wall)
17¾ x 18⅛ x 76 in.
(45 x 46 x 193 cm)
Courtesy Sperone Westwater,
New York

PAGE 89
Untitled, 1992
Beeswax, slabs of granite
108⅝ x 100⅜ x 204¾ in.
(276 x 255 x 520 cm) overall
Private collection
Installation: Museo Communale
d'Arte Moderna, Ascona, 1992

PAGE 91
Untitled, 1991–99*
Beeswax, wood
(6 small beeswax pieces and
1 ziggurat on 3 wood shelves)
24½ x 17¾ x 267¾ in.
(62 x 45 x 680 cm) overall
Private collection
Installation: Carré d'Art—Musée
d'art contemporain de Nîmes, 1999

PAGE 93
Untitled, or *Staircase (Treppe)*, 1999*
Beeswax
56¼ x 44⅞ x 21¼ in.
(143 x 114 x 54 cm)
Collection Robert and Marguerite
Hoffman, Dallas
Installation: Sperone Westwater,
New York

PAGE 95
*Für einen anderen Körper (For
Another Body)*, 1988
Beeswax, wood, and brick
construction, stucco
Interior: 135⅞ x 63 x 153⅝
(345 x 160 x 390 cm)
Installation: Hamburger Bahnhof,
Berlin, 1988

PAGES 96 and 97
*Somewhere Else—La Chambre des
certitudes*, 1997*
Exterior and interior views
Beeswax, wood
Interior: 127½ x 30 to 50 x 191 in.
(324 x 78 to 23 x 485 cm)
Installation: Carré d'Art—Musée
d'art contemporain de Nîmes, 1999

PAGE 99
Untitled, 1989
Interior view
Beeswax, wood
72⅞ to 148⅞ x 23⅝ to 35⅜ x
314½ in.
(185 to 378 x 60 to 90 x 800 cm)
Galerie der Stadt Stuttgart

PAGE 101
Wax Room, 1992
Interior view
Beeswax, wood
170½ x 53½ x 190⅞ in.
(433 x 136 x 485 cm)
Kunstmuseum Bonn

PAGE 102
Passage, 1992
Besswax, wood
311 x 205½ in. (790 x 522 cm)
Private collection
Installation: capcMusée d'art
contemporain, Bordeaux, 1992–93

PAGE 103
Wall (Wand), 1990
Beeswax, wood
167⅝ x 129½ in. (426 x 329 cm)
Private collection
Installation: The National Museum
of Contemporary Art, Oslo, 1990

PAGE 105
You Will Go Somewhere Else, 1995*
Beeswax, wood
(6 beeswax ships on wood
scaffolding)
157½ x 31½ x 512¼ in.
(400 x 80 x 1300 cm) overall
Courtesy Sperone Westwater,
New York
Installation: Sperone Westwater,
New York

PAGE 107
I Am Not Here (Ich bin nicht hier)
(detail), 1997
Beeswax, wood
(10 beeswax ships on wood
scaffolding)
185 x 33½ x 590¼ in.
(470 x 85 x 1500 cm) overall
Installation: Staatliche Kunsthalle
Karlsruhe, 1997

PAGE 109
Not Here (Nicht hier), 1996
Beeswax, wood
(7 beeswax ships and one beeswax
staircase, wood construction)
124 x 157½ x 149⅝ in.
(315 x 400 x 380 cm) overall
Installation: Galerie Chantal
Crousel, Paris, 1996

PAGES 110–13
I Am Not Here (Ich bin nicht hier),
1997–99*
Three views
Beeswax, wood
(10 beeswax ships on wood
scaffolding)
167½ x 33½ x 827½ in.
(425 x 90 x 2100 cm) overall
Installation: Kunsthaus Bregenz,
1999

PAGE 115
Nowhere—Everywhere, 1998*
Beeswax, wood
(2 beeswax ziggurats on wood
construction)
152 x 146⅞ x 29½ in.
(386 x 373 x 75 cm)
Courtesy Sperone Westwater,
New York
Installation: Sperone Westwater,
New York, 1998

PAGE 117
*There Is No Beginning and No End
(Es gibt keinen Anfang und kein
Ende)*, 1999*
Beeswax ziggurat, wood
244 x 51⅛ x 224½ in.
(620 x 130 x 570 cm)
Installation: Kunsthaus Bregenz,
1999

PAGE 119
*The Rice Meals for the Nine Planets
(or whatever the connections)
(Die Reismahlzeiten für die
neun Planeten [oder wie die
Zusammenhänge auch sein kön-
nten]),* 1983*
Oil pastel and pencil on paper
17 x 24 in. (43 x 61 cm)
Collection Johannes Cladders,
Krefeld, Germany

PAGE 120

Top:
The Rice Meals for a Stone, 1983*
Pencil on paper
11⅝ x 16½ in. (29.5 x 42 cm)

Bottom:
The Rice Meals for a Stone, 1983*
Pencil on paper
11⅝ x 16½ in. (29.5 cm x 42 cm)

PAGE 121
The Rice Meals for a Stone, 1983*
Oil pastel and pencil on paper
16½ x 11⅞ in. (42 x 30 cm)
Private collection

PAGE 122
The Rice Meals for a Stone, 1983*
Oil pastel and pencil on paper
20½ x 17 in. (52 x 43 cm)

PAGE 123
Untitled, 1983*
Oil pastel and pencil on paper
17 x 24 in. (43 x 61 cm)

PAGE 124
The Rice Meals for a Stone, 1983*
Oil pastel and pencil on paper
20 x 16⅛ in. (50.5 x 41 cm)

PAGE 125
Untitled, 1987*
Oil pastel and pencil on paper
35½ x 24½ cm (90 x 62 cm)
Private collection

PAGE 126
Untitled, 1994*
Oil pastel and pencil on paper
16½ x 11⅞ cm (42 x 30 cm)

PAGE 127
Untitled, 1983*
Oil pastel and pencil on paper
13 x 9½ in. (33 x 24 cm)

PAGE 128
Untitled, 1994*
Oil pastel and pencil on paper
16½ x 11⅞ cm (42 x 30 cm)
Private collection

PAGE 129
A Waxroom for a Mountain, 1994*
Oil pastel and pencil on paper
19½ x 15¾ in. (49.5 x 40 cm)

PAGE 130
Nowhere (Nirgendwo), 1995*
Oil pastel and pencil on paper
30 x 24½ in. (76 x 62 cm)
Private collection

PAGE 131
*The Room of Certitudes—Certitude
Is the Imaginary (La chambre des
certitudes—La certitude c'est
l'imaginaire),* 1995*
Oil pastel and pencil on paper
24½ x 30 in. (62 x 76 cm)

PAGE 132
Untitled, 1995*
Oil pastel and pencil on paper
13½ x 8½ in. (34.3 x 21.6 cm)
Courtesy Sperone Westwater,
New York

PAGE 133
Untitled, 1995*
Oil pastel and pencil on paper
24 x 18 in. (61 x 45.7 cm)
Courtesy Sperone Westwater,
New York

PAGE 134
You Will Go Somewhere Else, 1995*
Oil pastel and pencil on paper
13½ x 8½ in. (34.3 x 21.6 cm)
Courtesy Sperone Westwater,
New York

PAGE 135
Untitled, 1995*
Oil pastel and pencil on paper
24 x 18 in. (61 x 45.7 cm)
Courtesy Sperone Westwater,
New York

n. b. Chronology images are not
captioned.

BIBLIOGRAPHY

MONOGRAPHS

Asseldonk, Wilma van. *Wolfgang Laib*. With an interview with the artist by Martin Schwander. Tilburg: De Pont Foundation, 1993.

Avrilla, Jean-Marc. *Wolfgang Laib*. Bordeaux: capcMusée d'art contemporain, 1992.

Cladders, Johannes. *Wolfgang Laib*. Venice: Biennale di Venezia, German Pavilion, and Mönchengladbach: Städtisches Museum Abteiberg, 1982.

Farrow, Clare. *Wolfgang Laib. A Journey*. Ostfildern-Ruit: Series Cantz, 1996.

Hutchinson, John. *Wolfgang Laib*. Dublin: The Douglas Hyde Gallery, 1992.

Kawaguchi, Reiji. *Wolfgang Laib*. Tokyo: Kanransha Gallery, 1991.

Kern, Hermann. *Wolfgang Laib*. Munich: Kunstraum München, 1978.

Krempel, Ulrich. *Wolfgang Laib. Zwei Orte*. Weimar: Castle Belvedere, and Ostfildern-Ruit: Series Cantz, 2000.

Menegoi, Simone, and Federico Ferrari. *Wolfgang Laib*. Milan and Venice: Gallery Milleventi, 1999.

Müller, Hans-Joachim. *Wolfgang Laib/Benjamin Katz*. Basel: Edition Gallery Buchmann, 1989.

Osterwold, Tilman, Johannes Cladders, Hans-Joachim Müller, and Harald Szeemann. *Wolfgang Laib*. Stuttgart: Württembergischer Kunstverein, and Ostfildern-Ruit: Edition Cantz, 1989.

Rowell, Margit. *Wolfgang Laib*. With an interview with the artist by Suzanne Pagé. Barcelona: Fundació Joan Miró, 1989.

Samsonow, Elisabeth von. *Wolfgang Laib*. With an interview with the artist by Rudolf Sagmeister. Bregenz: Kunsthaus Bregenz, 1999.

Schmidt, Katharina. *Wolfgang Laib. Milchsteine und Blütenstaub*. Baden-Baden: Annemarie und Will Grohmann Stipendium, Baden-Baden: Staatliche Kunsthalle, 1981.

Schrenk, Klaus, Kerry Brougher, and Donald Kuspit. *Wolfgang Laib*. Bonn: Kunstmuseum, and Los Angeles: The Museum of Contemporary Art, and Ostfildern-Ruit: Edition Cantz, 1992.

———. *Wolfgang Laib: ich bin nicht hier*. With an interview with the artist by Kirsten Voigt. Karlsruhe: Staatliche Kunsthalle Karlsruhe, 1997.

Schwander, Martin. *Wolfgang Laib*. With an interview with the artist by Schwander. Lucerne: Kunstmuseum Luzern, 1990.

Szeemann, Harald. *Wolfgang Laib*. With an interview with the artist by Suzanne Pagé. Paris: ARC, Musée d'Art Moderne de la Ville de Paris, 1986.

———. *Wolfgang Laib*. Ascona: Museo Comunale d'Arte Moderna, 1992.

Tosatto, Guy. *Wolfgang Laib*. Rochechouart: Musée départemental de Rochechouart, 1989.

———. *Wolfgang Laib: Somewhere Else*. Nîmes: Carré d'Art, Musée d'art contemporain de Nîmes, and Ostfildern-Ruit: Cantz, 1999.

Wolfgang Laib. Basel: Edition Gallery Buchmann, 1988.

Wolfgang Laib. Blütenstaub von Löwenzahn. Munich: Kunstraum München, 1978.

BROCHURES

Armitage, Diane. *Radical Practice/Time Out of Mind (beauty in the extreme), Wolfgang Laib*. Santa Fe: The Center for Contemporary Arts, 1991.

Butler, Cornelia. *Wolfgang Laib: Simple Structures*. Des Moines: Des Moines Art Center, 1988.

Cottong, Kathy. *Wolfgang Laib. You Will Go Somewhere Else*. Chicago: The Arts Club of Chicago, 1998.

Farrow, Clare. *Wolfgang Laib*. Halifax: Henry Moore Sculpture Trust, Dean Clough, and London: Camden Arts Centre, 1994.

Pohlen, Annelie. *Wolfgang Laib*. London: Whitechapel Art Gallery, 1985.

Shutan, Suzan. *A Glimpse upon All That Is Necessary: The Work of Wolfgang Laib*. Des Moines: Des Moines Art Center, 1988.

CATALOGUES OF GROUP
EXHIBITIONS

1945 bis 1985, Kunst in der Bundesrepublik Deutschland. Berlin: Nationalgalerie, 1985, pp. 283, 289, 400.

3. Triennale der Kleinplastik. Fellbach: Triennale der Kleinplastik, 1986, pp. 196–97.

97 Kwangju Biennale: Unmapping the Earth. Essays by Harald Szeemann, Richard Koshalek, et al. Kwangju: Kwangju Biennale Press, 1997.

Ars '83 Helsinki. Helsinki: Ateneumin Taidemuseo, 1983. Vol. 1, p. 142; vol. 2, pp. 95–96.

Luis Barragán: Sitio Superficie. Mexico City: Antiguo Colegio de San Ildefonso, 1996, p. 17.

Bonfand, Alain, and David Dobbels. *Tu es pierre*. Vassivière, Limousin, 1986, p. 43.

Brüderlin, Markus. *Magie der Bäume*. Basel-Riehen: Fondation Beyeler, and Ostfildern-Ruit: Hatje, 1998, pp. 116–23.

Busine, Laurent. *Un Détail immense*. Charleroi: Palais des Beaux Arts, 1991, pp. 91–101.

Celant, Germano. *La Biennale di Venezia. XLVII Esposizione Internationale d'Arte. Future, Present, Past*. Venice: La Biennale di Venezia, and Milan: Electa, 1997, with text by the artist, p. 300.

Century 87. Amsterdam: Oude Kerk, 1987, pp. 126–27.

Città Natura. Rome: Palazzo delle Esposizioni and Fratelli Palombi Editori, 1997.

Chessa, Sivia, and Beatrice Merz. *Hortus Artis*. Turin: Orto Botanico, 1989, pp. 20–28.

Cladders, Johannes. *La Biennale. Arti visive '82*. Venice: La Biennale di Venezia, 1982, pp. 146–49.

Cladders, Johannes, and Annelie Pohlen. *Sixth Biennale of Sydney*. Sydney: Gallery of New South Wales, 1986, pp. 166–67.

Deutsch, Eckhart. "Anschauung und ästhetische Autonomie. Zum Problem religiöser Kunst." In *Bilder sind nicht verboten*. Düsseldorf: Städtische Kunsthalle, 1982, pp. 118–22.

Didi-Huberman, Georges. *Régions de dissemblence*. Rochechouart: Musée départemental de Rochechouart, 1990, pp. 58, 61.

Documenta 7. Kassel: Documenta 7, 1982, pp. 186–87, 372–73.

Epicenter. Ljubljana: Moderna Galerija, 1997, pp. 41–50.

Etrenature. Paris: Fondation Cartier pour l'art contemporain and Actes Sud, 1998, pp. 23–27.

Falls the Shadow. The Hayward Annual 1986. London: Hayward Art Gallery, 1986, pp. 96–97.

Farrow, Clare. *Kunstwelten im Dialog*. Cologne: Museum Ludwig and DuMont-Verlag, pp. 440–41.

Froment, Jean-Louis. *Même si c'est la nuit*. Bordeaux: Musée d'art contemporain, 1993.

———. *Les Pensées bleues*. Bordeaux: capcMusée d'art contemporain, 1993, pp. 22, 23, 31.

Gambrell, Jamey. *Carnegie International 88*. Pittsburgh: The Carnegie Museum of Art, and Munich: Prestel-Verlag, 1988, pp. 95–96.

Gamwell, Lynn. *A Century of Silence.* Binghamton: University Art Museum, State University of New York, 1993, p. 30.

Giloy-Hirtz, Petra. *Geistes Gegenwart.* Munich: Diözesanmuseum Freising, 1998, pp. 126–29.

Hall, Dieter. *Wolfgang Laib.* Zurich: Ink-Dokumentation 5, 1980, pp. 70–74.

Holsten, Siegmar. *Kosmische Bilder in der Kunst des 20. Jahrhunderts.* Baden-Baden: Kunsthalle Baden-Baden, and Tel Aviv: The Tel Aviv Museum, 1983, pp. 177, 179, 181.

Hübl, Michael. *Defacto.* Copenhagen: Charlottenborg, 1988, pp. 52–55.

Jäger, Joachim. "Beseelte Materie." In *Das XX. Jahrhundert. Ein Jahrhundert Kunst in Deutschland.* Berlin: Nationalgalerie and Nicolai-Verlag, 1999, pp. 318–19.

Kern, Hermann. *1. Ausstellung der Jürgen Ponto-Stiftung.* Frankfurt: Karmeliterkloster, 1980.

———. *Art allemagne aujourd'hui.* Paris: ARC, Musée d'Art Moderne de la Ville de Paris, 1981, pp. 278–81.

Krempel, Ulrich. *Figur. Natur.* Hannover: Sprengel Museum, Hannover, 1994, pp. 10, 42–43.

Kunst in Deutschland. Bonn: Kunst- und Ausstellungshalle, 1995, p. 104.

Kunst wird Material. Berlin: Nationalgalerie, 1982, pp. 58–61.

Magasin 3 Stockholm Konsthall pa Arken: Udvalgte vaerker fra samlingen/Selections from the Collection. Arken, Sweden: Museum for Moderne Kunst, 1997.

Matsumoto, Tohru. *Color and/or Monochrome.* Tokyo and Kyoto: The National Museum of Modern Art, 1989, pp. 54–58.

Onorato, Ronald J. *Wolfgang Laib.* Providence: University Art Museum, 1982, pp. 12–13.

Osterwold, Tilman. *Das Goldene Zeitalter: Die Geschichte des Goldes vom Mittelalter zur Gegenwart.* Stuttgart: Württembergischer Kunstverein, and Edition Cantz, 1991, p. 141.

Ouverture II. Turin: Castello di Rivoli, 1986, pp. 60–61.

Picazo, Glòria. *Orientalismos.* San Sebastian: KM. Kulturrurnea, 1998, pp. 182–87.

———. *LightSeed.* Tokyo: Watari-um, Museum of Contemporary Art, 1990, pp. 41–61.

———. *SkulpturSein.* Düsseldorf: Städtische Kunsthalle, 1986, pp. 119–24.

———. *Spuren, Skulpturen und Monumente ihrer präzisen Reise.* Zurich: Kunsthaus Zürich, 1985, pp. 127–32.

———. *Zeitlos.* Berlin: Werkstatt 88, and Munich: Prestel-Verlag, 1988, pp. 205–10.

Pohlen, Annelie. *Wechselströme. Kontemplation—Expression— Konstruktion.* Bonn: Bonner Kunstverein, 1987, pp. 28–31.

Rosc. Dublin, 1988, pp. 108–10.

Rowell, Margit. *Objects of Desire: The Modern Still Life.* New York: The Museum of Modern Art, 1997, pp. 218–19.

Saltz, Jerry. *New Locations.* New York: Wolff Gallery, 1987, pp. 5, 14–15.

Schneckenburger, Manfred. *Documenta 8.* Kassel: Documenta 8, 1987. Vol. 2: pp. 142–43; vol. 3: entry under *Wolfgang Laib.*

Scott, Sue. *The Edward R. Broida Collection: A Selection of Works.* Orlando: Orlando Museum of Art, 1998, pp. 92–93.

Signs of Life. Philadelphia: Institute of Contemporary Art, 1990, pp. 17 and 50.

Spirit + Place. Sydney: Museum of Contemporary Art, 1996, p. 61.

Szeemann, Harald. *4e Bienale de Lyon d'art contemporain. L'autre.* Lyon: Réunion des Musées Nationaux, 1997, pp. 112–13.

———. *De Sculptura.* Vienna: Messepalast, Wiener Festwochen, 1986, pp. 147–54.

———. *Einleuchten.* Hamburg: Deichtorhallen Hamburg, 1989, pp. 201–4.

———. *GAS, Grandiose Ambitieux Silencieux.* Bordeaux: capcMusée d'art contemporain, 1993, pp. 22–27.

Territorium Artis. Bonn: Kunst- und Ausstellungshalle, and Stuttgart: Hatje-Verlag, 1992, pp. 182–83.

Threshold. Oslo: The National Museum of Contemporary Art, 1990, p. 48.

Tosatto, Guy. In *La Bienale di Venezia.* Venice: La Bienale di Venezia, 1999, pp. 78–81.

BOOKS

Jean Bernier Gallery. 1977–98. Athens: Agra Publications, 1998.

Casterman, Geneviève. "Jouer avec les matières." In *Copain des peintres.* Toulouse: Milan, 1997, p. 130.

Cladders, Johannes. "Wolfgang Laib." In *Künstler, Kritisches Lexikon der Gegenwart.* Ausgabe 15. With an interview with the artist by Martin Schwander. Munich: WB-Verlag, 1991.

De Pont Foundation: De Collectie. Tilburg: De Pont Foundation, 1998, pp. 120–24.

Galerie mit Bleistift Fischer. 1967–92. Bielefeld: Edition Marzona, 1993, pp. 142, 216, 304.

Gamwell, Lynn, and Donald Kuspit. *Health and Happiness.* Ithaca: Cornell University Press, 1996, cover and pp. 62–63.

Garraud, Colette. "Wolfgang Laib." In *L'Idée de nature dans l'art contemporain.* Paris: Flammarion, 1993, pp. 150–57.

Igliori, Paola. *Wolfgang Laib.* In *Entrails, Heads & Tails.* New York: Rizzoli, 1992.

Kanransha. 1980–1992. Tokyo, 1992.

Kern, Hermann. "Kunst als Gestaltung des Gestaltlosen." In *Expansion.* Vienna: Biennale Vienna, 1979, pp. 69–97.

Laib, Wolfgang. In *The Bread and Butter Stone.* Dublin: The Douglas Hyde Gallery, 1997.

Le Thorel-Daviot, Pascale. "Wolfgang Laib." In *Petit dictionnaire des artistes contemporains.* Paris: Bordas, 1996, p. 149.

Levanto, Yrjänä. "Of the Rainbow and Other Debris." In *Nykytaiteen Lähteitä/Sources of Contemporary Art.* Helsinki: Museum of Contemporary Art, 1989, pp. 48–49.

Motanari, Elio. *Arte e persone a Venezia.* Venice: Editrice Bardi, 1995, p. 76.

Regel, Günther, et al. *Moderne Kunst: Schulbuch.* Stuttgart: Klett-Verlag, 1994, p. 13.

Simpson, Colin, and Donald Williams. *Art Now.* Sydney: McGraw-Hill, 1994, p. 152–53.

Thomson, Christian, and Christoph Schreier. *Aufbruch in die Neunziger.* Cologne: Dumont, 1991, p. 299.

Wardell, Michael. In *Australian National Gallery. An Introduction.* Canberra: Australian National Gallery, 1982, p. 117.

Weintraub, Linda. Interview with the artist in *Art on the Edge and Over.* Litchfield, Conn.: Art Insights, 1996, pp. 39–44.

ACADEMIC THESES AND STUDIES

Capossela, Mariangela. *Wolfgang Laib: Natura Paesaggio Spostamento.* Bologna: Accademia di Belle Arti, 1994–95.

Clavien, Marlène. *De Passage.* Geneva, 1997.

Engelhardt, Stephan. *Wolfgang Laib: Konstruktion des Werks und Konzept.* Vienna: Institut für Kunstgeschichte, Universität Wien, 1990.

Geway, Kitty. *Niet in de hemel maar op aarde: Doctraalscriptie Moderne Kunst.* Groningen: Institut voor Kunstgeschiedenis, Rijksuniversität, 1990.

Lauber, Maria. *In search for a place where snow never melts: Die Auseinandersetzung mit natürlichen Materialien in der zeitgenössischen Kunst am Beispiel von Andy Goldsworthy, Wolfgang Laib and Tony Cragg.* Freiburg im Breisgau: Philosophische Fakultät der Universität, 1995.

Melchior, Sigrid, and Charlotte Schulze. *Die Blütenstaubarbeiten Wolfgang Laibs: Hausarbeit zum Hauptseminar Farbe und Material in der Malerei der Moderne bei Prof. Monika Wagner.* Hamburg: Institut für Kunstgeschichte, Universität Hamburg, 1990/91.

Schmitz, Nathalie. *L'Utilisation de matières organiques premières dans l'oeuvre de Wolfgang Laib.* Strasburg: L'Université des Sciences Humaines, 1998.

Verreet, Isabelle. *Wolfgang Laib—Aspekte seines Naturverständnisses.* Munich: Institut für Kunstgeschichte, Universität München, 1991.

PERIODICALS AND NEWSPAPERS

Archer, Michael. "Installation Art." *The Unesco Courier,* December 1996, p. 32.

Arici, Laura. "Gelebte Achtsamkeit." *Neue Züricher Zeitung,* October 26, 1990, p. 27.

Artner, Alan G. "Laib Strives to Balance Inner, Outer Worlds." *Chicago Tribune,* November 23, 1990, p. 76, section 7.

———. "Natural Selection. *Chicago Tribune,* January 29, 1998, pp. 1, 12, section 5.

Avrilla, Jean-Marc. "A Wax Room in the Mountains." *Parkett,* no. 39 (1994): 88–91 (German text), 92–101 (English text).

Bartelik, Marek. "Wolfgang Laib, Sperone Westwater." *Artforum XXXIV,* no. 5 (January 1996): 82.

Beil, Ralf. "Wolfgang Laib, Paris, Galerie Crousel-Robelin." *Arte Factum,* February–March 1992, p. 45.

Bizot, Jean-François. "C'este quoi la force? C'este quoi la beauté?" *Acteul,* no. 72 (October 1985): 98–107.

Bode, Ursula. "Suggestive Botschaften." *Süddeutsche Zeitung,* January 12, 1993, p. 14.

Bona, Clara, and Elisabetta Pincherle. "Ho trovato l'America." *La Repubblica,* August 25–31, 1998, pp. 35–37.

Bonetti, David. "Gallery Watch: Obsession Meets Devotion." *San Francisco Examiner,* October 24, 1997, p. B-9.

Bonnefoi, Stéphane. "L'Ascendance selon Wolfgang Laib." *Midi Libre,* March 6, 1999, p. W7.

Bowyer, Bell J. "Wolfgang Laib." *Review,* May 15, 1998, p. 44.

Braet, Jan. "Het vision van een arts." *Knack,* no. 26 (June 27–July 3, 1990): 118–19.

Breerette, Geneviève. "La Nature tout entière sous la patte de Wolfgang Laib." *Le Monde,* April 3, 1999, p. 31.

Brougher, Kerry. "The Highlights: Wolfgang Laib." *The Contemporary.* Los Angeles: The Museum of Contemporary Art, 1992, p. 3.

Brown, Azby. "The Persistence of Life." *Asahi Evening News* (Tokyo), October 2, 1989.

Cafopoulos, Catherine. "Wolfgang Laib." *The Athenian 6,* no. 75 (January 1980).

Camper, Fred. "Powers of Subtraction." *Chicago Reader,* February 13, 1998, p. 30.

Casadio, Masiuccia. "Wolfgang Laib." *Casa Vogue*, December 1994, pp. 108–111, 174.

Catoir, Barbara."Blütenstaub und Körner." *Frankfurter Allgemeine Zeitung*, November 24, 1992.

Christofori, Ralf. "Milchstein, Bienenwachs und die unbesteigbaren Berge." *Frankfurter Allgemeine Zeitung*, August 5, 1999, p. 44.

Cladders, Johannes. "Aan de Rijsttafel van Stuifemeel." *Openbaar Kunstbezit* 6 (1987): 221–23.

Clot, Manuel. "La Casa del Extremo Silencio." *El Pais*, April 29, 1989.

Cooper, Dennis. "Art on the Amstel." *Art in America* 75, no. 10 (October 1987): 34.

Cotter, Holland. "Wolfgang Laib. Galerie Lelong." *Artnews* 88, no. 2 (February 1989): 144–46.

Couderc, Sylvie. "Wolfgang Laib, die vitale Kraft des künstlerischen Aktes." *Artefactum* 4, no. 18 (April/May 1987): 6–11.

Curtis, Cathy. "Wolfgang Laib." *Los Angeles Times*, November 25, 1988, part V, p. 20.

Davis, Douglas. "Post Post Art." *The Village Voice*, June 25, 1979, p. 41.

Davvetas, Demosthenes. "Wolfgang Laib, Interview with the Artist." *New Art Examiner*, no. 2 (January 1987): 30–32.

Debailleux, Henri-François. "Le Ciel n'est pas une peinture bleue" (interview). *Libération*, March 26, 1999.

De Domizio Durini, Lucrezia. "Bienale di Kwangju." *Tema Celeste*, no. 65 (October/December 1997): 58–59.

Denk, Andreas. "Tatalitbt von Sehen, Riechen und Hören." *Bonner General-Anzeiger*, November 7/8, 1992, p. 16.

Diehl, Carol. "Wolfgang Laib at Sperone Westwater." *Art in America* 86, no. 11 (November 1998): 126.

Dienst, Rolf-Günter. "Deutsche Kunst: eine neue Generation 6." *Das Kunstwerk*, December 1978, pp. 18–19, 37.

Dietrich, Christa. "Kunsthaus als Energiespeicher." *Vorarlberger Nachrichten*, July 9, 1999.

Drobnick, Jim. "Reveries, Assaults and Evaporating Presences: Olfactory Dimensions in Contemporary Art." *Parachute*, no. 89 (January/February/March 1998): 10–19.

Dunne, Aldan. "Life As a Bed of Pollen: Minimalist Art Gets its Francis of Assisi." *The Sunday Tribune* (Dublin), April 22, 1992.

Enneper-Klaes, Monika. "Zauberhafte Pollenteppiche." *Rhein-Sieg-Anzeiger*, November 6, 1992.

"Et Aussi . . . ." *Art Actuel* 1, no. 1 (March–April 1999): 27.

Farrow, Clare. "Wolfgang Laib: Beyond the Imagination. An interview by Clare Farrow." *Art and Design*, no. 36 (1994): 24–31.

———. "Wolfgang Laib: More Than Myself." *Parkett*, no. 39 (1994): 77–81 (English text), 82–87 (German text).

Fechner-Smarsly, Thomas. "Schwierige Arbeit der Kontemplation." *Die Tageszeitung* (Berlin), January 11, 1993.

Ferrari, Corinna. "Wolfgang Laib, una mostra a Milano." *Domus*, no. 581 (April 1978): 48.

"Five Artists from Germany Exhibit Works at de Saisset." *Silicon Valley Visitors Guide* (November 1987).

Freeman, Judi. "Still Life at MoMA." *Apollo*, October 1997, pp. 44–46.

Frenkel, Vera. "An Ordering Madness: The 40th Venice Biennale." *Vanguard*, December/January 1982–83, pp. 8–11.

Galloway, David. "Wolfgang Laib at Konrad Fischer." *Artnews* (February 1991): 159.

Gerbal, Yves. "Wolfgang Laib." *Arts Croisés*, April/May 1990, pp. 69–74.

Glintz, Claude. "Nature, culture, écriture à propos de Wolfgang Laib, Lothar Baumgarten et quelques autres." *Art Press*, October 1986, pp. 15–19.

Glueck, Grace. "When Is a Still Life Not a Still Life?" *Quarterly*, Fall 1997, p. 46.

"Goings On about Town." *The New Yorker*, February 15, 1993, pp. 16–17.

Gross, Roland. "Milch und Stein." *Rheinische Post*, December 29, 1992.

———. "Die Milch auf Marmorsteinen." *Kölner Stadt-Anzeiger*, November 28/29, 1990.

Haapaleinen, Riikka. "Elamantaiteilija Wolfgang Laib." *Taide Art Magazine*, May 1996, pp. 17–19.

Händler, Ruth. "Natürliche Fülle in kargen Räumen." *Art. Das Kunstmagazin*, July 1999, pp. 96–97.

Hecht, Axel. "Ein Fest der Stille und der Farben." *Art*, no. 6 (June 9, 1982): 132–35.

Herbstreuth, Peter. "Wolfgang Laib—Kunsthaus Bregenz." *Kunstforum* 147 (September/November 1999): 437–38.

———. "Teilhabe am Vollkommenen." *Der Tagesspiegel* (Berlin), August 22, 1999.

Hinton, Susan. "A Counterbalance to Neoexpressionism." *Artweek*, November 14, 1987.

Hofleitner, Johanna. "Das Einfachste ist auch die größte Herausforderung." *Die Presse*, July 16, 1999.

Hohmeyer, Jürgen. "Ernte im Hochmoor." *Der Spiegel* 36, no. 20 (May 17, 1982): 246–47.

Hübl, Michael. "Askese des Abundanten. Wolfgang Laib." *Kunstforum* 80 (July–September 1985): 108–15.

———. "Das Jahr danach." *Kunstforum* 88 (March/April 1987): 267–73.

Hufschlag, Inge. "In Bregenz bringt Beton die Fantasie zum Blühen." *Handelsblatt*, July 16/17, 1999, p. 61.

Hulten, Pontus. "Territorium Artis, Kunst und Ausstellungshalle, Bonn." "Flash Art News," *Flash Art* (January/February 1993): 132.

Huser, France. "Lait et sang, Wolfgang Laib—Bruce Nauman." *Le Nouvel Observateur*, October 31, 1986.

———. "Wolfgang Laib." *Le Nouvel Observateur*, December 7–13, 1989, pp. 33, 36.

Illés, Vera. "Mooi, maar niet mooi gemaokt." *Else vier*, January 2, 1993, pp. 68–69.

Inoue, Shoji, "Wolfgang Laib." *Chunichi Shimbun*, November 16, 1996.

Jäämeri, Hannele. "Elämän voima-aineet." *Suomen Kuvalehti*, August 30, 1996, p. 31.

Jakkola, Leena. "Kun Maito on kannista ja puhuttelevaa." *Demari*, September 5, 1996.

Kent, Sarah. "Space Invaders." *Time Out London*, December 14–21, 1994.

Kief, Dieter. "Poetische Kraft der Imagination." *Badisches Tagblatt*, July 20, 1999.

Kimoto, Sakae. "Wolfgang Laib." *Bijutsu Techno*, January 1990, pp. 58–69.

Kiviriuta, Marja-Terrtu. "Olen poliittinen taitei-lija." *Helsingin Sanomat*, September 3, 1996.

Klapproth, Micheline. "Herausforderung auf die Hektik." *Luzerner Tagblatt*, October 6, 1990.

Kramris, Eva. "Askese und Fülle mit Blütenstaub und Reis." *Luzerner Nachrichten*, October 6, 1990.

Kreis, Elfi. "Konzentrat der Stille." *Der Tagesspiegel* (Berlin), April 21, 1988.

Kölgen, Birgit. "Seelenvolle Kunst aus Milch und Blütenstaub." *Westfälische Rundschau*, November 6, 1992.

———. "Meditation und Blütenstaub." *Schwäbische Zeitung*, July 14, 1999.

Kuspit, Donald. "Wolfgang Laib at Galerie Lelong." *Artforum* XXVII, no. 6 (February 1989): 127.

———. "Wolfgang Laib at Sperone Westwater." *Artforum* XXXI, no. 9 (May 1993): 102.

Lacagnina, Salvatore. "Wolfgang Laib." *Tema Celeste* XVI, no. 74 (May/June 1999): 86–87.

Laib, Wolfgang. "The Passageway: A Project for *Artforum* by Wolfgang Laib." *Artforum* XXVII, no. 8 (April 1989): 136–39.

———. "Ce qui importe pour la vie future (What is important for future life)." *Artpress*, April 1995, p. 27.

Lambirth, Andrew. "Things Fall Apart." *Independent Saturday Magazine*, October 1997, pp. 32–35.

Larson, Kay. "Wolfgang Laib." *New York Magazine*, November 24, 1986.

Lascault, Gilbert. "Pollen jaune, calme, calme. . . ." *La Quinzaine Littéraire*, October 31, 1986.

Lavonen, Kuutti. "Ars 83 on siitepolya." *Helsingin Sanomat*, October 12, 1983, p. 22.

———. "Wolfgang Laib." *Helsingin Sanomat*, December 27, 1986, p. 20.

Lay, Franz Joseph. "Bienenwachsturm führt in geistige Höhen." *Südkurier*, July 31, 1999.

Le Goff, Jean-Pierre. "Wolfgang Laib." *Kanal Magazine*, January/March 1987, pp. 70–71.

Lepik, Andres. "Laibs Demut." *Neue Züricher Zeitung*, December 29, 1992.

Leske, Marion. "Läßt sich das verkaufen?" *Die Welt*, January 2, 1993.

Levin, Kim. "Wolfgang Laib." *The Village Voice*, November 26, 1986.

———. "Ethnoeccentricity: Lothar Baumgarten and Wolfgang Laib." *The Village Voice*, November 22, 1988, p. 95.

Lillington, David. "Famous for Sprinkling Pollen on Gallery Floors." *Time Out London*, November 30–December 7, 1994, p. 4.

Linder, Gisela. "Draußen Spektakel, drinnen Stille." *Schwäbische Zeitung*, December 2, 1998.

Lotz, Corinna. "Art & Artists: Still, but Very Real." *Socialist*, October 1997, p. 10.

Mack, Gerhard. "Blütenstaub, Wachs und Milch-Kunst als Spiegel der Natur." *Stuttgarter Zeitung*, July 29, 1999.

———. "Mit Laib und Seele im Dienste der Natur." *Cash*, no. 29 (July 23, 1999): 32.

Mahoney, Robert. "Group Show." *Tema Celeste*, November/December 1990, p. 59.

———. "Wolfgang Laib." *Arts Magazine*, May 1991, p. 99.

McEwen, John. "Some Boxes Are Better Left Closed." *The Sunday Telegraph* (London), January 8, 1995, p. 8.

McEvilley, Thomas. "Medicine Man: Proposing a Context for Wolfgang Laib's Work." *Parkett*, no. 39 (1994): 104–9 (English text), 110–17 (German text).

McKenna, Kristine. "Wolfgang Laib: Nature and Nurture." *Los Angeles Times*, November 9, 1990.

———. "Flower Power." *L.A. Style Magazine*, January 1993, pp. 28–29.

Meier-Grolman, B. "Da sieht einer den Blütenstaub und schüttet Milch auf Marmorsteine." *Südwestpresse*, June 8, 1982.

Meinhardt, Johannes. "Wolfgang Laib." *Kunstforum* 105 (January/February 1990): 352.

Meister-Klaiber. "Blütenstaub auf dem Boden." *Südwestpresse*, July 30, 1999.

Melkonian, Neery. "Wolfgang Laib: Art and Remedy." *Artspace*, January/April 1992, p. 41.

Meneguzzo, Marco. "Con Laib il romantico il polline si fa colore." *Avvenire*, May 23, 1992.

Millet, Catherine. "Unmapping the Earth." *Art Press*, no. 230 (December 1997): 64–65.

Morschel, Jürgen. "Milch und Blütenstaub." *Süddeutsche Zeitung*, December 1, 1978.

———. "Wolfgang Laib." *Das Kunstwerk*, February 1979, p. 92.

Müll, Willi. "Massiv und fragil zugleich, allemal aber schön." *Giessener Allgemeine*, November 21, 1992.

Müller, Dorothee. "Meditationsstätte." *Süddeutsche Zeitung*, November 10, 1989, p. 45.

Müller, Hanno. "Unbesteigbar fragile Berge." *Thüringer Allgemeine*, August 7, 1999.

Müller, Hans-Joachim. "Sensibilissmus und die Natur." *Die Zeit*, February 19, 1982, p. 40.

———. "Milch und Blütenstaub: Wolfgang Laib in der Galerie Buchmann." *Basler Zeitung*, December 30, 1987.

———. "Wolfgang Laib neues 'Wachshaus' in der Basler Galerie Buchmann." *Basler Zeitung*, July 18, 1989.

Newmann, Cathy. "Pollen." *National Geographic* 166, no. 4 (October 1984): 518–19.

Nochlin, Linda. "Objects of Desire: The Modern Still Life. MoMA." *Artforum* 36, no. 2 (October 1997): 91–92.

"Object of Desire: The Modern Still Life. Hayward Gallery." *Art Monthly*, October 1997, pp. 38–39.

Okada, Kiyoshi. "Wolfgang Laib." *Mainichi Shimbun*, November 21, 1996.

Olejarz, Harold. "Wolfgang Laib." *Arts Magazine* 53, no. 9 (May 1979): 37.

Ottmann, Klaus. "The Solid and the Fluid: Bartlett, Laib, Kiefer." *Flash Art*, no. 123 (Summer 1985): 48–49.

———. "Die Malerei im Zeitalter der Angst: Die Kunst der Achtziger Jahre—Eine Beschreibung." *Kunstforum* 80 (July–September 1985): 46–49.

———. "True Pictures." *Flash Art*, no. 132 (February/March 1987): 90–91.

———. "Wolfgang Laib" (interview). *Journal of Contemporary Art* 1, no. 1 (Spring/Summer 1988): 90–96.

Pasanen, Kimmo. "Wolfgang Laib." Finnish translation of an interview with the artist by Gemma Piñana, "Wolfgang Laib en el 'Cuadrado del Arte' de Nîmes." *Critica de Arte*, March 1999.

Patner, Andrew. "Wolfgang Laib: You Will Go Somewhere Else." *Chicago Sun-Times*, February 2, 1998.

Peak, Stephanie. "Wolfgang Laib at Sperone Westwater, NY, October 1995." *Rant and Rage*, no. 1 (1996): 40–41.

Pietrouiusti, Cesare. "Wolfgang Laib, Alfonso Artiaco." *Flash Art* (Summer 1992): 126–27.

Philadelphy, Ursula. "Der Staub des Lebens." *Der Standard*, August 9, 1999.

Pohlen, Annelie. "Cosmic Visions from North and South." *Artforum* XXIII, no. 7 (March 1985): 76–81.

———. "Steizeit—Endzeit—Meditationszeit, von Laib zu Beuys zu Knoebel mit einem Seitensprung zu Lechner." *Kunstforum* 62/64 (July 1983): 346–48.

———. "Wolfgang Laib, Städtisches Museum Mönchengladbach." *Artforum* XXII, no. 1 (September 1983): 82.

Ponti, Lisa. "Wolfgang Laib." *Juliet*, no. 31 (April/May 1937): 20.

Rainer, Wolfgang. "Der Duft von Wachs und Blütenstaub." *Stuttgarter Zeitung*, October 13, 1989.

Rautio, Persi. "Uuras taiteiliga lentää kukasta kukkaan." *Nyt-Helsingin Sanomat*, August 30, 1996.

Réguier, Philippe. "Laib, une vie de moine." *Le Journal des Arts*, March 19–April 2, 1999.

Reinke, Klaus. "Ritueller Oberbau." *Handelsblatt*, November 13/14, 1992, p. 6.

"Report from Korea: Kwangju Bienale." *Bijutsu Techo* 49, no. 748 (November 1997): 189–204.

Reust, Hans Rudolf. "Wolfgang Laib: Kunstmuseum." *Artscribe*, March/April, pp. 80–81.

Richard, Frances. "Wolfgang Laib: Sperone Westwater." *Artforum* 37, no. 2 (October 1998): 125.

Richter, Wolfgang. "Marmor, Milch und Bienenwachs." *Salzburger Nachrichten* (July 9, 1996).

Rose, Matthew. "New York Wrap-up. Galerie Lelong: 'The Bulge, It's Called a Meniscus.'" *ArtNews* 90, no. 7 (September 1991): 84–85.

Russell, John. "Wolfgang Laib." *New York Times*, March 27, 1981, p. C17.

———. "Wolfgang Laib—Robert Ryman—Ian Wilson." *New York Times*, May 24, 1985, p. C19.

———. "Thirteen Sculptors." *New York Times*, November 20, 1987.

Saunders, Wade, and Anna Rochette. "Wolfgang Laib at Maeght Lelong." *Art in America* 75, no. 1 (January 1987): 130.

Saurisse, Pierre. "Wolfgang Laib, Alchimiste du Volatil." *Beaux Arts*, April 1999.

Schenker, Christoph. "Wolfgang Laib, Bordeaux." *Kunstforum* 88 (March/April 1987): 298–99.

Schmid, Karlheinz. "Kunsthaus Bregenz: Wolfgang Laib." *Kunstzeitung*, no. 36 (August 1999): 9.

Schmidt, Katherina. "Materie + Form. Zeitgenössische Steinskulpturen, Malerei, Grafik." *Zürich ETH*, 1983.

Schön, Wolf. "Urstoff der Natur." *Rheinischer Merkur*, November 13, 1992.

Schwarz, Michael. "Erfahrungsräume." *Daidalos*, no. 41 (September 1991): 67.

Schwarze, Dirk. "Kunst als Lebensvollzug." *Hessische/Niedersächsische Allgemeine*, April 3, 1982.

Schwendener, Martha. "Art, Reviews: Wolfgang Laib, *Nowhere-Everywhere*." *Time Out New York*, no. 140 (May 28–June 4, 1998): 56.

———. "Wolfgang Laib at Sperone Westwater." *Flash Art*, no. 183 (November/December 1935): 127–28.

Semin, Didier. "A Piece by Wolfgang Laib at the Centre Pompidou." *Parkett*, no. 39 (1994): 70–73 (German text), 74–76 (English text).

Seth, Nikki Ty-Tornkins. "Art East and West." *Sunday Observer* (Bombay), February 10, 1985, p. 19.

Sherman, Mary. "German Sculptors Provoke, not Preach." *Chicago Sun-Times*, June 18, 1983, p. E17.

Smith, Roberta. "Wolfgang Laib." *New York Times*, November 7, 1986, p. C26.

———. "Wolfgang Laib." *New York Times*, November 25, 1988.

Sommer, Gerlinde. "Kosmische Komponente des Blütenstaubberges." *Thüringische Landeszeitung*, July 31, 1999.

Soutif, Daniel. "Laib plus fort que Kirkeby." *Libération*, January 8, 1986, p. 30.

———. "L'Etre et le néon, Wolfgang Laib et Bruce Nauman." *Libération*, November 25, 1986, p. 32.

Stachelhaus, Heiner. "Staub gelber Blüten." *Neue Rhein-Zeitung*, December 4, 1992.

Stevens, Mark. "Art: Bee-ing and Nothingness." *New York Magazine*, June 8, 1998, p. 104–5.

Tallman, Susan. "Wolfgang Laib at Sperone Westwater." *Art in America* 79, no. 6 (June 1991): 137–38.

Tatransky, Valentin. "Wolfgang Laib." *Arts Magazine* 53, no. 7 (March 1979): 33.

Testa, Gemma de Angelis, and Giuliana Setari. "L'enigma di Vercruysse e la spiritualità di Laib." *Il Giornale dell'Arte*, March 1999.

Thomas, Mona. "Laib, l'esprit du lieu." *Beaux Arts*, May 1989, pp. 38–43.

Tompkins, Calvin. "A Question of Human Presence." *The New Yorker*, June 1997, pp. 104–206.

Trimarco, Angelo. "Il mito ha una casa di cera." *Il Mattino*, April 6, 1992.

Uhde, Robert. "Leuchtende Stille." *Tain,* no. 3 (May/June 1998): 26–31.

Van Winkel, C. H. "Wolfgang Laib, Lothar Baumgarten en de geest van Joseph Beuys." *Metropolis M,* May/June 1990, pp. 26–33.

Vogel, Maria. "Wenn Blütenstaub zu Kunst wird." *WB Woche,* October 19, 1930.

Voigt, Kirsten. "Je andersartiger die Dinge sind, desto revolutionärer wirken sie" (interview). *Badisches Tagblatt,* October 18, 1997.

Wei, Lilly. "Wolfgang Laib at Sperone Westwater." *Art in America* 83, no. 11 (November 1995): 103–10.

Wells, John. "Wolfgang Laib." *Arts Magazine* 53, no. 7 (March 1979): 2.

Weskott, Hanne. "Wolfgang Laib und Thomas Schütte, Preisträger der Jürgen-Ponto-Stiftung 1980." *Kunst-forum* 31 (January 1980): 243–45.

Withers, Rachel. "Preview: Wolfgang Laib, Carré d'Art." *Artforum* 37, no. 5 (January 1999): 53.

"Wolfgang Laib." *Hsing Shih Art Monthly* (Taipei), 1992, cover and pp. 74–79.

"Wolfgang Laib: Sperone Westwater." *New York Contemporary Art Report* 1, no. 1 (May 1998): 72–63.

Zimmer, William. "Wolfgang Laib." *Soho News* 8, no. 27 (April 1–7, 1981): 47.

Zwez, Anneliese. "Meditative Räume." *Berner Rundschau,* November 6, 1992.